AF833715

India Studies in Business and Economics

The Indian economy is one of the fastest growing economies of the world with India being an important G-20 member. Ever since the Indian economy made its presence felt on the global platform, the research community is now even more interested in studying and analyzing what India has to offer. This series aims to bring forth the latest studies and research about India from the areas of economics, business, and management science, with strong social science linkages. The titles featured in this series present rigorous empirical research, often accompanied by policy recommendations, evoke and evaluate various aspects of the economy and the business and management landscape in India, with a special focus on India's relationship with the world in terms of business and trade. The series also tracks research on India's position on social issues, on health, on politics, on agriculture, on rights, and many such topics which directly or indirectly affect sustainable growth of the country.

Review Process

The proposal for each volume undergoes at least two double blind peer review where a detailed concept note along with extended chapter abstracts and a sample chapter is peer reviewed by experienced academics. The reviews can be more detailed if recommended by reviewers.

Ethical Compliance

The series follows the Ethics Statement found in the Springer standard guidelines here. https://www.springer.com/us/authors-editors/journal-author/journal-author-helpdesk/before-you-start/before-you-start/1330#c14214

Susan Thomas
Editor

Insolvency and Bankruptcy Reforms in India

Springer

Editor
Susan Thomas
Jindal Global Business School
O. P. Jindal Global University
Sonipat, Haryana, India

ISSN 2198-0012 ISSN 2198-0020 (electronic)
India Studies in Business and Economics
ISBN 978-981-16-0853-7 ISBN 978-981-16-0854-4 (eBook)
https://doi.org/10.1007/978-981-16-0854-4

© The Editor(s) (if applicable) and The Author(s), under exclusive license to Springer Nature Singapore Pte Ltd. 2022
This work is subject to copyright. All rights are solely and exclusively licensed by the Publisher, whether the whole or part of the material is concerned, specifically the rights of translation, reprinting, reuse of illustrations, recitation, broadcasting, reproduction on microfilms or in any other physical way, and transmission or information storage and retrieval, electronic adaptation, computer software, or by similar or dissimilar methodology now known or hereafter developed.
The use of general descriptive names, registered names, trademarks, service marks, etc. in this publication does not imply, even in the absence of a specific statement, that such names are exempt from the relevant protective laws and regulations and therefore free for general use.
The publisher, the authors, and the editors are safe to assume that the advice and information in this book are believed to be true and accurate at the date of publication. Neither the publisher nor the authors or the editors give a warranty, expressed or implied, with respect to the material contained herein or for any errors or omissions that may have been made. The publisher remains neutral with regard to jurisdictional claims in published maps and institutional affiliations.

This content of this book is for research purposes and must not be used as a guide for taking or recommending any action or decision, commercial or otherwise. Views expressed are those of the authors. Neither Insolvency and Bankruptcy Board of India (IBBI) nor the author will be responsible for any damage or loss to anyone, of any kind, in any manner arising therefrom. The Code, Rules, and Regulations relevant to the matter are available at www.ibbi.gov.in.

This Springer imprint is published by the registered company Springer Nature Singapore Pte Ltd.
The registered company address is: 152 Beach Road, #21-01/04 Gateway East, Singapore 189721, Singapore

Foreword

Ease of entry, operation and exit are most essential for creating an enabling environment for sustainable business. When a business becomes unviable, there must be an option for a graceful exit. Failure of a business could be on account of different reasons such as competition, external crisis, disruptive technology, or even mismanagement. Freedom of exit is crucial, as it enables maximization of value of assets of the corporate debtor (balancing the interests of all stakeholders) and releases the resources to be put to better economic use.

In India, while a lot had been done with respect to promoting the ease of doing business by doing away with license raj and inspector raj and simplification of procedures for setting up business, exit remained time taking and cumbersome, until the enactment of the Insolvency and Bankruptcy Code, 2016 (IBC). Prior to that, the insolvency law was highly fragmented and ineffective. With the introduction of the IBC there has been palpable improvement in the repayment behavior of corporate borrowers. Successful resolutions also led to significant reduction in NPAs. The outcomes of IBC have been noteworthy on several fronts—the time taken for and cost of insolvency resolution; the percentage of recovery; the speed of implementation; and development of a new cadre of resolution professionals. Government too has been proactive in addressing various implementation issues, including delays in resolution. It brought as many as five amendment bills, all of which were passed by the Parliament and upheld by the apex court.

I had the privilege of being closely associated with this journey, both as the Union Secretary of Corporate Affairs (from October 2017 to May 2020) and as the Chairperson of the Insolvency Law Committee, which acted as the standing committee for reviewing the insolvency law and making recommendations to the Government from time to time. While a lot has been done a lot more is in the offing, especially with respect to the MSME sector, individual insolvency, strengthening the institution of resolution professionals, capacity development of committee of creditors, cross-border insolvency and introduction of prepacks.

The report of the Bankruptcy Law Reforms Committee formed the basis of the new insolvency law in India. Since then, a lot of new developments have taken place. I am happy to note that this book undertakes an in-depth diagnosis and evaluation of the Code, and focuses on the challenges that lie ahead, including plausible solutions, some of which were presented and discussed at the IBBI-IGIDR Research Conference held in August, 2018, of which I was a part. I would like to compliment the authors as well as the editor for bringing out such a comprehensive publication on the subject of insolvency.

New Delhi, India
December 2020

Injeti Srinivas
Chairperson
International Financial Services Centre Authority

Acknowledgements

This book was born out of the discussions and deliberations that arose in the years after the Insolvency and Bankruptcy Code (2016) started operating as the new legal framework to resolve corporate insolvencies in India. The IBC, as the law has come to be called, was a structural change compared to how things were done. It led to an eruption of discussions and deliberations through a plethora of seminars and conferences across the country, with a mixture of academics, policymakers, and practitioners, participating with full engagement and commitment. The work presented in the book is an attempt to capture some of the important issues and ideas that gripped the intellectual debates of the day.

Some of the chapters in this book were presented and debated at the IBBI-IGIDR-FICCI insolvency and bankruptcy reforms workshop that was held in Mumbai in April 2018, and the IBBI-IGIDR insolvency and bankruptcy reforms conference, which was held in New Delhi in August 2018. These events were generously supported by the Ministry of Finance and with enthusiastic participation by the Ministry of Corporate Affairs and the newly created Insolvency and Bankruptcy Board of India, the IBBI. Anirudh Burman, Sagar Goyal, Ganapathi Narayanamoorthy, Deepak Panda, and Rajeswari Sengupta offered comments and suggestions that helped to strengthen our understanding of the new law, and so helped to improve the quality of this work. Other chapters arose from other discussions and observations of issues raised in similar events, as well as in the public domain.

This work has also benefitted from rich discussions with the very long list of academics and the practitioners who have long been a part of the discourse on bankruptcy reforms in India. Dr. M. S. Sahoo, former Chairperson of IBBI, kindly and generously gave his time to review and comment on the chapters in the book. Thanks also go to Injeti Srinivas, ex-Secretary at the Ministry of Corporate Affairs, Gyaneshwar Singh of Ministry of Corporate Affairs, P. P. Chaudhary, Minister of State for Law and Justice and Corporate Affairs, Subash Chandra Garg and Shashank Saksena of Ministry of Finance, Justice M. M. Kumar of the National Companies Law Tribunal, Justice Kannan Ramesh of Singapore Supreme Court, Sudarshan Sen from the Reserve Bank of India, K. R. Saji Kumar, Mamta Suri, Ritesh Kavdia, and Navrang Saini of the Insolvency and Bankruptcy Board of India, and Chinmaya Goyal of NITI Aayog.

Among industry experts, we would like to thank Nikhil Shah of Alvarez & Marsal, Harish Chander and Rashesh Shah of Edelweiss, Ravi Chachra of Eight Capital, Dhananjay Kumar and Richa Roy of Cyril Amarchand Mangaldas, Sapan Gupta of Shardul Amarchand Mangaldas, Nilang Desai and Suharsh Sinha of AZB&Partners, Sumant Batra of Kesar Dass B. & Associates, Harish Pais of Trilegal, Anuj Jain of BSRR&Co, Badri Narayan of Third Eye Capital, Surya Mahadev of Multiples Alternate Asset Management and Srikrishna Dwaram of True North Managers LLP, Anurag Das of International Asset Reconstruction Company, Harsh Vardhan of Bain Advisors, Shaildra Ajmera, Abizer Diwanji, and Dinal Shah of EY, P. R. Ramesh of Deloitte, Venkattu Srinivasan of Kotak Mahindra Bank, Rajnish Kumar of State Bank of India, Shuva Mandal of Tata Sons, Bhargavi Zaveri of the Chennai Mathematical Institute and the Finance Research Group, Venkatesh Panchapagesan of IIM Bangalore, Yesha Yadav of Vanderbilt Law School, Surya Prakash from Daksh, Alok Prasanna from Vidhi Centre for Legal Policy, Somasekhar Sundaresan, Montek Singh Ahluwalia, and A. S. Chandiok.

FICCI, Eight Capital, E&Y, Kotak Mahindra Bank, Alvarez&Marsal, and Trilegal generously provided financial support for enabling the discussions through various forums that enrich the chapters of this book.

Last but not the least, I thank the team from Springer—Nupoor Singh and Sagarika Ghosh—who gave this work the opportunity to be published, and for having the tireless patience and gentle persistence in dealing with our busy schedules and following up so diligently. I am similarly very grateful for the time that Rajesh Gupta and Sudhakar Shukla of the IBBI have generously given to proof-read the manuscript and for the depth of their review. This compilation would have been the poorer but for their hard work.

Finally, any book project cannot grow well without the understanding of the families and partners of those who are immersed in the task of its creation. I thank my family for their understanding.

April 2022

Susan Thomas
Research Professor of Business
Jindal Global University

Senior research fellow
XKDR Forum

Contents

Editor and Contributors

About the Editor

Dr. Susan Thomas is a Research Professor of Business at the Jindal Global Business School and Research Fellow at XKDR Forum. She has worked on problems such as designing the stock market index, real-time risk management system for the clearing corporation, and the use of call auctions. She has had various policy engagements with the Ministry of Finance, including being a member of the Standing Council of the competitiveness of the Indian Financial Sector (2013 onwards), and the Bankruptcy Legislative Reforms Committee (2014–2015). She led the research secretariat for the Bankruptcy Law Reforms Committee which conceptualised the Insolvency and Bankruptcy Code.

Contributors

Datta Pratik Advocate, New Delhi, India

Feibelman Adam Sumter Davis Marks Professor of Law at Tulane Law School, New Orleans, LA, USA

Felman Josh J.H. Consulting, Pune, India

Marwah Varun Associate at Shardul Amarchand Mangaldas & Co., Delhi, India

Nayak Aditi Aakriti Shantiniketan, Noida, India

Ravi Aparna Samvad Partners, Bengaluru, India

Regy Prasanth V. Aakriti Shantiniketan, Noida, India

Sane Renuka National Institute of Public Finance and Policy, New Delhi, India

Shaikh Gausia Public Policy Researcher and Industry Expert, Mumbai, India

Sharma Anjali Public Policy Researcher and An Industry Expert, Mumbai, India

Thomas Susan Jindal Global Business School, and Senior Research Fellow at XKDR Forum, Mumbai, India

Acronyms

AA	Adjudicating Authority
AAL	Amtek Auto Limited
ABA	American Bar Association
ABG	ABG Shipyard Limited
ACCC	Australian Competition and Consumer Commission
ACL	Australian Consumer Law
ADR	Alternative Dispute Resolution
AFT	Accelerated Failure Time
AIC	Akaike Information Criteria
AIF	Alternative Investment Funds
AIL	Alok Industries Limited
AOTA	Association of Travel Agents
AOUSC	Administrative Office of the United States Courts
AQR	Asset Quality Review
ARC	Asset Reconstruction Company
ATOL	Air Travel Organizer's Licence
BAPCPA	Bankruptcy Abuse Prevention And Consumer Protection Act, 2005
BIFR	Board for Industrial and Financial Reconstruction
BLRC	Bankruptcy Law Reforms Committee
BPSL	Bhushan Power & Steel Limited
BSL	Bhushan Steel Limited
CA	Companies Act
CAG	Comptroller and Auditor General
CAP	Corrective Action Plan
CBIBSFC	Central Bureau of Investigation, Bank Securities and Fraud Cell
CCI	Competition Commission of India
CD	Corporate Debtor
CDR	Corporate Debt Restructuring
CIRP	Corporate Insolvency Resolution Process
CLB	Company Law Board
CMIE	Centre for Monitoring Indian Economy

CoC	Committee of Creditors
CPC	Civil Procedure Code
CPSC	Consumer Product Safety Commission
CVC	Central Vigilance Commission
DIPP	Department of Industrial Policy & Promotion
DRT	Debt Recovery Tribunal
EIEL	Era Infra Engineering Limited
EOI	Expression of Interest
ESIL	Essar Steel India Limited
ESL	Electrosteel Steels Limited
EU	European Union
FC	Financial Creditor
FCA	Financial Conduct Authority
FDA	Food and Drug Administration
FDMC	Financial Data Management Centre
FRG	Finance Research Group
FSLRC	Financial Sector Legislative Reforms Committee
FTC	Federal Trade Commission
GAO	Government Accountability Office
GNPA	Gross Non-Performing Assets
GRR	Global Restructuring Review
HC	High Court
IAC	Internal Advisory Committee
IAUK	Insolvency Act, UK
IBA	Indian Banks' Association
IBBI	Insolvency and Bankruptcy Board of India
IBBI-IGIDR	Insolvency and Bankruptcy Board of India-Indira Gandhi Institute of Development Research
IBC	Insolvency and Bankruptcy Code
IBCAO	The Insolvency and Bankruptcy Code (Amendment) Ordinance
ICAI	Institute of Chartered Accountants of India
ICR	Interest Cover Ratio
ICSI	Institute of Company Secretaries
ICWAI	Institute of Cost Accountants of India
IGIDR	Indira Gandhi Institute of Development Research
ILC	Insolvency Law Committee
IM	Information Memorandum
IP	Insolvency Professional
IPA	Insolvency Professional Agency
IPE	Insolvency Professional Entities
IRDAI	Insurance Regulatory and Development Authority of India
IRP	Insolvency Resolution Process
IRPCPAR	Insolvency Resolution Process for Corporate Persons (Amendment) Regulations
IU	Information Utilities

JAL	Jaiprakash Associates Limited
JIA	Judicial Impact Assessment
JIL	Jaypee Infratech Limited
JLF	Joint Lenders Forum
JPE	Judicial Performance Evaluation
JSL	Jyoti Structures Limited
KCC	Kisan Credit Cards
KYC	Know Your Customer
LIL	Lanco Infratech Limited
LRC	Legislative Reforms Committee
LRFCA	Law Reform (Frustrated Contracts) Act, 1943
MCA	Ministry of Corporate Affairs
MFI	Micro Finance Institution
MIEL	Monnet Ispat & Energy Limited
MSME	Micro, Small and Medium Enterprises
NBFC	Non-Banking Finance Company
NCDRC	National Consumer Disputes Redressal Commission
NCLAT	National Company Law Appellate Tribunal
NCLT	National Company Law Tribunal
NHB	National Housing Bank
NI	Negotiable Instruments Act, 1881
NITI	National Institution for Transforming India
NPA	Non-Performing Assets
OC	Operational Creditor
OECD	Organization for Economic Co-operation and Development
P2P	Peer-to-Peer
PACER	Public Access to Court Electronic Records
PCA	Prompt Corrective Action
PFRDA	Pension Fund Regulatory Development Authority
PIA	Provisional Insolvency Act, 1920
PPI	Prepaid Payment Instruments
PSB	Public Sector Bank
PTIA	Presidency Towns Insolvency Act, 1909
RBI	Reserve Bank of India
RDDBFIA	Recovery of Debt Due to Banking and Financial Institution Act, 1993
RERA	Real Estate Regulatory Authority
RP	Resolution Professional
S4A	Scheme for Sustainable Structuring of Stressed Assets
SA	Stamp Act, 1899
SARFAESI	Securitisation and Reconstruction of Financial Assets and Enforcement of Security Act, 2002
SBI	State Bank of India
SC	Supreme Court
SCA	Singapore Companies Act, 2017
SCB	Standard Chartered Bank

SCC	Supreme Court of Canada
SDNY	Southern District of New York
SDR	Strategic Debt Restructuring
SEBI	Securities and Exchanges Board of India
SGA	Sale of Goods Act, 1979
SGD	Singapore Dollar
SICA	Sick Industrial Companies (Special Provisions) Act, 1985
SIP 16	Statement of Insolvency Practice 16
SRO	Self-Regulatory Organizations
TCPS	Trial Court Performance Standards
UK	United Kingdom
USA	United States of America
USBC	U.S. Bankruptcy Code, 2012
YoY	Year-over-Year

An Overview

Susan Thomas

In May 2016, the Insolvency and Bankruptcy Code (IBC) was passed by the upper house of the Parliament in India. It was a sea change in dealing with firm failure in India (Bankruptcy Law Reforms Committee 2015). The IBC was the last in a long list of legal and regulatory changes that Indian policymakers have attempted to resolve firm financial stress, in a timely and predictable manner. As with bankruptcy reform everywhere, the key insights of the bankruptcy process are (a) To shift control of the distressed firm to creditors, who then choose how best to proceed; (b) To move swiftly, so as to reduce the costs imposed upon society through the bankruptcy process; (c) To improve the incentives of borrowers and lenders, and (d) To improve the resource allocation, and thus, invisibly improve the working of economy, in innumerable debt transactions which may never actually go into the bankruptcy process (Sengupta et al. 2017; Ramann et al. 2015).

As with any major reform, there were gaps between the law as designed and the law as enacted. The institutional apparatus that emerged in the enforcement of the law was untried and untested. Once the law was enacted, a diverse array of cases started flowing through the new processes. Different sections of the law were tested for the first time, and many flaws were uncovered of the new insolvency resolution mechanisms. The IBC represented a major realignment of the power structure between borrowers, lenders, managers of firms and shareholders. While it represented a *predictable* allocation of losses from business failure, there were inevitably those who lost from the reform, and who were incentivised to be critical of the law. But there were also others who benefited from the reform and who were incentivised to champion the law. When all these elements came together with the operationalisation of

S. Thomas (✉)
Jindal Global Business School, and Senior Research Fellow at XKDR Forum, Bombay, India
e-mail: sthomas.entp@gmail.com

© The Author(s), under exclusive license to Springer Nature Singapore Pte Ltd. 2022

S. Thomas (ed.), *Insolvency and Bankruptcy Reforms in India*,
India Studies in Business and Economics,
https://doi.org/10.1007/978-981-16-0854-4_1

the IBC, it generated a great deal of debate, and intellectual engagement, from the diverse participants of the Indian bankruptcy ecosystem.

This book represents some of that intellectual debate and discussion during the early years of the IBC. The chapters in this book reflect the thought process of researchers and thought leaders who were part of the design as well as the drafting of the law and were involved in the early years as practitioners and as policy thinkers.

Special forms of forbearance for resolving insolvency were temporarily brought into place during the pandemic of 2020. Once these were moved out of the way, India would get back to the main question of how firm and individual insolvency should be dealt with. This book represents a contribution towards that debate.

1 The Questions Addressed by the Chapters of This Book

Chapter 2 describes some of the most visible cases which occupied the headlines immediately after the IBC was enacted. This chapter, "The RBI–12 cases under the IBC", by Josh Felman, Varun Marwah and Anjali Sharma, looks at the journey of 12 large cases chosen by the RBI to be filed under the new law.

This was a unique situation for insolvency resolution for several reasons. The first reason was that it was the banking regulator, and not the lender, which selected the cases to be put into insolvency resolution. The second reason was that the magnitude of these insolvencies were large by the size of the debt under dispute. The claims admitted in each of these cases were one or two orders of magnitude higher than the other cases filed under the law. Put together, the amount to be resolved was nearly a quarter of the existing non-performing assets of the banking system. Finally, all the 12 cases began their IBC journey on the same date. For the newly operationalised IBC and its infant institutions, the cumulative entry of 12 large, long-distressed firms was a large shock, and one that merits careful analysis.

The authors study the progress of these 12 insolvencies, and show us how the fledgling insolvency system responded when faced with unprecedentedly large and complex cases. They find that this presents a cautionary lesson for policymakers about 'premature load-bearing' when developing new legal frameworks. As the authors point out, premature load-bearing when juxtaposed with weak institutions can generate an 'organisational rout'. Another key insight from this chapter concerns the ways in which the limitations of banking regulation have hampered the bankruptcy reform.

Chapter 3, which is titled "Real estate insolvencies and the status of home buyers", is authored by Gausia Shaikh and Anjali Sharma, who take a closer look at the insolvency of real-estate developers. Unlike in the case of dealing with advances against future delivery of goods and services when the business goes into distress, there is no standard way of dealing with advances made for the delivery of homes when the developer becomes insolvent before the homes are delivered.

This becomes more complicated when the customers involved are treated as 'consumers' because they have entered into a transaction to purchase a house. If there are a large number of home-buyers who are viewed as having paid a large proportion of their lifetime savings towards such advances, it introduces a political economy dimension over and above the financial and business aspects of the insolvency. The authors show how such issues have influenced the behaviour of various participants in the IBC process, to the extent of triggering changes in the nascent law itself.

Both these early chapters highlight the importance of the 'invisible infrastructure' surrounding the reform of interest (in this case, the bankruptcy reform), that shapes and limits the possibilities of a reform. One such institution is the National Companies Law Tribunal or NCLT. The NCLT is the adjudicating authority under the IBC, and is one of the structural pillars on which the operationalisation of the law rests. Aditi Nayak and Prasanth Regy examine the performance of the NCLT in Chap. 4 titled "Performance of Company Law Tribunals in India".

From the start, there were concerns about how the relatively young NCLT would manage the workload of both the IBC and the Companies Act. In their analysis, the authors find that the NCLT had significant delays in dealing with its workload. This is very similar to the other parts of the legal system in India, despite the lack of historical backlog of cases at the NCLT. Traditionally, the solution proposed has been to increase the strength of the judicial bench.

The authors suggest that while the addition of judicial members may help to reduce delays at the NCLT, there could be more immediate efficiency gains in reducing delays from process-related problems, such as delays arising from wasteful hearings at the tribunals. They suggest that support for the judicial members must be improved through higher quality and better trained support staff.

Another proposal that they make concerns better information technology (IT) systems. There has been a continuing effort in India to improve the technology systems available at courts. What has been missing is the human resource element in integrating such systems structurally into the judicial process. This seems to suggest that there is need to first carry out a deeper examination of the prevailing judicial culture, in order to understand how to best effect change in performance through these various solutions.

Another piece of institutional preconditions for the success of the bankruptcy reform lies in the systems for information access during insolvency resolution. Such systems serve to capture, record and readily access information related to the firm and its insolvency. The IBC makes the collection and dissemination of this information the statutory responsibility of the Insolvency and Bankruptcy Board of India or IBBI, which is the regulator under the new law. In Chap. 5, which is titled "A maximalist approach to data under IBC", Adam Feibelman and Renuka Sane point out that the IBBI is likely the first regulator in India which has been created with an explicit responsibility regarding the development of information systems.

Given the lack of precedence of such a task within India, it is difficult to examine how well the required information systems have been developed and deployed under the IBC. Instead, the authors present an analogy of bankruptcy data systems that have been developed in the U.S. This includes a narrative on how these systems are used to give comfort and confidence to participants about the insolvency process. It also helps to measure the changes that has been brought about by the new law, both in terms of financial outcomes, and in terms of economic outcomes more broadly. The authors propose a framework within which to create an insolvency and bankruptcy data-set for India. They describe the types of data that the system can generate, the challenges in gathering and disseminating such data, and the comparative advantages that the IBBI and the tribunals of the NCLT have, in doing so.

When a new law is operationalised, it often triggers behavioural changes among those that it applies to. In the case of the IBC, this includes the behaviour of the various creditors in the economy, particularly the formal financial creditors such as banks and non-banking finance firms, and the debtors. It is well acknowledged that an effective law for insolvency and bankruptcy resolution nudges creditors and debtors to arrive at a consensus on how to resolve impending or existing financial stress, without taking recourse to legal processes.

Whether the IBC allows creditors and a financially stressed debtor to reach an out-of-court resolution that can then be sanctified by the law has been one of the most lively discussions in this area. One process through which an out-of-court settlement is done is referred to as a 'Prepack'. In Chap. 6 which is titled "Prepacks under the IBC: a tussle between speed and fair process", Aparna Ravi asks how feasible the prepack is in India within the IBC as a statute. The author examines the provisions of the IBC and finds that prepacks are possible under the law as it was originally passed.

The analysis finds, however, that prepacks under the IBC can only be conducted over a long time horizon, because of time requirements at various stages of the resolution process as prescribed by the law. The author also finds that subsequent amendments to the law, that were independently implemented to solve resolution bottlenecks in specific cases (within the set of the RBI-12 cases discussed earlier), made it harder to enable a prepack under the IBC. This serves as a sombre reminder that amendments related to some actions and functions of the law are likely to have unintended consequences for other actions under the law. Thus, amendments to a provision in the law need to be done while taking into consideration all other provisions in the law.

The need for a holistic appraisal of amendments is particularly important given the broad mandate of the IBC. This is a single legal framework for the resolution of insolvency for all persons in India, even though only the sections related to the insolvency of corporate entities have been operationalised. The part that deals with the insolvency of individuals are yet to be notified.[1] The flow of the IBC processes for individual insolvency resolution runs parallel to that for corporate insolvency resolution.

Renuka Sane points out, in Chap. 7 titled "The way forward for personal insolvency", that the domain and the scope of a resolution framework for individual insolvency are very different from corporate insolvency. The author points out that these differences will emerge in the design of the specific rules and regulations which

[1] This holds for all sections of the individual insolvency provisions, other than those related to the sections on individuals as personal guarantors to corporate debt. Sections related to corporate guarantors were notified and operationalised by the first quarter of 2020.

will be part of the operationalisation of the individual insolvency provisions of the IBC. More importantly, for the law to be used at the scale that is required by the rapidly growing base of individual borrowing in India, the institutions of the adjudicating authority, the information utilities, and the insolvency practitioners need to be strengthened and made robust at a different scale and has been pace than done for corporate insolvency resolution ecosystem.

The chapters thus far focused on examining the law and various aspects of the issues that arose as it was operationalised. From a careful reading of these chapters, it becomes apparent that an assessment of how the IBC has performed in these early years would conclude that it did not work well, either for a rapid resolution of financial distress of the borrowing firms, or for good recovery for lenders.

In Chap. 8 titled "Value destruction and wealth transfer under the Insolvency and Bankruptcy Code, 2016", Pratik Datta uses concepts from legal and economic theory on insolvency, to study the impact of the provisions of the IBC on the likely trade-offs that creditors, and debtors, will consider under the law. The author presents the challenge of designing a law that can differentiate between insolvent firms with a viable business, and those where the business model is fundamentally nonviable. Without this feature, the legal framework for insolvency resolution could result in economic value destruction.

Another challenge for the law is to ensure that there is no discrimination between different types of creditors in insolvency resolution. The presence of discrimination is seen as a source of wealth transfer. When the IBC is evaluated from the perspective of how well it solves these challenges, the author finds that there are issues which can improve the law from the perspective of resolving these problems. Outside of amending the law, the crux of resolving these issues lies in building robust valuation of insolvent firms, both as a going concern and in liquidation.

2 Looking Ahead

As the IBC matures, and the ecosystem that has developed around it reaches a steady state stage of behaviour and activity, there are three more aspects that the alert reader can glean from the various chapters of this book.

The outlook for recovery rates The recovery rate obtained in the first wave of cases at the IBC was relatively poor. This is generally seen as reflecting (a) Gaps in the law and (b) Limitations of the institutions that evolved during its implementation. However, there is a third and important reason which shaped these outcomes also. When the IBC was enacted, there was a substantial stock of *aged* distressed firms, where the default had taken place well before the date that the case was filed under the IBC. For instance, the insolvency filings in first quarter of 2017 were cases that had been mandatorily transferred from the erstwhile Board of Industrial and Financial Reconstruction and the Debt Recovery Tribunals. These were firms that have been derelict and defunct for many years, for which no recovery is viable. It is often said that a defaulted firm is akin to a melting ice cube. The long delays, which had elapsed after default, had led to value destruction. The low recovery rates in the early years of IBC also reflect the domination of these difficult cases in the case load.

In steady state, the IBC will receive cases of fresh default; e.g. there may be a delay of as little as a few days between the date of default and the date of IBC filing. The true performance of the IBC will only be revealed when recovery rates for *these* (fresh default) cases is seen.

Changes in creditor and debtor behaviour under the IBC In any country, only a small fraction of defaults actually show up at the bankruptcy court. For a lender or a borrower, every formal bankruptcy process involves rigidity of process and costs of lawyers. Hence, in every country, bankruptcy filings are avoided as much as possible, and the desired path is a private negotiation under the shadow of the bankruptcy laws and courts.

By this reasoning, many cases are being negotiated outside of the bankruptcy court, under the shadow of the IBC. Through this, the institutional reform is generating an economic impact that runs beyond the narrow measurement of the recovery rate.

When the bankruptcy process is evolving, there is a greater chance that a borrower or lender will end up making errors of judgement about what the bankruptcy process will do. This will lead to a higher probability of mistakes in the negotiation, leading to a higher probability of going to the bankruptcy court. Over time, as expectations about the IBC become more realistic, these asymmetries of perception will decline, and more cases will be resolved through negotiation.

The behaviour of large financial lenders such as banks—i.e. behaviour in renegotiation—are influenced by financial regulation. Many elements of financial regulation in India have flaws, which induce inefficient behaviour by lenders. Certain lenders are also shaped by the threat of the agencies. The combination of regulators and agencies are an important force that serves to increase the probability of bankruptcy process instead of negotiation, and of faulty behaviour by a lender regarding the use of the IBC.

These elements emphasise that a narrow bankruptcy reform can only deliver limited gains. The full gains from the IBC will emerge from the transformation of financial laws which change the working of financial regulators, and from similar ambitious reforms of the agencies.

The research community and the policy process The path to improved policy frameworks lies in an analytical research discourse that engages in a process of debate, where many kinds of criticism are in the public sphere and a consensus develops, which guides the future steps in reform.

A key ingredient in this is an active policy community, which includes academic researchers, policymakers and practitioners. This community should be able to build and analyse data-sets with equal access, be able to measure the maladies, and evolve hypotheses concerning root cause analysis. These communities do not emerge easily; building and nurturing them is a long-term process. But it is the capabilities of this community, and the quality of discourse, that will enhance the quality of the Indian bankruptcy reform.

References

Bankruptcy Law Reforms Committee (2015) The report of the Bankruptcy law reforms committee volume I: rationale and design. Technical Report, Ministry of Finance. http://ibbi.gov.in/BLRCReportVol1_04112015.pdf

Ramann S, Sane R, Thomas S (2015) Reforming personal insolvency law in India. http://www.igidr.ac.in/pdf/publication/WP-2015-035.pdf, url date = 2020-06-28

Sengupta R, Sharma A, Thomas S (2017) Evolution of the insolvency framework for non-financial firms in India. India Development Report

An Early Examination of the RBI–12 Cases Under the IBC

Josh Felman, Varun Marwah, and Anjali Sharma

1 Introduction

India undertook a fundamental reform of its insolvency regime when it passed the Insolvency and Bankruptcy Code (IBC) in May 2016. This reform was carried out in the backdrop of a large and growing problem of Non-Performing Assets (NPAs) in the banking sector. While improving the *ease of doing business* was the primary motivation in the early days of the reform process, since its operationalisation, policy and popular discourse have been viewing the IBC as the main strategy for resolving the banking sector NPA problem.

In May 2017, less than six months after the corporate insolvency provisions of the IBC became operational, the Government of India, amended the *Banking Regulation Act, 1949*, to give the RBI the power to *direct banks* to initiate IBC proceedings against firms that had defaulted on bank loans. The RBI used this power to identify 12 large firms, which accounted for approximately 25% of the banking system NPAs,[1] for referral to the IBC. In July and August 2017, banks filed IBC petitions against these firms in the insolvency court, the National Company Law Tribunal (NCLT). In all

[1] NPAs identified at that time. The lack of suitable recognition of NPAs has been a concern in Indian banking.

The opinions expressed in this chapter are the authors' own and not that of their employers.

J. Felman (✉)
J.H. Consulting, Pune, India
e-mail: joshfelman@gmail.com

V. Marwah
Associate at Shardul Amarchand Mangaldas & Co., Delhi, India

A. Sharma
Public Policy Researcher and An Industry Expert, Mumbai, India

© The Author(s), under exclusive license to Springer Nature Singapore Pte Ltd. 2022
S. Thomas (ed.), *Insolvency and Bankruptcy Reforms in India*,
India Studies in Business and Economics,
https://doi.org/10.1007/978-981-16-0854-4_2

of the 12 cases, these petitions were admitted and Corporate Insolvency Resolution Process (CIRP) began.

These 12 cases, often referred to in popular discourse as the RBI-12, were significantly more complex than the cases that had been coming to IBC till then, or compared to the cases that came subsequently. By the design of the RBI identification process, these were the largest NPA accounts of the banking system, identified as being in stress from as far back as 2013–2014, and for which, prior resolution efforts had not yielded any positive outcomes.

The IBC was a recently implemented law whose design was a structural shift from existing bankruptcy and debt recovery mechanisms. This structural shift was a deliberate policy choice, since it was widely accepted that the pre-IBC framework had failed to deliver on outcomes. From a policy perspective, bringing the largest, most complex stressed accounts of the banking system to the IBC was a risky strategy. These cases were encumbered with the issues and challenges of the earlier regimes, and it wasn't clear whether the new law, with its nascent jurisprudence and its fledgling institutional set-up, would be able to deal with these cases in the manner that the IBC envisaged. There was a possibility that fundamental elements of IBC design would get eroded under the burden of these cases.

There were also risks from the perspective of the RBI-12. The IBC design created a sequential choice between insolvency resolution and liquidation. If a company could not be resolved, it would get liquidated. The CIRP was the process for determining this choice, and its outcome depended on many factors that were not in control of the company or its creditors. For instance, there may not be any resolution applicants interested in submitting resolution plans. Or even if there were resolution plans, the Committee of Creditors (CoC) as a group could not get the requisite threshold of votes to agree on one plan.

These challenges were exacerbated by the fact that many of the procedures under the IBC, for submission and evaluation of resolution plans, for voting by CoC and so on were evolving as the resolution process was going on. It was as though the detailed rules of the game were being made up as the game was being played.

The strategy of bringing the RBI-12 to the IBC has led to what can best be described in the policy literature as 'premature load-bearing'.[2] From the perspective of reform and capacity building premature load-bearing can cause the limited capability that has been created to collapse. In turn, this can place in jeopardy, future capability creation both in terms of nature and scope.

The coming of these cases to IBC has had one significant positive impact. It has brought sharp focus on two elements critical to the insolvency reform agenda. The need to build the institutional infrastructure for the IBC, and the need to align key elements of financial sector policy and business policy with the IBC. Elements such as (1) state capacity to distinguish business failure from fraud, (2) the incentive problems of public sector banks (PSBs), (3) robustness of banking regulation and (4) an enabling environment for non-bank finance, including for stressed assets finance and other such reforms are critical to the success of insolvency reform. A commitment

[2] See Pritchett et al. (2010) and Pritchett and de Weijer (2010).

to a long term, coordinated reform agenda, along with a reform road map are required from the government, its agencies and the gamut of regulators. On the face of it, these agencies have shown great alacrity in resolving the various road blocks the IBC has run into. But their responses to fit an immediate requirement may lead to deviations from the key design principles of the law over the medium to long term.

In this chapter, we undertake the ambitious task of documenting how the RBI-12 have progressed under the IBC, as well as the manner in which the IBC ecosystem has evolved in response to these cases. This task is made specially challenging by the fact that for most of the 12 cases, even after a year of having been admitted to IBC, the resolution process is still underway. Almost on a daily basis, there are critical developments that continue to take place. This makes this exercise a work in progress, which can only conclude when these cases complete their insolvency resolution process with finality.

The chapter is divided into five sections. In Sect. 2 we set out the context of the IBC reform process, and highlight the key design features of the IBC. This is subsequently used as a reference point to evaluate how the RBI-12 have progressed under the IBC. Section 3 documents details of these 12 firms and compares them with other firms in IBC. Section 4 describes the progress of the RBI-12 under the IBC, with specific focus on whether these cases have adhered to the key design elements of the new law, and how the IBC ecosystem has evolved in response to these 12 cases. Section 5 discusses the success of the IBC in dealing with banking sector NPAs and the recent developments in this regard. It concludes with some thinking on the way forward for the IBC.

2 The Evolution of Insolvency Reform in India

A coherent and effective legal and institutional framework for resolving insolvency has been a missing piece in the Indian economic landscape for several decades. At the start, there were two legal mechanisms for collective action by creditors, winding up under *Companies Act, 1956* and rehabilitation under *Sick Industrial Companies Act, 1985* (SICA). Both suffered from delays and low recovery rates.[3] Over time, the use of these mechanisms declined, with fewer than 300 to 400 new cases being filed each year. In 2014, *World Bank Doing Business Report, 2014* ranked India 121 amongst 189 countries on the *Resolving Insolvency* parameter, with a recovery rate of 25.6 cents to the dollar and more than four years to recovery.

In the absence of functioning collective action laws, debt recovery laws such as *Recovery of Debts due to Banks and Financial Institutions Act, 1993* (RDDBFI Act) and *Securitisation and Reconstruction of Financial Assets and Enforcement of Security Interest Act, 2002* (SARFAESI), which worked at the level of individual

[3] Sengupta et al. (2017) find that winding-up proceedings took anywhere from 4 to 15 years to get completed, while SICA became a refuge for defaulting companies seeking to escape recovery action from creditors.

creditors and individual credit contracts, became the mainstay of creditors' rights. However, these laws were accessible only to a specific class of creditors, banks and some Financial Institutions (FIs). Other creditors only had access to the over-burdened civil court system for recovery. Even so, RDDBFI Act and SARFAESI had low recovery rates, in the range of 13–20% for several years.

Given the poor state of debt recovery, the RBI set up schemes for multi-creditor action such as Corporate Debt Restructuring (CDR) and Strategic Debt Restructuring (SDR) for banks to collectively take action on loan accounts of stressed firms. Schemes such as CDR found momentum when the RBI provided regulatory forbearance in the form of lower loan loss provisioning requirements to accounts restructured under the scheme.[4] However, these schemes did little to structurally address the problem of stress in firms that had received these loans from banks.

India suffered from what the *Economic Survey (2015–2016)*, describes as the *chakravyuha* challenge for the economy:

> Over the course of six decades, the Indian economy moved from 'socialism with limited entry' to 'marketism without exit.

Firms in India had no credible, functioning mechanism through which to resolve their stress. In 2011, the Indian economy entered into a phase of business cycle recession.[5] The banking sector witnessed increased stress, mainly on account of corporate loan NPAs.[6] These NPAs were high relative to the lending portfolio of banks and relative to their risk capital.[7] In 2013, a Credit Suisse report found that 10 of the largest Indian corporate houses, which accounted for 13% of the total system debt, were stressed.[8] In 2016, Credit Suisse estimated that Rs. 13,40,000 crore or 39% of the system debt was in stressed firms. For banks that had lent to these firms, corporate stress manifested as bank stress. In 2016, stressed advances[9] of banks were nearly 11% of their total advances.

---

[4] RBI/2008–2009/143 DBOD.No.BP.BC.No.37 /21.04.132/2008–2009; Prudential Guidelines on Restructuring of Advances by Banks, August 27, 2008. These guidelines specified that restructured assets would attract a lower provisioning requirement.

[5] Pandey et al. (2017) find a slowdown in both domestic demand and global demand for Indian exports from mid-2011 to 2012.

[6] In two reports, Reserve Bank of India (2013, 2016), the banking sector regulator (RBI) expresses concern about the health of sectors such as Iron & Steel, Textile, Infrastructure, Power generation and Telecommunications. Lindner and Jung (2014) find that corporate stress can explain a large part of India's banking NPAs. They also find that growing corporate stress, would exacerbate NPAs, could weaken India's banks, most notably at a time when they have to increase capital levels under BASEL III.

[7] Sengupta and Vardhan (2017) refer to this period as the second banking crisis, which is ongoing. The first banking crisis in their analysis is the 1997–2002 period. In this period too, the Indian banking system was weighed down by high levels of NPAs.

[8] Gupta et al. (2013). Here, stress was defined by debt servicing pressures and declining interest cover ratios.

[9] Stressed advances are the sum of gross NPAs and their restructured standard advances. Restructured advances are those that have gone through some restructuring but have not been recognised as NPAs. Restructured advances are included in stressed advances because slippages from restructured advances to NPAs are significant.

Table 1 Coverage and performance of creditors rights mechanisms in India

Mechanisms	Coverage	Recovery rate (%)	Avg. time (Years)	Case load (New case flow)	Cases outstanding
Collective action laws					
Winding up (CA, 1956)	Firms incorporated under the Companies Act	25.6[a]	4 to 15	353[b]	5,079[c]
Rescue (SICA)	Industrial firms that are sick[d]	–	5.1	62[e]	487[f]
Debt recovery laws					
DRT (RDDBFI)	Loans of Rs. 1 mn or more given by banks and specified FIs	13.6[g]	2 to 3	25,147[h]	95,537
SARFAESI	Secured loans of Rs. 1 lakh or more given by banks and NHB approved HFCs	13.2[i]	–	143,000[j]	–
Regulatory mechanisms					
CDR	Loans by CDR forum members, mainly domestic banks and NBFCs	–	4 to 8	44[k]	209[l]

Source MCA, RBI, DRT, BIFR, World Bank, CDR Cell
Recovery rate, Avg. time, Case load: is calculated as the average of 3 years.
Cases outstanding for the last period for which data is available
[a]Recovery rates according to the World Bank Doing Business survey 2015
[b]Average volume of new cases in FY 2013–2014 and FY 2014–2015
[d]The terms ‘industrial company’ and ‘sick’ specified in *SICA, 1985*
[e]Average volume of new cases coming to BIFR in 2012, 2013, 2014
[f]Pendency as of December, 2014
[g], [h]Average recovery rate during 2014–2017
[i], [j]Average volume of new cases during 2014–2017
[k]Average volume of new cases during 2011–2013
[l]Pendency as at 2013 end

The period from 2013 to 2018 witnessed two distinct phases in the policy strategy for dealing with this stress: rescheduling (*Phase 1*) and legal strategy (*Phase 2*).

Phase 1: Rescheduling Until 2015, the government and the RBI’s solution to banking sectors’ increasing NPAs was to deploy a series of RBI sponsored out-of-court restructuring programs. The 5/25 scheme, the CDR and the SDR were all part of this strategy. Most of these schemes involved banks giving relief to corporate borrowers by changing the terms of their bank debt, typically by increasing the tenure of loans or by giving relief on interest rates. In effect, the policy approach was to reschedule or push the problem to a future date in the hope that corporate stress would resolve itself over a period of time.[10]

There were two reasons for the adoption of this strategy. The first was that the legal system for corporate insolvency resolution and debt recovery was broken (Table 1). It was believed that lenders were likely to achieve better outcomes by negotiating with defaulting corporate borrowers on a restructuring platform, than by taking them to court. The second was the lack of capital made available to PSBs from the government, which was the dominant owner of the banking sector. For example, under the *Indradhanush plan* of 2015, the government committed Rs. 70,000 crore of capital and required PSBs to raise Rs. 1,10,000 crore from the market. This was far short of what the PSBs needed to deal with the stress in their balance sheets (Sengupta and Sharma 2017a). Given the limitations on capital, and the surge in NPAs post-2015, PSBs had little choice but to reschedule their stressed corporate loans, in a manner that made their balance sheets appear healthy. The RBI sponsored schemes enabled this *extend and pretend mechanism* by giving regulatory forbearance in the form of lower loan loss provisions to loans restructured under these schemes.

The rescheduling strategy temporarily postponed the recognition of the full scale of the NPA problem for banks, but in the process exacerbated the problem of underlying corporate stress by delaying resolution.[11] By 2015–2016, when the use of this strategy waned, around Rs. 15,00,000 crore of corporate debt was stressed without resolution.[12]

Phase 2: the legal strategy By April 2015, RBI withdrew the regulatory forbearance on restructured assets. In July, 2015, it initiated an Asset Quality Review (AQR), a move that forced banks to recognise their NPAs and make suitable provisions for them. As a result of the AQR, many corporate loans that banks had previously categorised as restructured loans moved to the NPA category. The stress in banks' books continued to rise and by April 2017, RBI had placed 11 of the 21 PSBs under its Prompt Corrective Action (PCA) framework (Reserve Bank of India 2017c).

In January 2017, the IBC provisions for corporate insolvency resolution became operational and a *legal strategy* for resolving corporate stress became available. However, the IBC was a fledgling law accompanied by a nascent institutional machinery. It was unclear whether this new law could handle the burgeoning problem of corporate stress that had built up over time. This was not the first

---

[10] Sengupta and Vardhan (2017) find that while this strategy had worked during the 1997–2002 banking crisis, it is unlikely to work in the current banking crisis, given the scale of corporate sector stress, and the economic conditions accompanying it.

[11] Ahamed and Mallick (2017) found that schemes such as CDR helped banks while Jain et al. (2016) found that firms that went through CDR did not perform well subsequently relative to firms that did not go through CDR.

[12] Authors' calculation using data from the CMIE Prowess database showed that 1,850 firms with debt of Rs. 14,70,000 crore did not have the cash-flows to sustain even interest payments on their debts in both FY 14–15 and FY 15–16.

instance when India had deployed a legal strategy to deal with corporate stress. There had been three previous efforts:

1. *SICA, 1985*, which created the Board for Industrial and Financial Reconstruction to rehabilitate eligible firms, within particular sectors,
2. *RDDBFIA, 1993*, which created the Debt Recovery Tribunals to enable banks to recover their debts that were greater than Rs. 0.1 crore and
3. *SARFAESI, 2002*, which created a recovery procedure that allowed banks to seize collateral to recover secured loan dues, without prior approval of courts.

In each of these instances, the legal strategy failed to deliver results for several reasons (Sengupta et al. 2017).[13] First, the implementation infrastructure did not keep pace with the case load, creating procedural delays (Regy and Roy 2017). Second, litigation and judicial interpretation of key provisions of these laws eroded many of their core features (van Zweiten 2012). Finally, there was little clarity on the interface of these laws with other laws of the country. Conflicting judgments by different courts created inconsistent case laws, and incentives for 'forum shopping' (Ravi 2015).[14]

But despite the poor experiences with prior legal strategies and despite the fact that the IBC was a new untested law, policy and public discourse actively projected the IBC as the primary tool for resolution of distressed corporate debt, and consequently the NPAs of the banking system (Kundu 2016; Mehta 2016).

Phase 3: IBC Genesis The IBC was a comprehensive legal framework for insolvency resolution of non-financial firms.[15] Besides being a structural reform, it was also one that was executed at an extraordinary pace. The deliberations of the Bankruptcy Law Reforms Committee, the expert committee that designed and proposed the IBC, started in March 2015 and by December 2016 India had a functional insolvency law for non-financial firms. The entire process, from start to finish, was completed in around 20 months, a considerable feat given that it included:

- Designing and drafting the IBC, a procedural law with 255 sections in its final form.
- Enacting the law in Parliament.

[13] Desired results of deploying a legal strategy for resolution or recovery are (1) improved recovery rates, (2) lowering of time to resolution/recovery and (3) procedural certainty with respect to resolution/recovery.

[14] Forum shopping is where multiple legal and judicial fora exist and every party uses the one that is aligned to its objective. For instance, in the same case a company may prefer to use *SICA, 1985* whereas banks may prefer to use *SARFAESI, 2002*.

[15] Section 2 of the IBC lays down its applicability. Sections 3(7) and 3(8) together limit the scope of this law to corporate debtors who are not financial service providers. Section 3(17) defines the scope of inclusion of financial service providers.

Table 2 Comparing insolvency reform process timelines across countries

Country	Committee process		Law enactment
	Committee formed	Report submission	
India	BLRC—March, 2015[a]	Volume 1 and Volume 2 of the BLRC Report—November, 2015	IBC May, 2016
UK	Cork Committee on Insolvency Law Review—1977	Report of the Committee on Insolvency Law and Practice—1979	Insolvency Act, 1986
Singapore	Insolvency Law Review Committee—2010	Report of the Insolvency Law Review Committee—2013	Companies (Amendment) Act, 2017

[a]The BLRC was constituted in November, 2014. Its initial mandate was to suggest amendments to the insolvency and bankruptcy provisions under the Companies Act, 2013. It was tasked with designing a single, comprehensive insolvency resolution law for all entities and individuals in March 2015

- Creating the infrastructure for its implementation,[16]
- Operationalising the law.

This pace is extraordinary when compared to similar structural reforms of the corporate insolvency regime in other countries. In the UK, the reform process which culminated in the enactment of the *UK Insolvency Act, 1986*, took nearly a decade to complete. Similarly, the reform process in Singapore started in 2010, and the change to the law made in 2017 (Table 2).

The rapid pace appears to have been driven by two factors. First, the government's focus on improving India's ranking in the *World Bank Ease of Doing Business Survey*, where on insolvency resolution, India's performance was far below peer countries (Table 3). The second factor was the burgeoning problem of banking NPAs, whose primary source was corporate stress. The IBC design and implementation process took place in the context of a growing policy acknowledgement that existing mechanisms were ineffective and that legal reform of the insolvency resolution system could be a tool for resolving corporate stress, and consequently bank stress.

3 The RBI-12 Cases Under the IBC

While the IBC was positioned as a legislative reform that would tackle the NPA problem of banks swiftly, few cases were filed by banks in its first six months (Table 4).

[16] The IBC is unique in proposing the design and structure of four institutions that are required for its functioning. These include: (1) the Insolvency and Bankruptcy Board of India (IBBI), the regulator, (2) the National Company Law Tribunal (NCLT), the adjudicating authority for corporate insolvency resolution, (3) Insolvency Professionals (IPs) and Insolvency Professional Agencies (IPAs) and (4) Information Utilities (IUs), credit data repositories.

Table 3 Resolving insolvency in the Doing Business project: a global comparison

	2014				2018			
	Rank[a]	Time (Years)	Recovery rate (Cents to $)	DTF[b] (%)	Rank	Time (Years)	Recovery rate (Cents to $)	DTF (%)
India	121	4.3	25.6	32.43	103	4.3	26.4	40.75
China	78	1.7	36	55.31	56	1.7	36.9	55.82
Korea, Rep.	15	1.5	82.3	88.02	5	1.5	84.7	89.33
Brazil	131	4	19.5	51.13	80	4	12.7	47.46
Russia	55	1.9	43.2	59.21	54	2	40.7	57.83
Singapore	4	0.8	89.7	74.82	27	0.8	88.7	74.31

Source World Bank Doing Business Project

[1]Rank as per the *World Bank Doing Business Report, 2014*. Not comparable to the rank in *World Bank Doing Business Report, 2014* due to a change in methodology. However, measures such as time and recovery rate are comparable. DTF has been reported as per the 2018 methodology and is hence comparable

[b]Distance to frontier score captures the gap between the economy's performance and the frontier, a measure of best practice. The frontier is the best performance on the indicator across all economies since 2005, or the third year in which data for the indicator were collected. For the resolving insolvency parameter in 2018 Norway is the frontier economy

Perhaps banks were waiting to see the initial performance of the new law or there was a lack of clarity amongst banks on the use of RBI specified regulatory schemes[17] versus the IBC. Alternatively, the incentives of banks may not have been aligned with the time bound resolution process offered by the IBC as it would accelerate their provisioning burden.

Whatever may have been the reason, the government felt the need to solve this problem by amending the *Banking Regulation Act, 1949*.[18] Through this amendment the government authorised the RBI to issue directions to banks to refer cases to IBC. A speech made by the RBI Governor on 9th August, 2017 clarified the motivation behind the Ordinance:

> The size and nature of the NPA problem necessitated concomitant measures to signal intent and commitment of the Government and the Reserve Bank to meet the challenge squarely. The IBC was in place but the required action in respect of the large stressed accounts was not forthcoming on the part of banks and JLFs. Part of the inertia may have to do with the initial days of the IBC; but part of it was also the typical (and severe) agency and moral hazard problems of not resolving NPAs when the banking sector is majorly government-owned.

On 22 May, 2017, through a press release RBI announced the constitution of an Internal Advisory Committee (IAC), comprising RBI Independent Board Members,

---

[17] Even in May 2017, the RBI was issuing notifications with details on the use of regulatory mechanisms such as the S4A and JLF (Reserve Bank of India 2017d).

[18] *Banking Regulation (Amendment) Ordinance, 2017* enacted on 4th May 2017.

Table 4 Cases admitted under the IBC: Jan-2017 to Dec-2017

Month	Total cases admitted	Filed by			RBI-12 admitted
		Debtor	Non-banks	Banks	
Jan-17	4	3	–	1	–
Feb-17	8	4	4	–	–
Mar-17	13	10	3	–	–
Apr-17	27	11	15	1	–
May-17	30	5	14	11	–
Jun-17	36	15	16	5	–
Jul-17	49	5	28	16	7
Aug-17	71	9	39	23	3
Sept-17	87	17	53	17	–
Oct-17	41	3	27	11	–
Nov-17	48	9	28	11	–
Dec-17	56	1	38	17	–
Total	470	92	265	113	10[a]

Source IBBI public announcement of CIRP
[a]Era Infra Engineering was admitted in May, 2018
[a]For Jaypee Infratech Limited, the CIRP started in August, 2017. Subsequently, it was restarted in August, 2018

to formulate the criteria for selecting cases to be referred to IBC.[19] Through another press release on 13 June, 2017,[20] RBI disclosed the selection criteria used by the IAC for identifying cases:

> The IAC also arrived at an objective, non-discretionary criterion for referring accounts for resolution under IBC. In particular, the IAC recommended for IBC reference all accounts with fund and non-fund based outstanding amount greater than Rs. 5000 crore, with 60% or more classified as non-performing by banks as of 31 March 2016. The IAC noted that under the recommended criterion, 12 accounts totaling about 25 per cent of the current gross NPAs of the banking system would qualify for immediate reference under IBC.

Using this criteria, 12 firms were identified and the RBI directed one of their PSB lenders to refer them to IBC. These cases came to be identified in popular discourse as the *RBI-12*. *Essar Steel*, one of the RBI-12 firms, challenged the constitutional validity of the 13 June, 2017 press release in the Gujarat High Court contending that RBI's selection of 12 cases was arbitrary and the selected firms had not been given a chance to be heard. With some critical remarks about the conduct of the RBI, the Gujarat High Court upheld the validity of the press release.[21] This cleared the way for the 12 cases to be admitted by the NCLT (Table 5). The early legal challenge to RBI's actions was instructive as a sign of things to come. The RBI-12 firms, while being

[19] Reserve Bank of India (2017b).

[20] Reserve Bank of India (2017a).

[21] *Essar Steel India Limited and Ors. versus Reserve Bank of India and Ors.*

the largest NPA accounts for banks, were also amongst the largest firms in India. The stakes involved in their insolvency resolution process were high for a range of stakeholders. For the promoters, the risk was of losing their firms. For all creditors, the risk was low recoveries but more specifically for PSBs the risk of their decisions in such large cases coming under the scrutiny of the three Cs—the CAG, CVC and CBI also existed. For employees, suppliers and a range of other stakeholders the risk was the possibility of a liquidation outcome. Many of these stakeholders, and even potential resolution applicants of these firms, had the capacity to litigate.

Tables 5 and 6 lay down information that helps us better understand the RBI-12 firms. These firms came from sectors such as metals, construction and textiles which had been in stress from 2013.[22] 70% of the total borrowings of the RBI-12 firms came from the six steel and metal sector firms. In 2016, The RBI had found this sector as having the highest stressed advances ratio (46.3%) amongst the various industrial sub-groups. Eight of these firms had been under the SDR scheme of the RBI, while three others had group firms that had been under SDR. One firm *Amtek Auto* had a reported case of bond default in 2015 (Economic Times 2015).

It is useful to compare the RBI-12 cases with other cases in IBC to put into context what the entry of these cases meant in terms of the pressures on the capacity of this ecosystem. Table 7 shows that the RBI-12 firms were very different from the other IBC firms in their size, indebtedness, and degree of stress.

- The median size of a RBI-12 firm was 38 times that of an non-RBI firm.
- The median debt (borrowing + current liabilities) of a RBI-12 firm was around Rs. 14,900 crore while that of non-RBI firm in IBC was Rs. 570 crore.
- RBI-12 firms' leverage was more than three times that of a non-RBI firm.
- 10 out of the 12 RBI-12 firms had positive operating profit but this was insufficient to cover their interest costs suggesting that much of their debt was unsustainable. For nearly half of the non-RBI firms, there were sustained operating losses suggesting business non-viability.
- Many of the RBI-12 firms were generating operating cash suggesting the ability to sustain themselves for a while during the insolvency process. Most of the non-RBI firms did not demonstrate this ability. A time bound process, hence, was more critical for the non-RBI firms than for the RBI-12 firms.

Table 8 presents the IBC outcomes for the non-RBI and the RBI-12 cases as of Quarter 3 (Q3) of 2018. It shows that liquidations have been the dominant outcome for non-RBI firms, with an average time of around 270 days to arrive at the outcome. It also shows that for nearly half of the non-RBI firms, an average time of 460 days has elapsed with no outcome in this period of time. Given that the RBI-12 insolvency

---

[22] The RBI in (Reserve Bank of India 2016) notes that

> Within the industrial sector, a few sub-sectors, namely; Iron & Steel, Textile, Infrastructure, Power generation and Telecommunications; have become a cause of concern in recent times. (Para 2.36)

Table 5 The RBI-12

Name	Industry	CIRP start	Prior restructuring
Bhushan power and steel	Steel	Jul-17	SDR
Bhushan steel	Steel	Jul-17	
Electrosteel steels	Steel	Jul-17	SDR
Essar steel	Steel	Aug-17	Group company Essar Projects in SDR
Jyoti structures	Metal products	Jul-17	SDR
Monnet Ispat and energy	Metal products	Jul-17	SDR
Era infra engineering	Construction	May-18	Winding up petitions pending in Delhi High Court
Jaypee infratech	Construction	Aug-17. Restarted Aug-18.	Parent company JAL, group company Jaiprakash Power in SDR
Lanco infratech	Construction	Aug-17	Group company Lanco Teesta in SDR
ABG Shipyard	Transport	Aug-17	SDR
Amtek auto	Auto ancillaries	Jul-17	Bond default, Sept-15
Alok industries	Diversified cotton textile	Jul-17	SDR

Source CMIE Prowess, IBBI, Credit Suisse India Corporate Health Tracker, 16 February 2017

cases had been in financial stress prior to their being admitted under the IBC, the time to outcome has been much longer. Five cases have had an outcome and the average time to outcome is far in excess of the prescribed timelines. The remaining seven cases have been continuing for more than 500 days as of the end of 2018. The recovery rates for RBI-12 and non-RBI cases also vary (Table 9) with the non-RBI cases seeing a far lower recovery rate than the RBI-12 firms.

4 Challenges that the RBI-12 Presented to IBC

Bringing the RBI-12 cases to IBC at such an early stage of its life-cycle appeared to be akin to asking *too much, too soon* of the law and its ecosystem. This is a well-discussed problem in the public policy literature where reforms that require significant capacity building are often subjected to *premature load bearing* (Pritchett et al. 2010; Pritchett and de Weijer 2010). In asking fragile ecosystems to move forward too quickly, even when it is desirable, there is a risk that the nascent capability of the system can collapse, even to the extent of jeopardising future capacity building. This literature

Table 6 The financial health of the RBI-12

Name	Borrowing (Rs. crore)	Bank Borrowing (% of Borr)	Debt/Equity (Times)	Operating profit (Rs. crore)	Interest Expense (Rs. crore)	$ICR < 1$ from	Incremental Provision[a] (Rs. crore)
ABG Shipyard	7,420	83	9.2	171	940	FY 14	2,459
Alok Industries	19,929	75	4.6	2,744	3,290	FY 16	5,999
Amtek Auto	7,602	46	1.7	704	805	FY 15	1,413
Bhushan power and steel	35,465	76	28.3	1,921	2,268	FY 15	10,735
Bhushan steel	43,405	68	10.5	2,481	3,480	FY 15	11,841
Electrosteel steels	10,226	75	10.9	57	614	FY 11	3,077
Era Infra Engg	7,412	66	6.1	–49	746	FY 14	1,946
Essar steel	34,112	69	14.5	1,738	4,787	FY 11	9,406
Jaypee Infratech	9,046	2	1.5	999	1,139	FY 16	80
Jyoti structures	2,900	96	18.9	180	383	FY 15	1,113
Lanco infratech	7,244	82	4.8	83	880	FY 14	2,376
Monnet Ispat	8,042	59	6.5	–26	743	FY 15	1,897
Total	1,92,805	68	12.6	11,000	20,074		52,342
Steel sector firms	1,34,151	71	16.2	6,351	12,274		38,069
Steel sector (as % of total)	70	73		58	61		73
Construction sector firms	23,702	46	3.4	1032	2,765		4,402
Construction sector (as % of total)	12	8		9	14		8

Source CMIE Prowess
All financial variables are reported as the average of the variable for the period FY 14 to FY 17
[a]Incremental provisions that banks may be required to make if the firm went into liquidation. The computation assumes that banks have made provisions for 60% of the bank advances to these firms, and once liquidation is ordered will have to make an additional provision for the remaining 40%. There may be subsequent write-backs on completion of the liquidation process, based on recoveries made

Table 7 RBI-12 versus other firms in IBC

		Non-RBI			RBI-12		
Variable	Unit	Median	25th P	75th P	Median	25th P	75th P
Size							
Size[a]	Rs. crore	259	114	1,074	9,956	6,451	25,250
Indebtedness							
Debt (Borr + CL)[b]	Rs. crore	567	157	1,618	14,896	13,249	37,793
Borr	Rs. crore	226	63	720	8,544	7,418	23,474
Bank Borr/Borr	%	79	56	91	70	64	77
CL	Rs. crore.	284	69	723	6,999	4,422	12,011
D/E	Times	2.4	1.5	4.8	7.9	4.7	11.8
Tangible assets							
NFA	Rs. crore	80	19	197	7,882	1,251	16,343
NFA/TA	(%)	25	9	46	52	13	56
Working capital							
NWC (CA - CL)[c]	Rs. crore	-33	-191	11	–2,942	–4,417	354
Curr ratio[d]	(Times)	0.8	0.4	1.2	0.5	0.3	1.0
Cash holding							
Cash	Rs. crore	6	1	20	133	107	181
Cash to Op exp[e]	Months	0.3	0.2	0.7	0.6	0.4	0.9
Profitability							
Op profit	Rs. crore	1	–15	18	442	76	1,784
Op profit/Sales	%	1.8	–18.1	6.9	13.7	3.8	21.2
PBT	Rs. crore	–21	–115	0	–1,046	–1,897	–729
PBT/Sales	%	–18.1	-61.1	0	–24.6	–39.9	–15.3
RoA	%	–7.2	–17.6	0	–5.1	–8.7	–4.1
Debt service							
Int exp/Sales	%	10.0	3.5	25.6	29.3	26.6	44.2
ICR[f]	Times	0.4	–0.5	1.4	0.6	0.2	0.8
Borr/Op profit	Times	9	5	18	18	12	38
(+ve firms[g])							

Source CMIE Prowess, IBBI. All financial variables are computed as the average of FY14 to FY17 data

[a]Size = $(Total\ assets + Sales)/2$

[b]Debt = $(Total\ borrowings + Current\ liabilities)$

[c]Net working capital = $(Current\ assets - Current\ liabilities)$. Negative NWC indicates that the firm requires working capital finance

[d]Current ratio = $(Current\ assets/Current\ liabilities)$. A ratio less than one indicates stress, as short-term assets are not adequate to cover short term liabilities

[e]Cash to Op. exp = $(Cash \times 12)/Opearting\ expense$. It tells us the number of months of operating expenses that cash balances will cover

[f]Interest cover ratio = $(PBDITA/Interest\ expense)$. A value less than 1 indicates stress

[g]$Borrowing/Operatingprofit$ is computed for the 76 non-RBI firms that have positive operating profit and the 10 RBI firms that have positive operating profit. It gives the number of years that it will take the firm to pay off its outstanding borrowings using its current operating profit, assuming no additional interest is charged

[h]Asset turnover = *Sales / Average total assets*

Table 8 Status of IBC cases admitted between Jan 2017 to Dec 2017, as of Q3, 2018

	Non-RBI (avg time (days))				RBI (avg time (days))			
Admission month	Cases admitted	Liquidation order[a]	Resolution plan[b]	Ongoing cases[c]	Cases admitted	Liquidation order	Resolution plan	Ongoing cases
Jan-17	4	2 (302)	1 (187)	1 (683)	–	–	–	–
Feb-17	8	6 (304)	1 (279)	1 (659)	–	–	–	–
Mar-17	13	9 (295)	2 (234)	2 (632)	–	–	–	–
Apr-17	27	15 (330)	5 (314)	7 (607)	–	–	–	–
May-17	30	17 (301)	5 (231)	8 (583)	–	–	–	–
Jun-17	36	18 (279)	2 (260)	16 (546)	–	–	–	–
Jul-17	42	17 (259)	4 (314)	21 (515)	7	–	4 (322)	3 (513)
Aug-17	68	24 (278)	12 (301)	32 (488)	3	1 (384)	–	2 (498)
Sept-17	87	27 (247)	7 (272)	53 (455)	–	–	–	–
Oct-17	41	21 (248)	2 (285)	18 (427)	–	–	–	–
Nov-17	48	14 (257)	1 (237)	33 (393)	–	–	–	–
Dec-17	56	19 (229)	2 (257)	35 (366)	–	–	–	–
Total	460	189 (270)	44 (279)	227 (459)	10	1 (384)	4 (322)	5 (507)

Source IBBI
[a]Liquidation status update as at 31 October 2018
[b]Resolution status update as on 30 September 2018, based on IBBI newsletters
[c]For cases where the process is ongoing the figure in brackets represents the time elapsed from date of admission till 15 December 2018

Table 9 Recovery rates in IBC

	Cases resolved (No.)	Claims admitted (Rs. crore)	Resolution Value (Rs. crore)	Recovery rate (%)
RBI-12	4	92,817	48,117	51.8
Non-RBI	42	28,232	8,455	29.9
Total	46	121,049	56,572	46.7

Source IBBI Newsletter Q1, Q2 and Q3 2018

differentiates organisational form from organisational functionality, pointing out that the former can be built much faster, creating the illusion of organisational capability. Organisational functionality, on the other hand, is harder to create and requires time and effort before it can be put to rigorous and sustained use.

The evidence presented in this chapter suggests that this may have been the case with the IBC ecosystem under the pressure of the RBI-12 cases. The organisational form of the new institutions that the IBC required—the regulator, the court, a cadre of intermediaries—had all been put in place in just six months, between May 2016 when the IBC was enacted and December 2017 when it was made operational. It is likely that these nascent organisational forms were not prepared for the nature and range of complexities that the RBI-12 cases would impose on them. In this review, we highlight a few of the larger pressures on this new ecosystem, and present some evidence on both the development of the RBI-12 cases as well as on the IBC.

4.1 Section 29A: The Dilemma of Promoter Involvement

Indian firms have traditionally retained the notion of the *promoter*. Promoters are typically the entrepreneurs who started the company, and at least in the public discourse, have the ultimate accountability for its performance and its liabilities. Soon after the RBI-12 cases came to IBC, public discourse turned to questioning whether promoters of insolvent firms should be allowed to re-gain control of their firms through the IBC process.

The IBC process visualised that equity holders would cede control of the company to creditors during the CIRP. Then, the *Committee of Creditors* (CoC) was given full powers to approve or reject resolution plans or bids that were received, including the power to reject any plans that promoters might submit. Despite this, policymakers felt the need to create an explicit exclusion for promoters in that prevented them from participating in the CIRP process, either directly or indirectly. The rationale for this was that promoters had let these firms become insolvent, and so should not be allowed to retain control while banks and other stakeholders suffered significant losses. State ownership of large parts of the banking system further complicated matters. It was felt that allowing promoters to retain control was akin to a *tax payer bail-out of crony capitalists*.

This led to the addition of Section 29A to the IBC.[23] Section 29A created wide ranging exclusions for promoters and any persons *connected* to them from the IBC process (Sengupta and Sharma 2017b). The definition of connected persons was so wide that even Asset Reconstruction Companies (ARCs) and Alternative Investment Funds (AIFs) that had invested in stressed loans appeared unlikely to qualify as resolution applicants.

Section 29A also created *threat of disqualification* as a tool to be deployed strategically to litigate or delay IBC proceedings. While its difficult to say whether Section 29A led to a reduction in the pool of possible applicants for firms in IBC, it can be said that it contributed to significant delays to the process.

The first round of delays came about because there was uncertainty about which cases this provision would apply to, new cases that were filed or cases where the resolution period had not been completed. In the interest of conservatism, participants in the various CIRPs relied on the latter interpretation. A host of litigation to determine the 29A eligibility of resolution applicants were started, and for the RBI-12 cases this began just when they were nearing their 180 day timeline. The legal question of 29A eligibility caused timelines in nearly all RBI-12 cases to be extended to the 270 day limit.

---

[23] Section 29A was inserted in the IBC through the *IBC (Ordinance), 2017* promulgated on 23 November 2017. Section 29A was introduced through the extraordinary tool of an Ordinance, instead of waiting for Parliament to convene and for it to be introduced as an amendment bill. The timing and the pace at which it was put into place suggest that Sect. 29A may have been triggered by reports that the promoters of *Essar Steel* with other investors had submitted a resolution plan for their company.

To clarify some of the ambiguity surrounding Section 29A, in early 2018, the Insolvency Law Committee (ILC) set up by the government proposed amending Section 29A to explicitly exclude from the disqualification of two categories of participants: (1) financial entities such as banks, AIFs and ARCs, and (2) resolution applicants that may have acquired firms through the IBC CIRP process. A third exemption from Section 29A was carved out by exerting a new provision, Section 240A. This provision allowed promoters of Micro, Small and Medium Enterprises (MSMEs) to submit resolution plans for their own firms. This was done so that MSMEs do not get liquidated solely because of lack of resolution interest.

But these amendments did not alleviate the implication of Section 29A on the RBI-12 cases or the other large cases in IBC. In the RBI-12 cases, resolution interest initially came mainly from promoters and from *strategic investors* with little or no resolution interest from pure play financial investors.[24] The following description of events in the case of *Essar Steel* is a useful illustration of this problem (Tables 10 and 11).

The resolution path of Essar Steel

The resolution of *Essar Steel* has been an unsettling precedent for the IBC.

Two resolution applicants (AreclorMittal and Numetal) litigated up to the Supreme Court to establish their eligibility as resolution applicants and to oppose the other's eligibility alongside. The Supreme Court found both to be ineligible under Section 29A, and offered both firms the opportunity to settle their existing dues as a way to become eligible applicants.

ArcelorMittal had previously deposited the amount due in an escrow account. However, Numetal's ineligibility was founded on the principle of *lifting the corporate veil* which revealed that the promoter of Essar Steel was part of the Numetal bid. For Numetal to become eligible, the promoter would have to pay off their dues to banks. If this was feasible the company may not have entered IBC at all. For these reasons, the CoC selected the ArcelorMittal resolution plan as the winning bid for *Essar Steel*. In response, the promoter family offered to repay the entire debt of *Essar Steel*. Under this situation, several operational creditors objected to the ArcelorMittal resolution plan since this plan did not cover all their dues unlike the plan offered by the promoter family or Numetal. This effectively created two sides in the resolution of *Essar Steel*: (1) the creditors whose dues were not accounted for in the winning ArcelorMittal resolution plan such as operational creditors and creditors such as Standard Chartered Bank, which claimed unequal treatment as a secured financial creditor, and (2) the CoC with the financial creditors who selected the ArcelorMittal resolution plan.

As a consequence of these actions, a range of complex legal issues have arisen from this case. Solutions for these have been offered by the court and by policymakers. But with many of these solutions being driven by narrow objectives without a deeper analysis of their impact on the broader IBC ecosystem, the solutions appear to have added to procedural uncertainty. Such uncertainty, in turn, leads to a dilution of the

[24] Strategic investors are firms in the same industry or business area who have a strategic business interest in the insolvent firm.

Table 10 Resolution plans received for the RBI-12

	Plans received	Resolution applicants
ABG Shipyard	1	Liberty House
Alok industries	1	Reliance Industries Ltd and JM Financial ARC combine
Amtek auto	2	(1) Liberty House Group, and (2) Deccan Value.
Bhushan power and steel	3	(1) Tata Steel, (2) JSW Living Pvt Ltd and (3) Liberty House submitted bid after deadline.
Bhushan steel	2	(1) Tata Steel and, (2) JSW Living Pvt Ltd.
Electrosteel Steels	4	(1) Renaissance Steel India Pvt Ltd, (2) Tata Steel, (3) Vedanta Ltd and (4) Edelweiss Alternative Asset Advisors Pte acting as the investment advisor of EISAF II and EC Holdings, with support of Edelweiss ARC.
Era Infra Engineering	1	Suraksha ARC.
Essar Steel	3	(1) Mauritius based Numetal, led by (Russian) VTB Bank, (2) ArcelorMittal India Pvt Ltd. and 3) Vedanta Ltd.
Jaypee infratech	3 (during first round)	(1) a consortium of Kotak Realty Fund and Cube Highways, (2) Adani Group and (3) Lakshadweep Pvt Ltd., a JV between Suraksha ARC and Dosti Realty.
Jaypee infratech	4 (during second round)	(1) NBCC, (2) a consortium of Kotak Investment, (3) Cube Highways, (4) Suraksha group
Jyoti structures	1	High networth individuals led by Sharad Sanghi, CEO of Netmagic.
Lanco infatech	1	Thriveni earthmovers
Monnet Ispat	1	AION-JSW consortium

Source based on company filings with stock exchanges and media reports

Table 11 Outcomes for RBI-12 cases under the IBC

	Outcome	Claims admitted (Rs. crore)	Resolution value (Rs. crore)	Recovery rate (%)	Implied haircut (%)
Amtek auto	Resolution	12,605	4,334	34.4	65.6
Bhushan steel	Resolution	56,022	35,571	63.5	36.5
Electrosteel steels	Resolution	13,175	5,320	40.4	59.6
Monnet Ispat	Resolution	11,015	2,892	76.0	24.0
Total	Resolution	92,817	48,117	51.8	48.2
Lanco infratech	Liquidation	53,158	–	–	–

Source IBBI

focus of the law on timely resolution and outcomes that are based on the collective commercial wisdom of creditors.

4.2 *Repeated Failure of Time Bound Resolution*

The IBC design had time bound resolution as a core objective. This objective has seen the most dilution over time, specially in the context of complex cases such as the RBI-12. We find this to be so in three instances where the IBC clearly provided a timeline:

1. Time to admit an insolvent case
   A 14-day timeline was prescribed by the IBC for admitting or dismissing CIRP applications. However, this has been diluted by the Supreme Court judgement that has held this time to be *directory not mandatory*.[25] In the RBI-12 cases, we see that this timeline was being consistently breached even before the Supreme Court order (Table 12).
2. Time to resolve insolvency
   Section 12(1) of the IBC prescribes a timeline of 180 days for completion of the insolvency resolution. Section 12(3) allows for this time to be extended by one instance of an additional 90 days, to allow a maximum period of 270 days for CIRP completion. However, the intent of the legislature was for this extension to be and exception rather than the rule.[26] Instead what we observe is that the 270 day

[25] *Surendra Trading Company vs. Juggilal Kamlapat Jute Mills Company Ltd. and Ors.*

[26] Section 12(3) of the IBC states:

> If the Adjudicating Authority is satisfied that the subject matter of the case is such that corporate insolvency resolution process cannot be completed within one hundred and eighty days, it may by order extend the duration of such process beyond one hundred and eighty days by such further period as it thinks fit, but not exceeding ninety days:

timeline has become the norm. In fact, the principle of adherence to prescribed timelines stands diluted in entirety, particularly in the RBI-12 cases, where even the 270 day limit has been exceeded. Our review suggests that the first instance of delays started around the introduction of Section 29A. At this time, many of the RBI-12 cases were approaching their 180 day timeline. Timeline extensions were granted to parties to context or determine 29A eligibility. In some cases, after Section 29A, the process for seeking resolution plans was conducted afresh. Table 12 presents the timelines in RBI-12 cases by the specific stages of the CIRP process. It shows that delays started to build up at the point at which the final list of resolution plans had to be submitted by the RP to the CoC (T_6 in the table). In most cases, the NCLT does not record the reasons for granting of the timeline extension.[27]

3. If no resolution, liquidation
The IBC processes require a company to move into liquidation if a resolution plan is not arrived at by the CoC and approved by the NCLT at the end of the 180 or 270 day period. This was meant to deter parties seeking to delay CIRP proceedings and to incentivise all stakeholders to meet the procedural timelines. However, it is evident that this is not the case. Table 12 shows that both for the RBI-12 and the non-RBI cases, the 270 days timeline did not hold as a marker for the start of liquidation proceedings. This has been aided by the NCLT order in the *Bhushan Power* case that has excluded time taken for litigation from the 180/270 day limit. The National Company Law Appellate Tribunal (NCLAT) upheld this principle as well.

A range of reasons have contributed to the delays in IBC. These include: (1) capacity constraints at NCLT to deal with the volume of case flow, (2) frequent changes to the law and to regulations which add to procedural uncertainty and create opportunities for litigation and for delays, (3) adoption of principles of criminal justice such as the *right to be heard* to IBC, which is fundamentally a commercial law. This is also manifested in the high rate of admittance of appeals against NCLT judgments, and (4) the tilting of the balance between value and timeliness firmly in favour of value maximisation. Courts and policymakers have, time and again, signalled that value maximisation has a higher policy priority than adherence to timelines.

Provided that any extension of the period of corporate insolvency resolution process under this section shall not be granted more than once.

.

[27] We have reviewed the orders of extension for 5 cases where they are available: *Electrosteel Steels*, *Amtek Auto*, *Monnet Ispat*, *Jyoti Structures* and *ABG shipyard*. None of these have a reason for the extension of the timeline for resolution.

4.3 Anti-liquidation Bias

While the BLRC envisaged liquidation as one of the possible outcomes of the insolvency resolution process, policymakers and the courts have clearly stated their bias *for resolution* and *against liquidation*. There have been several instances where the NCLT has pushed for a resolution outcome, even when the CoC had failed to gather the required vote in favour of a resolution plan. In the case of *Alok Industries*, the voting requirement of 75% was not obtained by the 270-day deadline and an application for liquidation was moved. Before the final liquidation could be passed, the *IBC (Ordinance), 2018* was promulgated and the voting threshold was lowered to 66%. In view of the lowered voting threshold, the NCLT called for a re-vote while recording that,

> ...in the interest of the company as well as its employees in view of main object of the IBC as also the very intent of legislature is for the revival of the company and its welfare.

This was a case where the company would have been liquidated, if adjudicated within the statutory timelines. Instead, the *IBC (Ordinance), 2018* was retrospectively applied to pull the company out of liquidation and into resolution. This retrospective application was challenged by a dissenting financial creditor at the NCLAT. In another instance, the CoC of *Lanco Infrastructure Limited* was granted time beyond 270 days by the NCLT for considering the sole resolution plan placed before it. Similarly, in the case of *Bhushan Power*, NCLAT allowed the resolution applicants to revise their financial offers one year after the case was admitted into CIRP, even though by design a liquidation order should have been made. In the case of *Jyoti Structures*, the NCLAT prohibited the NCLT from passing a liquidation order. In the case of *Jaypee Infrastructure Ltd.*, the Supreme Court started the CIRP of the company afresh after one year had elapsed from its first CIRP.

The bias against liquidation has been observed in the CoC decisions as well. In the case of *ABG Shipyard*, the CoC issued a fresh Expression Of Intent document (EOI) after nearly 270 days had elapsed. This was done to allow its sole resolution applicant to revise its resolution plan. Later, in the same case when the NCLT rejected the resolution plan that was submitted, instead of ordering liquidation, it ordered 'Liquidation as a Going Concern', a principle that had till then not been defined either in the IBC or in the Companies Act. The IBC amendment that lowered the CoC voting threshold for a resolution plan from 75% to 66% indicated that policymakers were not free from the anti-liquidation bias.

4.4 Lack of Commercial Consensus

The design of the IBC vested the CoC with the commercial decision of whether the company should be resolved or liquidated. To this effect the *Report of the BLRC* states that

Table 12 Timelines of the RBI-12 cases: expected vs actual

Company	T_0-T_1	T_1-T_2	T_1-T_3	T_1-T_4	T_1-T_5	T_1-T_6	T_1-T_7	T_1-T_8	T_1-T_9
Expected	14	3	14–90	30	75	115	135	165	180–270
ABG Shipyard	29	3	15	34	41	–[a]	258	290	NA[b]
Alok industries	19	1	14	29	72	–	–	–	NA
Amtek auto	-	5	17	29	–	225	225	266	361
Bhushan power & Steel	–	2	14	–	57	210	391	–	NA
Bhushan steel	23	0	14	–	73	–	205	–	293
Electrosteel steels	–	0	11	31	68	–	–	255	270
Era infra engineering	–	–	–	–	–	–	–	–	NA
Essar steel	-	3	14	33	–	–	–	–	NA
Jaypee infratech (1st round)	–	1	15	–	79	–	–	–	NA
Jaypee infratech (2nd round)	–	–	–	–	–	NA	NA	NA	NA
Jyoti structures	–	–	–	37	51	–	–	NA	NA
Lanco infratech	–	3	15	36	103	–	269	–	384
Monnet Ispat	–	7	20	–	65	-	228	–	364
Average	24	3	15	33	68	218	263	270	334

Filing of CIRP petition: T_0
Admission of CIRP petition: T_1
Public announcement of CIRP: T_2
Last date of submission of claims: T_3
First meeting of CoC: T_4
Invitation for EOI from potential resolution applicants: T_5
Final list of resolution applicants by RP to CoC: T_6
Receipt of resolution plans from resolution applicants: T_7
Submission of CoC approved resolution plan by RP to NCLT: T_8
Approval of resolution plan by NCLT: T_9
Updated as of 15 December 2018.
[a]—indicates that timeline data is not available.
[b] NA indicates that the case has not reached this stage

> The legislature and the courts must control the process of resolution, but not be burdened to make business decisions.
>
> The law must explicitly state that the viability of the enterprise is a matter of business, and that matters of business can only be negotiated between creditors and debtor. While viability is assessed as a negotiation between creditors and debtor, the final decision has to be an agreement among creditors who are the financiers willing to bear the loss in the insolvency.

Over the course of the two years since the IBC became operational, the CoCs have increasingly ceded this decision-making power to the judiciary. This has been aided by policymakers who have amended the law to widen the remit of judicial intervention in commercial matters. As an example, the original IBC design empowered the CoC to accept or reject resolution plans from any party. With Section 29A in place, a set of potential resolution applicants have been removed from the process completely. A popular perception is that this decision may have been driven by the concerns of the PSBs, who because of state ownership, would be seen to be *using tax payer money to bail out crony capitalists* if they voted in favour of a promoter led resolution plan.

Similarly, there has been a rise in the extent to which courts exercise their powers in adjudicating 29A eligibility. In the matter of an appeal by Arcelor Mittal in the case of *Essar Steel* at the Supreme Court, the Court remarked that the CoC's view on 29A eligibility is only *prima facie*, and it is NCLT that has the statutory mandate to adjudicate (Jain 2018).

In another instance, the IBC was amended to introduce Section 31(1), which gave wide powers to the NCLT to adjudge the *implementability* of a resolution plan, a decision which the BLRC had solely left to the CoC. The rationale offered for this amendment was that it would reduce potential appeals against resolution plans. The original design of the IBC was to allow procedural appeals against resolution plans and not substantive ones. Thus, the amendment did not appear to be consistent with the IBC design principle of a resolution based on the *commercial wisdom of CoC*.

There have also been other instances of the CoC ceding its decision making powers, not just to the courts, but also to non-statutory bodies such as the Indian Banks Association (IBA) and enforcement agencies such as the Central Vigilance Commission (CVC). The IBA had come up with a bid evaluation matrix which lays down common evaluation criteria for assessing resolution bids. The use of this matrix has become almost a norm, given that the CoC are dominated by banks. The evaluation matrix has a nearly standardised evaluation criteria across cases in a *one size fits all* manner. This is contrary to the notion that each company may have unique and specific issues associated with its insolvency. At the same time, the CVC guidelines on choosing the H1 bidder have become the norm, despite the fact that the H1 plan may not be the most optimal from a viability perspective. In fact, banks themselves have been asking policymakers to adopt an auction-like structure as a preferred method for deciding on resolution bids during CIRP, completely ruling out any scope for negotiated outcomes or even discussions with non-H1 resolution applicants.

4.5 The Errant Bidder

The *Amtek Auto* case raised a unique question for the IBC: how to deal with cases where the final resolution applicant does not adhere to the terms of the resolution plan? This had implications for the finality of the resolution process. After having successfully cleared all hurdles and obtaining a favourable order from the NCLT, the winning resolution applicant for *Amtek Auto*, *Liberty House*, defaulted on its commitment under the resolution plan. The NCLT ordered Liberty House to withdraw its resolution plan, and the CoC decided to proceed against Liberty House under the provisions of the IBC (Economic Times 2018).

Section 33(3) of the IBC envisaged a liquidation in case the terms of the resolution plan were not met. However, at the time of writing this review, the courts are yet to test the scope of this provision. The CoC of *Amtek Auto* applied to the NCLT seeking more time for consideration of fresh resolution plans, even though the IBC does not permit this. The decision of the court in this case may become a template for future action in similar cases. Given the anti-liquidation bias that prevails in the IBC ecosystem, it is likely that for the courts will allow the IBC process to be restarted.

Further, proceedings against *Liberty House* have been initiated under Section 74(3) of the IBC. But the outcome of these proceedings remain to be seen. This raises an important question on whether action can be taken against a resolution applicant that has defaulted on its commitment under the resolution plan. For instance, can default on a resolution plan be the basis for re-starting CIRP against the defaulting resolution applicant? The policy response to this question will have far reaching implications, affecting not just one case but the overall IBC process. Already, the IBBI is contemplating the introduction of a *earnest money deposit* type of design for resolution applicants. This may change costs and outcomes in the CIRP of many firms.

5 Some Learnings

There have been mixed results on how the RBI-12 cases have fared on some of the key objectives of the IBC. There are concerns around:

1. A lack of adherence to timelines: the prescribed 180 or 270 day timeline no longer holds sanctity.
2. A lack of predictability in outcomes: approved resolution plans have appeals pending. Liquidation does not get ordered when 270 days pass without a resolution plan being in place.
3. Widening gaps in commercial decision-making through amendments in the law: Section 29A has placed widespread disqualifications on parties who can submit resolution plans. Section 31(1) gives the courts the power to reject CoC approved resolution plans.

It may be argued that these concerns are temporary and that they will not be present in future cases as jurisprudence builds up under the law. However, since these concerns are similar to those observed in pre-IBC resolution regimes, it tends to support the expectation that these issues may persist. For instance, if non-adherence to timelines is because of inherent capacity challenges at NCLT, then as caseload increases in the NCLT, the observed delays in case resolution may continue as is or increase.

Similarly, taking away key decisions from the CoC may create incentives for the CoC to not take decisions when posed with a complex problem. This is a real possibility, given that PSBs, which have inherent constraints in decision-making, are likely to be the dominant force in decision-making in most CoCs. Further, placing the onus of taking commercial decisions such as ‘implementability of resolution plans’ on courts, which are far less equipped to deal with such decisions compared to the creditors, will hurt the confidence of market participants in the IBC process.

If resolving banking sector NPAs was a key reason for referring the RBI-12 cases to the IBC, then at first blush, the RBI-12 cases provide some support for the success of the IBC by way of standard measures of bankruptcy reform success which are 'Recovery rates', 'Time to recovery' and 'Ex-ante status of credit markets'.

The RBI-12 cases have delivered better recovery rates than the 25.6% that the *World Bank Doing Business Report, 2014* reported. This is largely based on resolution outcome in one case which is *Bhushan Steel* at 64%. The recovery rates have been in the range of 25–35% for 3 other cases that have been resolved. Further, these outcomes are observations from a specific industry (steel and metal products). In the remaining cases, only one resolution plan each was received among *ABG Shipyard*, *Alok Industries*, *Jyoti Structures*, *Laco Infratech*, and *Monnet Ispat*. Two plans were received for *Amtek Auto* but one was withdrawn. Three plans were received for *Jaypee Infra* of which none were approved by the CoC.

Similarly, the time taken for recovery in the IBC has been significantly less than under earlier regimes. However, for the RBI-12 cases, it has been in excess of the timeline prescribed under IBC.

Lastly, it remains too early to draw conclusions about the impact of IBC on the credit market landscape. We do observe a policy commitment to the IBC as the *only game in town*. The RBI, as the banking sector regulator, has been enthusiastic about having banks resolve their NPAs using the IBC. Indeed, the RBI has dismantled several of the earlier resolution mechanisms that were in place. However, the government as the majority shareholder of the public sector banks, seems to be more circumspect of the use of IBC to resolve NPAs. Reports suggest that the 'High Level Committee on Restructuring Stressed Assets and Creating More Value for PSBs' has recommended a five pronged resolution strategy where the resolution of small and mid-sized stressed assets of PSBs has been recommended to be done using IBC platform. But larger assets (greater than Rs. 500 cr.) has been recommended to be dealt with by an Asset Management Company structure.

Therefore, while using IBC as a legal strategy for resolving banking sector NPAs was a bold move, the learning from the RBI-12 cases is that resolution of corporate insolvency continues to be plagued with significant challenges and risks. If the IBC proves to be ineffective in resolving the NPA accounts in a timely manner, there is no 'plan B' to fall back upon. If it proves to be ineffective, this will suggest that one of the most important reforms undertaken by India in the recent period has failed (Shah 2018). Thus, it is important for policy makers to conduct a careful review of the life cycle of these first 12 large cases that have been put through the IBC, for a diagnosis of where the premise of the law has worked well and where it has not succeeded. These lessons will be useful to guide future reforms actions.

References

Ahamed MM, Mallick S (2017) Does regulatory forbearance matter for bank stability? evidence from creditors' perspective. J Financ Stab
Economic Times (2015) Amtek auto defaults on Rs 800 crore bond payment. online, https://economictimes.indiatimes.com/markets/bonds/amtek-auto-defaults-on-rs-800-crore-bond-payment/articleshow/49053448.cms
Economic Times (2018) Liberty house told to withdraw plan for Amtek auto subsidiary. online, https://economictimes.indiatimes.com/industry/banking/finance/liberty-house-told-to-withdraw-plan-for-amtek-auto-subsidiary/articleshow/66979726.cms
Gupta A, Kumar P, Shah K (2013) Indian financial sector, house of debt—revisited. Technical Report, Credit Suisse. https://plus.credit-suisse.com/u/C823ww
Jain M (2018) ArcelorMittal Vs Numetal: opinion of CoC on disqualification of a resolution applicant under S.29A Of IBC is only prima facie one, NCLT is the statutory authority to decide it: Nariman. J. online, https://www.livelaw.in/arcelormittal-vs-numetal-opinion-of-coc-on-disqualification-of-a-resolution-applicant-under-s-29a-of-ibc-is-only-prima-facie-one-nclt-is-the-statutory-authority-to-decide-it-nariman-j/
Jain S, Singh K, Thomas S (2016) Evaluating the impact of debt restructuring on firm performance. online, https://ifrogs.org/PDF/CONF_2015/sl_Jain_Singh_Thomas_2015.pdf
Kundu K (2016) Bankruptcy law: key to tackling the burgeoning NPA issue. online, https://www.livemint.com/Money/27jZJSt1N5qYoVRP4xjrxL/Bankruptcy-law-key-to-tackling-the-burgeoning-NPA-issue.html
Lindner P, Jung SE (2014) Corporate Vulnerabilities in India and banks' loan performance. IMF Working Paper
Mehta S (2016) How Bankruptcy law will curb bank NPAs. online, https://www.financialexpress.com/opinion/new-bankruptcy-law-will-curb-npas/309158/
Pandey R, Pattnaik I, Shah A (2017) Dating business cycles in India. NIPFP Working Paper 175
Pritchett L, de Weijer F (2010) Fragile states: stuck in a capability trap? world development report (2011), Background Paper
Pritchett L, Woolcock M, Andrews M (2010) Capability traps? the mechanisms of persistent implementation failure. Cente for Global Development, Working Paper No 234
Ravi A (2015) The indian insolvency regine in parctice—an analysis of insolvency and debt recovery proceedings. Economic and political weekly
Regy PV, Roy S (2017) Understanding judicial delays in debt tribunals. Technical Report 195, National institute of public finance and policy. http://macrofinance.nipfp.org.in/releases/RoyRegy2017_judicial-delay-debt-tribunals.html
Reserve Bank of India (2013) Financial stability report, June 2013. Technical Report, Reserve Bank of India
Reserve Bank of India (2016) Financial stability report. Technical Report, Reserve Bank of India
Reserve Bank of India (2017a) RBI identifies accounts for reference by banks under the insolvency and Bankruptcy Code. https://www.rbi.org.in/scripts/bs_pressreleasedisplay.aspx?prid=40743
Reserve Bank of India (2017b) Reserve Bank of India outlines the action plan to implement the banking regulation (Amendment) ordinance, 2017. https://www.rbi.org.in/scripts/BS_PressReleaseDisplay.aspx?prid=40518
Reserve Bank of India (2017c) Revised Prompt Corrective Action (PCA) framework for banks. Notification, https://rbi.org.in/Scripts/NotificationUser.aspx?Id=10921&Mode=0
Reserve Bank of India (2017d) Timelines for stressed assets resolution. https://www.rbi.org.in/Scripts/NotificationUser.aspx?Id=10957&Mode=0
Sengupta R, Sharma A (2017a) Bank recapitalisation: the myth around growth capital. online, https://blog.theleapjournal.org/2017/11/bank-recapitalisation-myth-around.html
Sengupta R, Sharma A (2017b) Understanding the recent IBC (Amendment) ordinance, 2017. online, https://blog.theleapjournal.org/2017/12/understanding-recent-ibc-amendment.html

Sengupta R, Vardhan H (2017) Non-performing assets in Indian Banks: this time it is different. Economic and Political Weekly
Sengupta R, Sharma A, Thomas S (2017) Evolution of the insolvency framework for non-financial firms in India. India Development Report
Shah A (2018) Sequencing issues in building jurisprudence: the problems of large bankruptcy cases. online, https://blog.theleapjournal.org/2018/07/sequencing-issues-in-building.html
van Zweiten K (2012) The demise of corporate insolvency law in India: the role of the courts. Oxford University, Technical Report

Real Estate Insolvencies and the Status of Home Buyers

Gausia Shaikh and Anjali Sharma

1 Introduction

For decades, India lacked a functioning and efficient framework for dealing with corporate insolvency that was accessible to all classes of creditors and debtors. In many sectors, this led to the emergence of financing structures that sought to correct the imbalance in creditor-debtor rights that existed. One such sector is the residential real estate development sector. Firms in this sector have relied substantially on advances from customers as a means of financing their projects. However, these customers have not earned returns on their advances. In the event of a delay or a default by the firm in delivering the residential units, these customers have had few remedies available.

When the Insolvency and Bankruptcy Code, 2016 (IBC) became operational, this issue came to the fore on account of insolvency proceedings of one such firm, *Jaypee Infratech*. *Jaypee Infratech* had residential projects under development in which it had sold units to customers and collected advances against these sales. In many cases, the delivery of these units was delayed for which customers had already filed cases in existing consumer forums against *Jaypee Infratech*. When the Corporate Insolvency Resolution Process (CIRP) under the IBC for *Jaypee Infratech* was initiated under the newly operationalised IBC, these customers were faced with three new uncertainties. The first was with regard to the status of their advances in the insolvency proceedings. It was unclear whether they would be treated as creditors and, if so, what type of creditors. The second was with regard to the status of their pre-existing cases before the consumer forums. Under the CIRP, the moratorium on legal proceedings against the corporate debtor had stayed the proceedings in these cases. The third was about

The opinions expressed in this chapter are the authors' own and not that of their employers.

G. Shaikh (✉) · A. Sharma
Public Policy Researcher and Industry Expert, Mumbai, India
e-mail: gausiagshaikh@gmail.com

© The Author(s), under exclusive license to Springer Nature Singapore Pte Ltd. 2022

S. Thomas (ed.), *Insolvency and Bankruptcy Reforms in India*,
India Studies in Business and Economics,
https://doi.org/10.1007/978-981-16-0854-4_3

the resolution outcome for these customers. It was very likely that, whether *Jaypee Infratech* got revived or liquidated under IBC, these customers would neither get the residential unit they had purchased, nor would they be able to recover the advances they had paid.

The IBC revealed a multifaceted problem in the resolution of *Jaypee Infratech*. One facet was the unique financing structure of residential real estate firms. Most of the firms were undercapitalised and used customer advances as a "filler" for their capital gap. The second facet was the manner in which these firms accounted for customer advances, and lack of due diligence by financial firms that extended credit to these firms about the true indebtedness of these firms. Another facet was the failure of contracts and consumer protection laws in providing timely and adequate remedies to the customers of these firms. Finally, there was the facet of how the IBC would deal with the highly emotive problem of "home-buyers", essentially customers of this firm being affected in a significant way by *Jaypee Infratech*'s insolvency.

It is not an uncommon practice for businesses to collect advances or prepayments from their customers against a promise of delivery of goods or services in the future. The question of what happens to these advances when the business becomes insolvent is what requires new policy thinking. This question assumes a different public policy dimension when these advances come from *a large number* of *consumers* who have used up a large proportion of their *lifetime income or savings* towards them. The response of the judiciary and of policymakers to this problem, so far, has been to create special dispensations for "home-buyers" in the IBC process. However, these actions have larger implications on other stakeholders in the IBC process, and on the evolution of the law.

Here, we evaluate the various issues brought forth by *Jaypee Infratech*'s insolvency. We also assess the current and future impact of the judicial and policy response to these issues on the various stakeholders, as well as on the IBC itself.

In order to do this, we first study the unique financing framework of the real estate sector in the pre-insolvency stage and observe the firm in the insolvency stage in Sect. 2. We then look at how the decision of classifying home buyers as financial creditors has affected the insolvency law in general and what are its implications on other industries and classes of creditors in Sect. 3. To place this discussion in a broader perspective, we undertake a cross-country analysis in Sect. 4 to understand how jurisdictions such as the U.K., U.S.A and Australia deal with consumers as creditors during the insolvency process and of the consumer protection regimes in these jurisdictions in Sect. 5. In Sect. 6, we delve into the issue of consumer protection under the Indian insolvency regime and critically analyse the Indian response to the home buyer problem. In Sect. 7, we attempt to provide a glimpse of a world without the amendment of the IBC and provide recommendations for how the problem of home buyers could have been dealt with differently.

2 The 'Uniqueness' of the Indian Real Estate Sector

Indian real estate firms continue to rely on traditional sources of finance. Be it bank loans or family-run businesses surviving on family incomes, the real estate sector has largely relied on limited sources of finance. This leads to firms being undercapitalised. In order to deal with such undercapitalisation, real estate firms depend on consumer advances for some of their long term, and mostly for their working capital requirements. But this excessive dependence on consumer advances raises its own issues.

While advances by home buyers constitute a large financing component for the firm, they have little or no rights as creditors. This is largely due to the nature of contracts entered into between them and the real estate firms. Until the registration of a Sale Deed under the *Registration Act, 1908*, the agreement entered into between home buyers and firms is an 'Agreement for Sale'. This Agreement for Sale is an agreement to enter into a Sale Deed and purchase immovable property at a future date. It is often understood as an 'agreement to agree' in the future. Until the registered Sale Deed, the home buyers have no security interest in the property, despite paying as much as 90% of the consideration as advances to the real estate firm. Further, unlike other forms of credit, there is no fixed tenure for the advances forwarded by the home buyers. The agreements do not specify a date on which the advances would be returned in case the real estate firm is unable to deliver the property to the home buyer. Also, unlike other creditors, home buyers do not receive any assured returns such as interest on the advances forwarded by them.[1] When we look at the outcome of a breach of agreement by the real estate firm, such agreements do not adequately protect the interests of the home buyers. The repayment of the advance itself is uncertain under such agreements.

Thus, there is an imbalance in the rights and claims of home buyers as creditors of a real estate firm. In the following Section, we delve deeper into these issues by studying them during the stages of (a) credit access by the firm, (b) financial distress of the firm and (c) insolvency of the firm.

2.1 *Credit Access*

The stage of credit access is the stage at which the home buyer decides to enter into an agreement for purchase of immovable property and to forward an advance to the real estate firm. At this stage, the home buyer faces the following issues:

- Home buyers do not undertake any specific credit assessment of the real estate firms. The financial condition or repayment ability of the real estate firm is usually not assessed by the home buyers. This is largely owing to the information asymmetry which exists between the firm and the home buyers.

[1] The exception being cases like *Nikhil Mehta and Sons versus AMR Insfrastrucure Ltd.*.

- Home buyers do not even have access to basic information about the real estate firm. This includes information such as the existence of a clear, undisputed and unencumbered title of the firm over the property in question. Anecdotal evidence suggests that most home buyers approach financial institutions for loans to fund the advances and then rely on such financial institutions to conduct due diligence of the real estate firm. However, when financial institutions conduct a due diligence before providing a home loan to a home buyer, they are primarily concerned with the repayment ability of the home buyer. Effort may not be put by the financial institution in ascertaining the financial condition and likelihood of project completion of the real estate firm. Therefore, such indirect credit assessment also fails and the information asymmetry continues.
- At the time of forwarding the advance, the home buyer does not acquire any security interest in the future property. Similarly, the financial institution which grants a loan to the home buyer also does not have any security interest over such property. Therefore, in case of default, neither the financier nor the home buyer has means of recovering the amount advanced.
- Despite the above risks, the home buyer has limited ability to negotiate the pricing of the property and the amount of advance to be forwarded.
- The agreement entered into between the home buyers and real estate firms is weak, in content and legality. It not only lacks adequate protection of the interests of the home buyers with an absence of a fixed tenure or clauses providing protection from insolvency, but it also has weak legal standing as it relates to future property and a future sale agreement. Upon a breach by the real estate firm, the only remedies available for the home buyers is to approach civil courts or consumer forums for relief. These proceedings are expensive and time-consuming.
- Home buyers also do not have the ability to monitor the use of funds forwarded by them to the real estate firm. Anecdotal evidence suggests that often, the finances from one real estate project are used for other projects or siphoning of funds takes place while the home buyers remain ignorant of the same.

One may question as to why despite each of the above issues, the average Indian household holds 84% of its wealth in real estate (The Household Finance Committee 2017). Apart from the innate desire of households to have a home of their own, one reason may be the incentives provided by the State for home purchasers. Be it tax breaks or rebates, home buyers have been incentivised to make home purchases. Even when residential property is sold, unless one is willing to make specific investment in government bonds, such sellers have to purchase new residential property to avoid the levy of 30% capital gains tax. However, while these incentives exist, there are not many protections accorded to the home buyers at the stage of credit access by real estate firms.

2.2 *Financial Distress*

As seen above, due to the information asymmetry between real estate firms and home buyers, there is little anticipation of financial distress of the firm. Therefore, when a firm does enter a state of financial distress, it comes as a shock to the home buyers and has its own issues. Some of these issues are as follows:

- Home buyers are unable to assess the business risks incurred by the real estate firms. Further, delays in real estate projects often arise out of delays in approvals from appropriate authorities. It is difficult for home buyers to judge whether the firm is in financial distress or merely awaiting approvals.
- Even if home buyers were to ascertain that the firm is in distress, they will not be able to monitor such distress owing to the information asymmetry between the parties. The home buyers do not have an open view of the profits, losses or general finances of the business of the firm. This also restricts them from ascertaining the level of distress that the firm is in, thereby adding to the uncertainty of completion of the project.
- For arguments sake, even if distress or the level of distress is somehow identified by the home buyers, they have limited options to deal with such distress. Their only options are consumer fora and civil courts, both of which suffer from delays.
- With no immediate relief from judicial fora, the home buyers are not even able to re-negotiate existing agreements owing to the distress situation. Therefore, leaving them without any remedies whatsoever.

Thus, home buyers are vulnerable to risk of the builder firm, right from the stage of credit assessment till the firm reaches a stage of financial distress.

2.3 *The Insolvency Stage*

Weak pre-insolvency rights of home buyers get aggravated at the stage of insolvency of the firm. Prior to the amendment of the law in 2018, home buyers were adjudged neither as operational creditors nor as financial creditors.[2] They were categorised, like all other consumers, as 'other creditors'. As 'other creditors' they did not have the right to trigger insolvency proceedings. They could merely submit claims during the insolvency resolution process. However, with the *Insolvency and Bankruptcy Code (Second Amendment)*, home buyers have now been classified as financial creditors under the law. We look at how this classification has affected the status of home buyers as regards the insolvency of the firm.

- The law as it stands today provides home buyers the right to trigger insolvency proceedings against the real estate firm.

[2] See *Col. Vinod Awasthy versus AMR Infrastructures Ltd.* and *Nikhil Mehta and Sons versus AMR Insfrastrucure Ltd.*

- As financial creditors, home buyers also have the right to vote in the Committee of Creditors (CoC). However, the extent of this right is proportionate to the claim of the home buyers. Further, the extent of their claim will also depend upon the resolution plan received. Therefore, in both these scenarios, there is a possibility that recovery of advance amounts will not be possible.
- While home buyers may have some enhanced rights in resolution, in liquidation, they continue to be unsecured creditors. As unsecured creditors, they fall below super priority creditors and secured creditors in the hierarchy of repayment.
- While the above depend on the formal process of insolvency under the IBC, there have been instances when the judiciary has deviated from the formal process. See Box for events in *Chitra Sharma and ors. versus Union of India and ors.*.
- In view of the above, it needs to be seen whether it is beneficial for home buyers to incur the costs associated with being financial creditors when they do not stand much to gain.

The journey of home buyers under the IBC

The issue of home buyers as creditors of a real estate firm first emerged out of the series of events in the case of *Chitra Sharma and ors. versus Union of India and ors.*. The following is a chronological account of these events.

- On 9 August 2017, an application for initiating insolvency proceedings against *Jaypee Infratech* was admitted by the Allahabad Bench of the National Companies Law Tribunal (NCLT).
- In response, the home buyers who had forwarded advances to *Jaypee Infratech* filed a writ petition before the Supreme Court of India (*Chitra Sharma and ors. versus Union of India and ors*). The petition challenged Sects. 14, 53 and 238 of the IBC.

  The home buyers contended that the CIRP of *Jaypee Infratech* adversely affects them in two ways. First, the moratorium under Sect. 14 of the IBC, along with Sect. 238, puts on hold cases that they have already filed before the consumer fora, and prevents any new cases of this nature to be filed. Second, if the outcome of the CIRP is liquidation of *Jaypee Infratech*, under the law at the time, home buyers would neither get the homes they have paid for nor a refund of their advances.

  In their petition, home buyers had sought two reliefs from the Court: (a) a stay on the CIRP of *Jaypee Infratech*, and (b) putting their claims on an even footing with those of financial creditors. Therefore, it may be said that the inception of the idea of preferential treatment of home buyers, emanated from this case.
- Observing a lacuna in the law regarding creditors who are neither operational nor financial, the insolvency regulator (Insolvency and Bankruptcy Board of India or IBBI) amended the *IBBI (CIRP) Regulations, 2017* to create a category of creditors called 'other creditors'. While these 'other creditors'

had the right to submit their claims during the CIRP, they did not have the right to initiate resolution.

- On 4 September 2017, post-hearing the writ petition, the Supreme Court stayed the order of the Allahabad NCLT until further orders by it. This meant that the CIRP which had begun on 9 August 2017 had suddenly been stayed within 30 days since its initiation. This led to a scenario wherein the interim resolution professional handed over the management of *Jaypee Infratech* back to the original management (Order dated 4 September 2017 in *Chitra Sharma and ors. versus Union of India and ors.*).
- On 11 September 2017, when this scenario was brought to the notice of the court, some radical directions were given by it.
  - The interim resolution professional was directed to regain control over the management of *Jaypee Infratech* and submit to the court, an 'interim resolution plan' within 45 days from the date of the order. He was further directed to make '*all necessary provisions to protect the interests of the home buyers*'. Under the IBC, there is no concept of an 'interim resolution plan'. Further, the law aims to place all creditors on an equal footing. This order of the apex court directed the interim resolution professional to ensure specific provisions being made for home buyers.
  - It further directed that the senior counsel and Advocate-on-Record in the matter participate in the meetings of the CoC '*to espouse the cause of the home buyers and protect their interests*'.
  - The Managing Directors of *Jaypee Infratech* as well as that of *Jayprakash Associates* were prevented from leaving the country without prior permission of the court.
  - In addition to the above, *Jayprakash Associates*, not being a party to the CIRP, was directed to deposit a sum of Rs. 2000 crores before the court. Restrictions were also imposed on the sale of assets by *Jayprakash Associates* to be able to make the deposit (Order dated 11 September 2017 in *Chitra Sharma and ors. versus Union of India and ors.*).
- Thereafter, on 22 November 2017, the court was informed that *Jayprakash Associates* was still attempting to deposit the money. It provided *Jayprakash Associates* with a timeline for disbursing the amount. Further, all independent and promoter directors were prohibited from alienating personal properties or assets. Taking it a step further, even properties and assets of such directors' immediate and dependent family members were prohibited from being transferred (Order dated 22 November 2017 in *Chitra Sharma and ors. versus Union of India and ors.*).
- In March 2018, the *Report of the Insolvency Law Committee* was released. This report called for the classification of home buyers as financial creditors, owing to the unique nature of the real estate sector whereby consumer advances are used by firms as a means of financing.

- On 16 May 2018, *Jayprakash Associates* was directed to deposit a further sum of Rs.1000 crores, post the receipt of the 16 April 2018 instalment. Further, in respect of the Rs.750 crores which had been deposited with the court, the court directed that the amount be disbursed on pro-rata basis amongst the home buyers (Order dated 16 May 2018 in *Chitra Sharma and ors. versus Union of India and ors.*).
- On 6 June 2018, the IBC was amended and home buyers were classified as financial creditors of a real estate firm (*IBC (Amendment) Ordinance, 2018*).
- On 9 August 2018, i.e. post one year since the admission of the insolvency petition in the Allahabad NCLT, the Supreme Court acknowledged the *IBC (Amendment) Ordinance, 2018* and gave the following directions:
  - In exercise of its powers under Article 142 of the Constitution of India, the court directed that CIRP of 180 days be re-initiated from the date of the order.
  - The CoC be re-constituted in light of home buyers being classified as financial creditors.
  - In addition to the 3 short listed bidders recognised during the earlier CIRP, fresh expressions of interests and revised bids be considered.
  - Owing to Sect. 29A of the IBC, *Jaypee Infratech* and *Jayprakash Associates* promoters were declared ineligible to participate in the CIRP.
  - The Reserve Bank of India (RBI), the Indian central bank, was allowed to direct banks to initiate insolvency proceedings against *Jayprakash Associates*.
  - The amount of Rs. 750 crores deposited with the court was to be transferred to the NCLT (Order dated 9 August 2018 in *Chitra Sharma and ors. versus Union of India and ors.*).
- Since then, the ordinance has been enacted as *Insolvency and Bankruptcy Code (Second Amendment)*, 2018.

3 Impact on the IBC Processes

The chronology of events shows that special provisions have been made in law and through judicial orders for home buyers as creditors of a real estate firm. While we have examined the impact of such changes on home buyers themselves, we now look at how these changes are likely to affect the IBC processes in the long run.

3.1 Impact on Timelines

Timely resolution is one of the key objectives of the IBC. The special treatment accorded to home buyers is likely to add to delays in the IBC processes.

- At the first instance, home buyers have been accorded the status of financial creditors by reading them as creditors whose debt has '*the commercial effect of a borrowing*' (Sect. 5(8)(f) of the IBC). This is likely to open a Pandora's box of creditors seeking to similarly place their debt under the category of one having the commercial effect of a borrowing. Creditors of firms who similarly rely heavily on consumer advances are most likely to seek classification as financial creditors. Decision-making on whether such other claimants' claims ought to be considered, will be time-consuming even at the stage of admission of a petition, if filed by such a claimant.
- Post initiation of CIRP, the home buyers, as financial creditors, will get a seat at the meetings of the CoC. Being large in number and new to the process of assessing the commercial viability of a company, it is possible that delays may take place in the CIRP. This may be due to the difficulty in obtaining consensus from a large number of creditors. While there is now a provision for appointment of an authorised representative in such cases, it is yet to be seen if this would affect the consensus problem.

3.2 Impact on CoC Decision-Making

Owing to the large number of home buyers as financial creditors, there is a need for an aggregation mechanism. Section 21 (6A) of the IBC makes a limited provision in this regard. It states that when a class of financial creditors exceeds a number specified, the interim resolution professional has to make an application to the NCLT, with a list of all financial creditors, containing the name of an insolvency professional to act as the authorised representative of such creditors. As an authorised representative, such representative has the right to participate and vote in meeting of the CoC. (S)he is duty bound to not act against the interest of the financial creditor and must always act in accordance with the prior instructions from the creditors (s)he represents.[3]

It may be argued that aggregation mechanisms are not a new phenomenon and have been operational especially with reference to bondholders. In Box we see how the aggregation mechanism for home buyers differs from that of the mechanism for bondholders.

---

[3] Section 25A of the IBC.

Bond holders v home buyers: aggregation mechanisms

While the *Insolvency and Bankruptcy Code (Second Amendment)*, 2018 has created an aggregation mechanism, it differs at various levels from the aggregation mechanism for bond holders.

- At the first instance, debenture trustees represent the bond holders right from the time of credit access, i.e. right from the execution of the debt agreement. The authorised representative under the IBC comes in only at the stage of meetings of the CoC.
- Since bonds are financial products, there is a high level of regulation of debenture trustees, along with mechanisms for rating of such trustees. Authorised representatives under the IBC do not have such level of regulation or rating.
- Debenture trustees also have a higher level of accountability and liability if they do not act in the best interests of the bond holders. While the IBC mandates that the authorised representative act in the interest of the financial creditor (s)he represents, there is no provision imposing any liability or penalty for not doing so.

In view of the above, it is yet to be seen how this provision is operationalised and how authorised representatives are regulated under the IBC.

Therefore, while attempts have been made to ease decision-making by consolidating home buyer interests, it is to be seen how it works in practice. At present, it does not solve the problem of ease of decision-making during CoC meetings. The issue of inability to assess the commercial viability of a company continues even when the authorised representative has been appointed. The representative itself is an insolvency professional who must act only in accordance with the specific instructions of the creditors. Further, the provision says that there will be one authorised representative for a 'class of creditors'. This may mean that one authorised representative will represent the interests of all home buyers, irrespective of their independent claims against the debtor. Consolidating such varied interests will also be a task for such representative and is likely to cause delays in the resolution process.

3.3 Impact on Procedural Litigation

As stated in respect of impact on timelines, the special treatment accorded to home buyers is likely to add to procedural litigation under the IBC. This begins right from the stage of other kinds of creditors, especially those who are consumers or operational creditors, who would want to identify their debt as having 'commercial effect of borrowing', to litigation on the authorised representative not representing the best interests of the home buyers. Further, there is a possibility that owing to smaller proportion of claims or limited scopes of resolution plans, home buyers are not likely to get the property or recovery of advances. This may lead to further litigation by aggrieved home buyers on similar grounds that led to amendments to the law—inability to recover their 'hard earned money' or obtain a home agreed to be bought.

In addition to the above, there are also cases pending before various High Courts in the country, challenging the IBC on the grounds that the classification in the law of financial and operational creditors is unconstitutional under Article 14 of the Constitution of India. While one such challenge has failed[4], other cases continue to be pending.

While we have seen the impact of the special treatment to home buyers on their rights and on IBC processes, there are implications and questions in respect of other industries as well. For instance, what about similar industries with high consumer advances and consequent imbalance of rights? The airline industry is an example. When firms are in distress, they seek more consumer advances for liquidity. For instance, reports of Jet Airways being in financial distress and of it providing heavy discounts on advance bookings provide one such picture.[5] Box shows how there is ongoing debate and discussion in the UK in respect of airline insolvencies and any special treatment which may be accorded to them.

Case study on airline insolvencies in the UK As an aftermath of the collapse of the airline Monarch in October 2017 in the U.K., the government worked on a review of norms concerning airline insolvencies. The review was aimed at ensuring minimum loss to consumers availing airline services. According to the *Airline Insolvency Review: Call for Evidence*, the questions placed before the review were as follows:

- What practical arrangements are needed to get passengers home if sufficient capacity does not exist in the market?
- How can passengers and the taxpayer be protected from the financial impacts of an airline failure?
- What changes need to be made to the current arrangements in light of the answers to the above, and to put them on a more commercial basis?

The need for review

Data suggests that on average, one in two people living in the UK will take a flight in any one year. (*Consumer Tracker Survey Wave 4*) This, coupled with and as a consequence of, the introduction of low-cost carriers, has led to a situation whereby the competition has led to various airlines being driven out of the market. In addition to the sluggish performance of the global economy and consumer reactions to recent terrorism and perceived political instability, the capital intensive nature and increasingly leveraged financing arrangements of

[4] *Akshay Jhunjhunwalla & anr. v. Union of India through the Ministry of Corporate Affairs & Ors.*, Calcutta High Court, W.P. No. 672 of 2017.

[5] Dubey (2018) and Bloomberg Quint (2018).

airlines add further risk (Department for Transport 2018). In such a scenario, all consumers, be it consumers who have made advanced bookings or consumers on board an airline which becomes insolvent, face a high risk of financial loss. The consequences of airline insolvency are as follows:

- Upon insolvency of an airline and suspension of its services, advance bookings by consumers become futile. In such a situation, they are compelled to either cancel their trip or to pay additional costs to buy tickets of another airline.
- There may also be a situation wherein the consumers are aboard an airline when the order of suspension of services is passed. This leaves the consumers stranded. Repatriation in such situations is an added financial burden on the consumers. At times, like in the case of *Monarch airlines*, the government arranges for repatriation. However, the domino effect of delays on this account are likely to cause further losses to consumers which they have to bear themselves (Department for Transport 2018).

Limited protections offered to aggrieved consumers are as follows:

- *ATOL* and package travel protection, which ensures that protected passengers can finish their holiday or receive a full refund in the event of an *ATOL* holder's insolvency.
- Travel insurance is another means of financial protection of consumers against airline insolvency.
- When payment for airline tickets has been made through a credit card, there are two options - the transaction may be reversed, subject to some limitations, or the card issuer can refund the transaction to the consumer, subject to certain conditions.
- Associations such as the International Air Transport Association facilitate repatriation of stranded consumers (Department for Transport (2018)).

However, these measures are subject to multiple terms and conditions with respect to the time and means of booking the airline ticket and may not always be available to all consumers.

Proposed step—Change the insolvency laws?

Most of the possible solutions discussed in the *Airline Insolvency Review: Call for Evidence* deal with the strengthening of the above-mentioned reliefs. The review also suggests that "*changes could also be made to place the emphasis on those administering an insolvent airline to ensure passenger welfare*". If this step is taken, it would be similar to the case of the home buyers in the post-2018 amendment scenario.

In the next Section, we look at how foreign jurisdictions such as the U.K., U.S.A. and Australia are treating consumers as creditors in corporate insolvencies.

4 Consumers as Creditors in Other Jurisdictions

4.1 U.K.

In this Section, we examine the rights available to consumers under the insolvency regime of the UK.[6] This examination adds to the arguments for special treatment contemplated towards a class of consumer creditors, being airline consumers as discussed in Box.

A consumer prepayment is defined as "*payment made by a consumer in advance of goods or services being provided.*" (UK Law Commission 2016). This prepayment may be of the entire amount of consideration as advance, paid by way of a deposit or a gift voucher purchased for a third party. Some of the protections available to aggrieved consumers are as follows:

- The credit card company may provide a refund to the consumer when the prepaid amount has been paid using a credit card.
- The administrator may honour gift vouchers or fulfil customer orders during a period of trading in administration.
- Where the business is sold as a going concern, the subsequent purchaser of the business may choose to honour the prepayments.
- If property in the goods has passed, then the consumer would be entitled to claim possession of them on payment of any balance to the insolvency practitioner (UK Law Commission 2016).

Other protections with which a business may protect consumer prepayments include trusts, insurance and bonds (UK Law Commission 2016). Each of these and the impact on consumer rights have been described below:

- **Trust**: Suppliers/service providers may place the advance amounts in a trust. In such cases, the beneficial interest of the amount lies with the consumer and the said amount belongs in its entirety to the consumer and not to the supplier/service provider. Therefore, for purposes of insolvency and bankruptcy, such amounts are kept outside the purview of the supplier/service provider's estate for distribution to creditors. However, if the funds kept by the supplier/service provider are insufficient, then the consumers will be paid off by means of pro-rata payments.
- **Insurance**: Insurance cover is commonly provided to buyers of new built property, solar panels and double glazing. This relief is often difficult, expensive and hedged with exclusions and conditions for other sectors (UK Law Commission 2016).
- **Bonds**: Commonly used in the travel industry, bonds guarantee payment of the agreed sum should a member of associations, such as the *AOTA*, becomes insolvent.

The above constitute some element of voluntary actions which keep the consumer prepayments outside the purview of the debtor's estate and consequently outside the

---

[6] In this Section, as in the earlier Sections, emphasis is on rights arising in respect of consumer prepayments and compensation/damages awarded to consumers.

insolvency proceedings. With specific reference to laws governing insolvency, *UK Insolvency Act, 1986*, as modified by the *Enterprise Act, 2002*, governs corporate insolvencies in UK. Under this present legal regime, consumer prepayments, when not subject to any of the protections mentioned above, are treated as general unsecured credit. Therefore, like in India, there is no preferential treatment provided to consumers in respect of insolvent corporate debtors.

As is evident, there are various protections available to consumers prior to insolvency and during insolvency. The U.K. also has efficient, timely and numerous mechanisms and remedies for consumer protection. This does not put the burden on the insolvency regime to provide for consumer protection.[7] Through the *Report on consumer prepayments on retailer insolvency*, the Law Commission has made certain recommendations in respect of consumer status in the insolvency hierarchy.[8] It is to be seen whether these recommendations are converted into law.

4.2 U.S.A

In this Section, we analyse the insolvency and bankruptcy laws in respect of consumers as creditors in the U.S.A. The law governing insolvency and bankruptcy in the U.S.A. is Title 11 of the *U.S. Code*. Chapter 5 of Title 11 enlists priorities given to certain creditor claims. Individual consumers, under this sub-paragraph, have unsecured claims to the estate of the bankrupt. According to this provision, such claims are ranked seventh in the list of claims. Valid claims for the purpose of this provision, are claims arising out of a deposit of money in connection with the purchase, lease, or rental of property or the purchase of services, when such property or service is yet to be delivered or provided. This provision applies to consumer prepayments. The sub-paragraph further clarifies that claims under it are to be allowed only to the extent of $2850 for each individual (Judicial Conference of the United States 2016).

While such claims are seventh in priority in case of liquidation, with respect to reorganisation of the corporate debtor, according to paragraph 1129(a)(9) of the *U.S. Code*, except when consumers have agreed otherwise, such claimants are to be paid cash equal to the allowed amount of the claim either on the effective date of the plan or in deferred payments of a value as of such effective date. Therefore, it can be said that the framework in the U.S.A does provide some protection to consumers even though in a limited way.

---

[7] See Sect. 5.

[8] See recommendations 4a and 4b from Chap. 10, *Report on consumer prepayments on retailer insolvency*.

4.3 Australia

In Australia, the *Corporation Act* governs insolvency of corporate debtors. The three most common corporate insolvency procedures are voluntary administration, liquidation and receivership. Consumers who have paid in full for goods or services to be collected or delivered later; or have paid a deposit, such as in a lay-by agreement or interest-free offer; or have bought a gift card or voucher and have not used it; or have returned a product and been issued a credit note; or have provided services or goods to the company; or have made loans to the company are categorised as 'unsecured creditors' under the law.

As an unsecured creditor, the consumer is required to register with the administrator or liquidator. In the hierarchy of distribution of funds, unsecured creditors are last in line. By virtue of being unsecured creditors, consumers rank extremely low in the distribution of the corporate debtor's estate.

The question of priority to consumers who have made prepayments was one of the points of consideration in the *General Insolvency Inquiry*. However, post reviewing the overseas experience, the committee did not favour a change in the law. The committee emphasised the importance of equal sharing and stated that priority provisions should be limited (Paragraph 771 of the *General Insolvency Inquiry*).

5 Consumer Protection Legislations

As is evident from Sect. 4, jurisdictions such as the U.K. and Australia do not make any special provisions for consumer creditors and the U.S.A. makes a limited provision for consumers. However, this does not mean that consumers are left helpless. These jurisdictions boast of adequate consumer protection norms which reduce the loss which may be caused upon the insolvency of a corporate debtor.

5.1 U.K.

The *UK Consumer Rights Act* is a legislation which provides for, among other things, the rights of consumers and the protection of their interests (Preamble to the *UK Consumer Rights Act*). The *UK Consumer Protection Act*, on the other hand, was enacted to make provisions for the liability of persons for damage caused by defective products, among other things.

The *Supply of Goods and Services Act, 1982* is similar to the *Sale of Goods Act, 1930* in India and defines the rights of consumers/purchasers/service recipients in respect of the supply of goods and services. It empowers the courts to grant remedies such as repair of damaged goods as well as reduction in the consideration amount for the relevant goods and services.

In addition, liabilities under torts also apply to consumers in the U.K.

Consumers in the U.K. may utilise three routes for obtaining relief in any consumer rights dispute:

1. In-house complaints mechanism, being the internal procedure established by the trader/service provider for dealing with consumer disputes;
2. Alternative Dispute Resolution (ADR) is a means of resolving disputes outside the court machinery by approaching a third party to decide upon the rights of the parties and
3. Court process, being remedies provided by civil courts such as county courts under various laws mentioned above.

The *Final report on resolving consumer disputes* released in April 2018 provides a comprehensive analysis of enforcement through ADR and the court process. The study focuses on various parameters to compare the two enforcement machineries, including time and cost of enforcement procedures. Some observations from the report are enlisted below:

- ADR procedures include mediation, conciliation, arbitration, adjudication and ombudsman schemes while county courts deal with consumer claims which go through three different tracks.[9]
- Of the sample of people surveyed for the report, 62% of the respondents found the ADR process simple, while 53% of the respondents found the court process to be simple.[10]
- In terms of time taken for completion of processes, the shortest duration for the completion of an ADR process was between one and four weeks (for 6% of the respondents) while the longest was more than nine months (for 13% of the respondents). Similarly, the minimum court case duration was less than four weeks (for 10% of the respondents) whereas the maximum was more than nine months (for 15% of the respondents). Further, while 50% of the court cases were disposed off between three to nine months, 41% of the ADR processes were completed in the same time frame.[11]
- In terms of the types of redress, 61% of ADR processes resulted in a favourable order for the consumers. Similarly, outcome of 60% of the court cases favoured the consumers.[12]
- In terms of monetary/financial awards/orders, 90% consumer respondents whose cases were solved in their favour received financial awards including compensation or refunds, whereas the corresponding number for ADR processes was 100%.[13]

As a consequence of these, consumer redressal is timely and efficient in the U.K.

[9] The three tracks are the small claim track, fast track claim and multi-track claim (Department for Business, Energy and Industrial Strategy 2018).

[10] Figure 12, *Final report on resolving consumer disputes*.

[11] Figure 20, *Final report on resolving consumer disputes*.

[12] Figure 25, *Final report on resolving consumer disputes*.

[13] Figure 26, *Final report on resolving consumer disputes*.

5.2 U.S.A

The primary legislation dealing with consumer protection in the U.S.A. is the *Federal Trade Commission Act*. Under this law, the Federal Trade Commission (FTC) is empowered to (a) prevent unfair methods of competition and unfair or deceptive acts or practices in or affecting commerce; (b) seek monetary redress and other relief for conduct injurious to consumers; (c) prescribe rules defining with specificity acts or practices that are unfair or deceptive, and establishing requirements designed to prevent such acts or practices; (d) gather and compile information and conduct investigations relating to the organisation, business, practices, and management of entities engaged in commerce; and (e) make reports and legislative recommendations to Congress and the public.[14]

The Bureau of Consumer Protection at the FTC is responsible for protection of consumers from fraudulent, deceptive and unfair business practices. The FTC can force wrongdoers to disgorge ill-gotten gains when it is able to objectively determine a clear violation of law and reasonably calculate the damages. For such restitution of the consumers, the FTC may use the court machinery to seek civil penalties (Waller and Acosta 2011). Other sanctions provided by the FTC include sanctions such as cease and desist orders. Other federal agencies responsible for consumer protection include agencies such as the *Consumer Product Safety Commission*, which is responsible for reducing injury or death caused by consumer products, and the *Food and Drug Administration*, which is responsible for food, drug, cosmetic and medical device safety. Further, at the state level too, there are statutes and regulatory authorities for addressing consumer protection issues.

In addition to the above, the law of torts also applies to consumers in the U.S.A. Negligence and product liability are the most common causes of action for torts against consumers. While negligence is 'omission to do something which a reasonable man, guided by those considerations which ordinarily regulate the conduct of human affairs would do, or doing something which a prudent and reasonable man would not do', product liability is the 'obligation or liability of the producer or supplier of goods and services in order to adjust for the loss associated with its utilisation, such as damage of property or personal injury'.[15] Remedies for both these torts may be sought from the civil courts, which may grant compensation to the aggrieved consumer. Post such compensation being ordered, the consumer becomes a creditor of the seller/service provider with respect to the compensation amount.

The *Uniform Commercial Code* is the other legislation which is applicable to all commercial transactions and therefore, also to transactions of sale of goods and may be used for obtaining monetary relief from a defaulting seller.

---

[14] The list of applicable legislations and powers of the FTC may be found at https://www.ftc.gov/enforcement/statutes.

[15] *Black's Law Dictionary*, https://thelawdictionary.org.

5.3 Australia

Consumer protection in Australia is a part of the *Competition and Consumer Act, 2010*. Schedule 2 of the *Competition and Consumer Act, 2010* contains the *Australian Consumer Law* (ACL) which commenced on 1 January 2011. The ACL is the principal law governing consumer protections matters in Australia.

Clause 36 of the ACL makes provisions in respect of consumer prepayments. It states that a person who accepts payment or other consideration for goods or services must supply all the goods or services either within the period specified by or on behalf of the person at or before the time the payment or other consideration was accepted; or if no period is specified at or before that time, within a reasonable time.[16] The clause also contains a note stating that a pecuniary penalty may be imposed upon contravention of this provision.

Therefore, consumer prepayments are protected under this clause. If a corporate debtor violates this clause, the consumer may approach the *Australian Competition and Consumer Commission* or the relevant state and territory consumer protection agencies.

It is noteworthy that these jurisdictions have not combined consumer protection and insolvency laws. Separate legal mechanisms with separate consumer protection objectives have been created. In the following Section, we look at consumer protection and insolvency in the Indian scenario.

6 Consumer Protection and Insolvency

During the pre-insolvency period, consumers as contributors to the business of a corporate debtor have a significant role to play, especially when it comes to advances paid by consumers. These advances are usually used by the corporate debtor for operations and regular business while amounts borrowed from financial institutions are typically used for long-term interests of such debtor.

Consumers are fundamentally different from others who pay advances to a corporate debtor. In most cases, consumer prepayments are towards purchases/services that will be used for consumption and not for profit making or risk taking. When the supplier firm becomes insolvent, consumers may not be aware of the insolvency event, the status of their claims in the resolution process, or have the financial and legal resources to pursue recovery. Often the quantum of such prepayments may be at its highest when insolvency proceedings commence, since companies try to push up their sales in the period preceding insolvency.

There also exists significant diversity in the nature, size and form of consumer advances across sectors. These could be for high-value purchases, such as homes, automobiles, electronic goods, or for smaller purchases such as travel, apparel, groceries or annual maintenance contracts for home appliances, home cleaning services

---

[16] Clause 36 of Schedule 2 of the *Competition and Consumer Act, 2010*.

and so on. There can also be implicit prepayments, such as airline miles, accumulated reward points or gift vouchers.

These characteristics, coupled with the sentimental value attached to credit forwarded by general members of the public who make advances for goods/services without a profit motive, attract an element of special treatment. However, there are various challenges when dealing with consumer claims in insolvency. Some of these challenges are as follows:

- Contracts entered into with consumers are not as robust as those with financial creditors or vendors and service providers. They often do not contain provisions for dealing with insolvency of the corporate debtor. This not only leads to a scenario where consumers are unaware of the reliefs available to them but also limits the reliefs available to consumers in case of insolvency of the corporate debtor.
- While independent consumer claims are mostly small in value, consumers are large in number as compared to other creditors of the debtor. Therefore, repayment of a small amount is pending in favour of a large group of recipients. This does not bode well for consumer interests as debtors are incentivised to deal with larger claims with a smaller set of creditors first. Claims of consumers tend to be ignored in the first instance.
- Legal proceedings, including insolvency and bankruptcy proceedings constitute a financial burden on litigating parties. Individual consumers might not have the ability to bear the legal and cost aspects of the insolvency process.

It is for this reason that most jurisdictions have specific laws for consumer protection. A few of these have been studied in Sect. 5.

While India also has similar laws and provisions under common law and in equity, the effectiveness of these laws is often poor in terms of the timeliness of the relief. Consumer forums have a timeline of three months recommended in the *Consumer Protection Act, 1986* for disposal of complaints. However, reports suggest that consumer forums are unable to adhere to these timelines, due to issues of capacity and infrastructure constraints (Ministry of Consumer Affairs 2013). Statistics show that in 2018, only 1911 applications were disposed off by the *NCDRC* while 20621 applications were pending before the forum. Of these pending applications, around 13000 applications are old pendencies carried forward from earlier years while the remaining arose from the applications filed in the year 2018.[17]

As is evident, problems of consumers start much before the firm enters insolvency. Therefore, there is a need to fix the underlying issue which is the consumer protection framework and better contract enforcement. In respect of home buyers, some efforts have been made in this regard. The Real Estate Regulation Act, 2016 (RERA) is one such example.

Various provisions of RERA provide for safeguards enacted to protect the interests of real estate consumers. Section 13 of the Act does not permit the promoter (being the builder/developer) to obtain any deposit or advance without entering into

[17] The statistics are as was accessed on 26 December 2018 at http://cms.nic.in/ncdrcusersWeb/dashboard.do?method=loadDashBoardPub.

a written agreement for sale which must be registered under the *Registration Act, 1908*. Section 18 then specifically provides for the return of the advance amount along with compensation. This Act also requires a promoter to give a declaration on affidavit that 70% of the amounts collected from the consumers will be deposited in a separate account to be maintained in a scheduled bank to cover the cost of the project and land cost and must be used only for that purpose (Sect. 6 of the RERA). The Act further imposes specific restrictions on the way that the amounts kept in the separate account are to be dealt with. Further, any complaints of the consumer have to be made to the RERA. Consumer protection legislations like RERA define consumer rights clearly and facilitate easier dispute resolution. These help in obtaining reliefs during the stage of financial distress itself.

These are remedies for the pre-insolvency stage. Insolvency is a specific problem where there are more claimants than resources. The IBC attempts to create a distribution mechanism which replicates, as far as possible, the pre-insolvency priority of claims. This is because there are certain *ex ante* effects of insolvency priority. What happens when one class of actors gets priority or preferential treatment over others? There is a corresponding class of actors who is aggrieved and feels unprotected or inadequately protected or even discriminated against. What does such discrimination lead to? It leads to discouragement from acting in a certain manner. Let us take the issue at hand. If a set of unsecured creditors, such as home buyers, get more rights in insolvency as financial creditors, other unsecured creditors will be disincentivised from forwarding credit to real estate firms. Financial institutions who know that owing to large-valued claims, home buyers with their seat on the CoC may cause hindrances in the resolution of a firm, they will also be discouraged from participating in the credit market for real estate firms. It is for this reason that classification of home buyers as financial creditors may have an adverse *ex ante* effect on the credit market for real estate firms. Further, the IBC was enacted with one objective in mind—timely resolution of firms. The entire design of the law is motivated by this objective. Introducing additional objectives such as consumer protection, as has been done in the case of home buyers, complicates this design.

7 Conclusion

The problems of the real estate sector and home buyers are a legacy problem. Years of flawed financing policies, weak contracts and consumer protection led the sector to the stage it is in today. In attempting to protect home buyers under the insolvency regime, the policymakers have taken one specific sector and a class of creditors within such sector and made changes which are likely to have system-wide implications. Even for home buyers themselves, their pre-insolvency rights remain the same while their rights in insolvency have changed.

Had we not resorted to these drastic measures, sector specific laws like RERA, once implemented completely, would have addressed most concerns of home buyers. Further, observing the trends under the IBC, contracting would have evolved to create a better balance of rights between parties in a real estate transaction. There would also be a pressure on the policymakers to improve the consumer protection framework. The real estate firms would also be constrained to adopt recapitalisation mechanisms. Since the *IBBI* had already created a class of 'other creditors' to record and address the claims of home buyers, the need to amend the law remains unclear.

It must also not be forgotten that the classification of creditors as financial and operational has itself been challenged on the grounds of being unconstitutional. Various proceedings are pending before High Courts such as the Madras High Court and the Gujarat High Court on this issue (Marwah 2017; Livelaw 2018). Therefore, there is a possibility that the distinction itself is done away with and then there would be no question of special carve outs for consumers such as home buyers. All creditors would then have similar rights, thereby rendering the amendment futile.

Various jurisdictions have toyed and continue to toy with the idea of making special provisions for a class of consumer creditors. However, as observed in this chapter, most jurisdictions refrain from creating such an exception. India has acted uniquely in response to the home buyers' issue, especially in light of constitutional challenges to the creditor classification and the purpose of the law being resolution of a firm and not consumer protection or recovery of debt. Only time will tell what the outcome of this drastic step of the policymakers will be. It will either be a lesson for the world on making a bold move or a lesson for India on learning from others' experience.

Author's note: Subsequent amendments related to home buyers in the IBC

Since the passing of the law and its operationalisation in 2017, there has been one significant development in the rights of home buyers under the IBC. This is the introduction of a new threshold for IBC applications filed by home buyers. Since December 2019, a home buyer initiated IBC application is to be filed jointly by the lesser of at least 100 home buyers OR 10% of the total home buyers under the real estate project.

In its 2020 report, the Insolvency Law Committee justified this amendment of the law by stating that in the original law, a single home buyer could put a real estate firm into insolvency even if there was a minor dispute. According to the committee, this had the potential to not only exert undue pressure on the real estate firm, but also to jeopardise interests of other home buyers who are not in favour of IBC proceedings. Therefore, lawmakers decided to limit the rights of a single home buyer and moved towards joint applications.

This limitation, in addition to the general increase in the monetary threshold for filing IBC proceedings from Rs.1 lakh to Rs.1 crore, could lead to a reduction in the number of IBC applications filed by home buyers.

References

Bloomberg Quint (2018) Jet airways is showering discounts this monsoon. online, https://www.bloombergquint.com/business/jet-airways-is-showering-discounts-this-monsoon#gs.GEwkHDtj

Department for Business (2018) Energy and industrial strategy. Resolving consumer disputes, Alternative dispute resolution and the court system. Technical Report

Department for Transport (2018) Airline insolvency review: a final report. Technical Report, Government of U.K., Great Minster House, 33 Horseferry Road, London SW1P 4DR

Dubey R (2018) Is jet airways, India's second largest airline, already insolvent? https://www.businesstoday.in/sectors/aviation/is-jet-airways-india-second-largest-airline-already-insolvent/story/281234.html

Judicial Conference of the United States (2016) Revision of certain dollar amounts in the Bankruptcy code. online, https://inthered.lexblogplatformthree.com/wp-content/uploads/sites/245/2016/02/Fed-Reg-Dollar-Amount-Adjustments-20161.pdf

Livelaw (2018) SC bars HC from hearing the constitutional validity of insolvency and Bankruptcy code or NCLT. 1, https://www.livelaw.in/sc-bars-hc-hearing-constitutional-validity-insolvency-bankruptcy-code-nclt/

Marwah V (2017) Insolvency code provisions challenged in the Madras High Court. online, https://barandbench.com/insolvency-code-provisions-challenged-madras-hc/

Ministry of Consumer Affairs (2013) Evaluation report on impact and effectiveness of consumer protection act, 1986. Technical Report, Government of India

The Household Finance Committee (2017) Indian household finance. Technical Report, Reserve Bank of India

UK Law Commission (2016) Report on consumer prepayments on retailer insolvency. Technical Report, Government of U.K

Waller JS, Brady Acosta R (2011) Consumer protection in the United States: an overview. Eur J Consum Law

Performance of Company Law Tribunals in India

Aditi Nayak and Prasanth V. Regy

1 Introduction

The Indian judicial system is seen to be unable to deliver timely justice. Many courts are unable to make much progress in reducing their immense backlog, or even to keep pace with inflow of new cases. In this chapter, we offer a framework to analyse judicial performance, and in particular judicial delays, using the National Company Law Tribunal (NCLT) as an example.

We begin in Sect. 2 with a quick sketch of the NCLT. In Sect. 3, we study the concept of 'judicial performance'. We survey the legal and economic literature to understand the indicators that have been used to measure it. We also propose a mathematical model that seeks to explain the duration of petitions in terms of the features of the petition as well as the workload of the tribunal. In Section 4, we use a new dataset to examine how the NCLT has performed against the selected indicators. We test the validity of the mathematical model against this dataset. This enables us to estimate the duration of petitions based on factors such as the type of the petition, the bench, the pendency and the rate of inflow. In Sect. 5, we try to diagnose the problem in the light of the empirical findings and make recommendations on the way forward, and we conclude in Sect. 6.

[1]Law Commission of India (2014).

The authors would like to acknowledge the valuable comments of two anonymous referees, as well as of Mr Vijay Mahajan. The opinions expressed in this chapter and all remaining errors are the authors own.

A. Nayak · P. V. Regy (✉)
Aakriti Shantiniketan, Noida, India
e-mail: prasanthvr@gmail.com

© The Author(s), under exclusive license to Springer Nature Singapore Pte Ltd. 2022

S. Thomas (ed.), *Insolvency and Bankruptcy Reforms in India*,
India Studies in Business and Economics,
https://doi.org/10.1007/978-981-16-0854-4_4

2 A Description of the NCLT

The establishment of the NCLT was first recommended by the Eradi Committee[2] as a specialised agency to deal with matters relating to rehabilitation, revival and winding-up of companies. In line with the recommendations, the Companies Act (1956) was amended to provide for the establishment of the NCLT and its appellate body, the National Company Law Appellate Tribunal (NCLAT). However, these provisions were found to be partly unconstitutional, leading to much legislative and judicial back-and-forth.

Eventually, NCLT was constituted with effect from June 1, 2016, under the Companies Act, 2013. It was vested with the powers to handle all matters under the Companies Act which were previously handled by the Company Law Board (CLB) and the High Courts. Upon the enactment of the Insolvency and Bankruptcy Code, 2016 (IBC), which also vested jurisdiction in the NCLT, all winding-up petitions handled by the High Courts, and matters handled by the erstwhile Board of Industrial and Financial Reconstruction (BIFR) under the Sick Industrial Companies (Special Provisions) Act, 1985 (SICA), were also transitioned to the NCLT.

The powers of the NCLT are exercised through several *benches* of the tribunal that are constituted by notification by the Ministry of Corporate Affairs (MCA). As of this writing, NCLT benches have been established at 13 locations, each bench exercising jurisdiction over one or more states. The Principal Bench is located at New Delhi and is presided over by the *President* of the NCLT. Each bench comprises of two members, one judicial and one technical member, or if specifically provided, a single judicial member. The judicial members are serving or retired judges, or lawyers. The tribunal also has a *Registrar*, who oversees the administrative functioning of the NCLT and is the custodian of the records of the tribunal.

The NCLT is a quasi-judicial body. It is not bound by the procedure laid down in the Civil Procedure Code (CPC), and can determine its own procedure. There are two levels of appeals. The first is to the NCLAT against an order passed by the NCLT, and the second is to the Supreme Court against the order of the NCLAT.

2.1 Workload

The NCLT adjudicates upon matters under the erstwhile Companies Act, 1956, the extant Companies Act, 2013, and the IBC.

Companies Act The matters handled by the NCLT under the Companies Act can be broadly categorised into the following types: cases pertaining to share capital and debentures; cases pertaining to the management, administration and accounts of companies; cases involving the exercise of NCLT's powers to order investigations into and adjudicate upon the affairs of companies; cases seeking sanction

[2] Department of Company Affairs (2000).

of schemes of compromise, arrangement and amalgamation of companies; cases seeking relief against oppression and mismanagement, or of class action, and finally, cases of winding-up.

Insolvency petitions The IBC, which came into effect on May 28, 2016, lays down a process, called the Corporate Insolvency Resolution Process (CIRP), for the resolution of an insolvent firm.[3] An application for initiating the CIRP may be filed before the NCLT by a Financial Creditor (FC), an Operational Creditor (OC) or by the Corporate Debtor (CD).[4] The IBC prescribes that the NCLT must apply or reject the application within 14 days. If the application is accepted, the IBC prescribes that the CIRP must be completed within 180 days, extensible by 90 days.

In addition to the application to initiate the CIRP, various other applications may also be filed before the NCLT under the IBC. These include applications seeking extension of the period for completion of the insolvency process, for approval of the resolution plan, for ordering liquidation, etc.

The NCLT workload also comprises of interlocutory applications (such as: for stay, direction and condonation of delay), as well as various miscellaneous applications.

3 Judicial Performance Measurement

> The growing criticism of the judiciary for its alleged lack of accountability is now taking its toll. ...Judicial accountability is inseparable from judicial independence. The challenge before the nation is how to secure judicial accountability without impairing judicial independence.
>
> N. R. Madhav Menon[5]

> It is in the interests of the judiciary to actively co-operate with government in the development of appropriate performance measures. Abdication of judicial responsibility for the identification and development of appropriate court performance measures seems to me to pose the greatest threat to the institutional independence of the courts between now and 2020.
>
> Wayne Martin, Chief Justice, Western Australia[6]

In this section, we consider the concept of judicial performance, and its measurement. The questions we attempt to answer are: are there objective measures of

---

[3] The IBC also deals with personal insolvency, but those provisions have not been notified yet.

[4] An OC is a person who has extended credit in the form of goods or services to the debtor. This includes trade credit, wages, taxes, etc. The term CD refers to the debtor company itself.

[5] Menon (2008).

[6] Martin (2008).

judicial performance which are widely accepted? If yes, what are they, and how can we use them? We also look at it from an India-specific angle, where the delays that pervade the rest of the judicial system have now spread to the NCLT as well.

3.1 Can Court Performance Be Measured?

There is one school of thought that claims that most of the important matters regarding the performance of courts are not measurable. Spigelman (2006) says:

> …there are significant areas of public decision-making, and the law is one of them, in which there is no measurable indicator of quality, even at the level of defect rates or numbers of complaints. There is simply no escaping qualitative assessment for purposes of evaluation. What this means is that decision-making processes which are based only on quantitative measurement are so defective as to be irrational.

However, he does not object to the publication of statistics about matters such as delays and costs, 'which are both capable of assessment in quantitative terms and which provide information that is useful to the courts and the publication of which serves to enhance the accountability of the courts'. His objection is against attempts to measure the quality of judicial decision-making.

Such objections are not universal. For instance, the US judicial system has set up standards that seek to measure, among other things, matters relating to judicial quality, such as equality, fairness and integrity.[7] There is also a substantial academic literature on the how and why of court performance measurement, not only in law reviews but also in economics journals. The economics literature measures court performance for very different reasons as compared to the legal literature. Interestingly enough, the measures used in these two literatures turn out not to differ all that much. In the sections below, we discuss both perspectives.

3.2 The Legal Perspective

From a legal point of view, judicial performance needs to be measured in order to evaluate the judiciary against its values. Some of these values, and the measures used in the literature, are discussed below.

Accountability and transparency Citizens have an interest in judicial accountability. They have an expectation that courts, like any other public-funded agency, should account for their performance. Essentially, measurement of court performance is a way to assess what the taxpayer gets for his money.[8] This strand of judicial performance measurement focuses on measures such as the rate of disposal of cases, duration of cases, delays and backlogs.

---

[7] National Center for State Courts (1997).

[8] Dakolias (1999); Keilitz (2000); Martin (2008); Schauffler (2007).

Independence In the legal literature, there is a recognition that measurement of judicial performance is deeply linked to preserving judicial independence. In the absence of legitimate criteria for the evaluation of the judiciary, it might come to be evaluated against, say, allegiance to political ideologies, or popular sentiments. Thus, the criteria that are used for the evaluation of the judiciary can play an important role in preserving the independence of the judiciary. Most of the judicial literature uses surveys of judges, the bar and the citizenry to evaluate independence.[9]

Efficiency Many attempts have been made to characterise the efficiency of courts, such as why the output of some courts is higher than others, whether courts could 'produce' more justice using the available resources, and if courts that are more productive have achieved their productivity at the cost of quality.

These are not easy questions to answer, particularly because the judiciary produces multiple outputs using multiple inputs. Hence, the measurement of judicial administrative efficiency requires a sophisticated notion of 'efficiency'. Typically, in such studies, the inputs include parameters such as the number of judicial officers, their experience and qualifications, the rate of their turnover, the number of support staff and the sophistication of their support systems. The outputs include the number of dispositions and the fraction of cases that are delayed.[10]

Given the pervasive delays in the judiciary in India, administrative efficiency has been a particular focus of the academic literature here. Regy and Roy (2017) provide a rigorous definition of what constitutes judicial delay in the context of adjournments and demonstrate a method to measure such delays. They calculate that about 60% of the time taken in a sample of cases in Debt Recovery Tribunals was lost to avoidable delays. They create a typology of reasons for delay and attribute delays to one of the three parties involved in the case: the plaintiff, the defendant or the court itself. They find that while most delays were due to the Tribunal's willingness to grant requests for adjournments from lawyers, about 19% of the adjournments were necessitated by the Tribunal's own administration. Daksh (2016) conducted a time-and-motion study of four courts in Bengaluru. They found that about 54% of the sitting time of civil courts and 33% of that of criminal courts are spent on handling adjournments.

Often, efficiency is not easy to calculate because a large fraction of the cases studied might still be under process, and ignoring them can systematically bias the analysis. In such situations, many authors have applied survival analysis techniques to case durations or legal settlements.[11] In India, Datta et al. (2017) applied these techniques to cases at the Income Tax Appellate Tribunal.

Accessibility Accessibility is a multidimensional concept, and it includes distance to courts, as well as accessibility and affordability of legal services. Some jurisdictions use High Court fees as an instrument to reduce the inflow of cases. This

[9] Martin (2008); Posner (2006); Schauffler (2007); White (2001).

[10] Lewin et al. (1982); Palumbo et al. (2013); Rosales-López (2008).

[11] Fournier and Zuehlke (1996); Kessler (1996); Kondylis and Stein (2018); Kritzer and Anderson (1983).

might also deter frivolous litigation. For example, a reading of the *Rules of Court* in Singapore states that for an open court hearing in a District Court, the first day is free. The second day onwards, a fee of SGD 500 (about Rs 26,000) is charged. In the High Court, the amount can be as high as SGD 9,000 (about Rs 4.8 lakh) per day.

The argument can be a double-edged sword. Limiting access in this manner may improve efficiency, but at a cost. High Court fees create a judiciary that only the rich can afford. Efficiency is a means, not the end, and a society might choose so-called 'inefficiency' if it helps to achieve more important values, such as democracy and equality.[12]

In India, Baruah et al. (2018) conducted a nation wide survey to understand people's experiences with, and perception of, the justice mechanisms in India. The indicators they used include the duration and cost of litigation.

Predictability A well-functioning judiciary can provide certainty, coherence and consistency in law. An arbitrary judiciary is contrary to the rule of law, and affects overall predictability in the economic and political life of the country. Like many other judicial values, predictability is commonly measured through questionnaire surveys.[13] But attempts have also been made to evaluate predictability using textual analysis of orders.[14]

Merit While 'judicial merit' might seem to glide perilously close to the kind of measurement which Spigelman (2006) warns us away from, that has not stopped academic efforts to quantify and measure it. For instance, Choi and Gulati (2004) suggest that the US judicial appointments process can be made more objective by measuring the merit of judges using three measures: productivity, as measured by the number of opinions written; opinion quality, as measured by the number of citations outside the jurisdiction; and independence, as measured by the number of dissents and concurrences written.

3.3 The Economic Perspective

Well-functioning judiciaries promote a healthy economy by securing two essential prerequisites of market economies: security of property rights and enforcement of contracts.[15] Much of the literature focuses on how the speed of adjudication, its cost and the enforcement of judicial orders, impacts the economy.[16] Some of the literature also focuses on parameters such as judicial independence.[17] The measurement of

[12] Botero et al. (2003); Spigelman (2006).

[13] Weder (1995).

[14] Wagner and Petherbridge (2004).

[15] Messick (1999).

[16] Beck et al. (2006); Coviello et al. (2018); Djankov et al. (2008); Johnson et al. (2002); Kumar et al. (1999); Ponticelli and Alencar (2016).

[17] Porta et al. (2002).

judicial performance can help shed light on the incentives of the judges. For instance, Schneider (2005) investigates the dispute resolution and the law-making functions of the German labour courts by measuring the productivity (related to the number of finished cases) and the confirmation rate (how often decisions are upheld in appellate court), to determine how career opportunities of judges shape judicial performance.

India scores very poorly (ranking 163 out of 190 countries) on the World Bank's Doing Business ranking for 'Enforcing Contracts', which measures the time and cost for resolving a commercial dispute.[18] Given the delays in the Indian judicial system, many authors have investigated its impact on the economy. Chemin (2010) finds that when courts became faster due to reforms in the CPC, it led to fewer breaches of contract, encouraged investment, and facilitated access to finance. Visaria (2009) finds that the introduction of specialised Debt Recovery Tribunal (DRT) in India (and the consequent faster disposition of credit recovery cases) increases loan repayment and lowers the cost of credit. Lilienfeld-Toal et al. (2012) study the same reform, and tease out further insights. While the faster enforcement due to the DRT might have led to an overall increase in credit, there is a differential impact on borrowers: larger borrowers got access to more credit and smaller borrowers, less. Chakraborty (2016) uses the pendency ratio (the ratio of the pending cases to all the cases in a year) as a measure of judicial quality and finds that firms in states with better judicial performance produce higher output. Ahsan (2013) also uses the pendency ratio as a measure of judicial efficiency.

3.4 Performance Measurement in Some Jurisdictions

Many countries have well-established systems for measuring court performance. In this section, we look at three jurisdictions: the United States, the European Union (EU) and Kenya.

European Union The EU focuses on three parameters of an effective justice system: efficiency, quality and independence.[19] The European Commission prepares Justice Scoreboards annually, comparing the performance of all 28 EU member nations along a number of indicators that measure these parameters. The objective is to assist the Member States in their efforts to create a more investment, business and citizen-friendly environment.

Kenya The Kenyan Judiciary has introduced a Judiciary Transformation Framework,[20] which emphasises performance management. A performance management committee, led by a senior judge, has been established, and a Directorate of Performance Management, with staff qualified in economics, statistics and business management, has been set up. In order to obtain baseline data, a case census

[18] World Bank (2019).

[19] European Commission (2018).

[20] Supreme Court (2012).

was conducted to establish the type and age of cases, as well as the resources available in each court. Kenya has also introduced a standardised data collection template to record the progress of cases.[21]

United States A commission to identify court performance standards was established in 1987.[22] The commission proposed Trial Court Performance Standards (TCPS), consisting of 22 standards under 5 broad areas: access to justice; expedition and timeliness; equality, fairness and integrity; independence and accountability; and public trust and confidence. Under these standards, 68 measures were selected. However, the adoption of these standards was limited, both because of their large number, and lack of clarity regarding their definition. Later, a simplified set of ten carefully defined measures (CourTools) was proposed, which have been broadly adopted.[23]
Apart from TCPS and CourTools, which are performance measures for courts, many jurisdictions also have performance measurement tools for individual judges, called Judicial Performance Evaluation (JPE) programmes. In 1985, the American Bar Association (ABA) established model standards for conducting JPE programmes.[24] These programmes rely largely on surveys of attorneys for feedback about a judge's performance on the bench.

In the case of the NCLT in India, only inflow and pendency seem to be reported in public.[25] These are the most commonly reported metrics for many courts. A few courts are also reported to have put performance evaluation systems in place.[26] While tracking the pendency and delay is very important, understanding the performance of the judiciary requires a richer and more sophisticated set of indicators. Recently, the NITI Aayog has also called for the introduction of a more sophisticated judicial performance index.[27] In the next following, we propose a set of measures based on the principles set out in the previous discussion.

3.5 *Performance Measures for the NCLT*

It might be best to start with a small set of indicators that are well thought out, rather than an unmanageably large number of indicators. If necessary, more can be added iteratively. We must also remember that the existing data quality may be quite poor. Attempts to measure too many indicators can lead to a heavy administrative burden. Measurement will be meaningless if the measures are poorly defined, or if the data

[21] Menzies (2015).
[22] Casey (1998).
[23] Schauffler (2007).
[24] American Bar Association (2005).
[25] Ministry of Corporate Affairs (2018a).
[26] Supreme Court of India (2017).
[27] NITI Aayog (2017).

is unreliable. It is also important that there is broad agreement within the judiciary itself about the importance of performance measures, their definition and the uses that they are put to. Else, performance measurement may be resisted from within, and even if data is collected and measures calculated, they will not be legitimate or useful.

In the light of the responsibilities of the NCLT (Sect. 2), and the economic as well as legal literature on the indicators of judicial performance (Sect. 3), we suggest that the judicial performance of NCLT can be measured through these indicators:

1. Duration,
2. Delays,
3. Pendency,
4. Outflow rate and
5. Cost.

These measures are relatively non-controversial and are tracked in many countries around the world. Some of these measures are well-accepted in India already. Each of these is discussed in more detail below.

Duration The duration of a trial is the time taken between the initial filing of the petition and its disposal.
It can be useful to further sub-divide the duration into two: administrative and judicial. The administrative duration measures how long it takes from the time the matter is first filed before the registrar, till the matter is listed before the bench. The judicial duration measures how long it takes from the time the matter is first listed before the bench, till a final order is passed.

Delay Delays are generally measured in two distinct ways. One way is to compare the duration of the case to a norm. If the case takes longer than the norm, it is said to be delayed, and the excess time taken is the delay. In India, many High Courts have brought case-flow management rules into effect. These rules prescribe that cases should be decided within a period that ranges between 9 months and 2 years.[28]
This method is simple, but blunt. Its utility depends on what the norm is, and how it is set. When time limits are prescribed in the law (as is the case of IBC, for instance), the determination of delay becomes easy. A drawback of this approach is that it cannot distinguish between cases that genuinely require more time, and cases that are delayed unnecessarily.
The second approach is to distinguish between those parts of the case which were judicially productive, and those which were not, and measure them both. This approach, demonstrated in Regy and Roy (2017), allows us to accurately calculate a lower bound on the judicial delay. While this method can give a more accurate picture of delays than the first method, it also requires much more granular data. The same approach can be used for the administrative time spent on the case, in order to evaluate administrative delays.

[28] Daksh (2017).

Both these methods have their advantages. The first method can easily give a gross measure. The second method gives us a detailed understanding of how delays arise in the system. This will reveal the frequent causes of delay, and help us devise ways to remove them. Given that judicial delays are so high in India, we should attempt to track the delays through both these methods.

Pendency Pendency is the stock of cases that have been filed, but not disposed of. Most Indian courts already report it. It is calculated as

$$P_{t+1} = P_t + I_t - O_t \quad (1)$$

where P_t = Petitions pending at the beginning of the time period,
I_t = Inflow of petitions during the time period,
O_t = Outflow of petitions during the time period and
P_{t+1} = Petitions pending at the beginning of the next time period.

Outflow Rate Pendency, by itself, is not helpful without the context given by the inflow or the outflow. High pendency might not be a problem if the cases require little time to dispose of, while even low pendency might be problematic if the pending cases are complex and time-consuming. In order to track the current performance of a court, we suggest that the *outflow rate* should also be reported. This is defined as the ratio of the outflow over a time period to the average pendency during that period.

The interpretation of the outflow rate is simple: it is the fraction of the workload that is disposed of in a certain time. For instance, if there are 1000 pending cases and, of them, 200 were disposed of in a month, the outflow rate would be 20% per month. Another way to think about it is that if no new petitions were filed, it would take 5 months for the tribunal to dispose of the existing workload.

Costs The cost of a trial in a court is a determinant of the accessibility of the court. As discussed earlier, a high cost can deter potential plaintiffs or defendants, even if they are on solid legal grounds. Contingent payment to lawyers could, to an extent, remedy this problem, but it is forbidden in India as stated in the 1975 Rules of the *Bar Council of India*.

The direct cost to the parties in the case generally consists of the charges payable to the court, and the fees charged by the lawyer. If court proceedings take a long time, the opportunity cost can be significant. For instance, the Economic Survey 2017–18 reported that 52 different infrastructure projects, amounting to a total of about Rs 52,000 crore, were stayed by various court injunctions, for an average period of 4.3 years.[29] Similarly, the World Bank's Doing Business report claims that the recovery rate in India is very low, just 26.5%.[30] This is part of the cost to the Indian economy due to judicial delay. For comparison, the number in Organisation for Economic Co-operation and Development (OECD) countries is 70.5%.

[29] Deptartment of Economic Affairs (2018).

[30] World Bank (2019).

The estimation of the cost must include the court fees, the fees charged by the lawyers and the indirect costs incurred by the parties.

3.6 *Modelling Duration in Court Proceedings*

In this section, we propose a model of court proceedings which can be used to characterise the time taken for the disposal of cases. We start with setting out some notation and some assumptions required for the modelling effort, as follows:

Notation Number of pending cases = n,
Time taken by each hearing = t (units: time),
Number of hearings per case = h,
Rate of net inflow of cases = r (units: per unit time) and
Total time to dispose of a case = T (units: same as t).

Assumptions We consider only the time taken by the judicial system, not calendar days. We trace the life of a new petition, from the time it is first filed, till the time it is disposed of. The number of hearings required for the pleadings, h, and the time taken per hearing, t, are outcomes of the given judicial procedures. They are properly random variables drawn from a bench-specific distribution, and here we take average numbers. The net inflow rate of petitions, r, is exogenous. While it is properly a function of time, it is an outcome of economy-wide phenomena, which are unlikely to vary fast. It may also respond to changes in disposal rate. Here, we take r to constant for each petition. This is supported by the trend of pendency against time in Fig. 2. After an initial period of adjustment, the plot is linear, implying that the net inflow is close to constant.

At the beginning of our analysis (time 0), our new petition is just added to the docket. Now, there are n petitions pending, with the new petition being the last in the queue. The new petition gets its first hearing after every petition before it in the queue has been heard once. Once the petition has had a hearing, it goes back to the end of the queue for its next hearing. When a petition reaches h hearings, the final order is passed.

The first hearing of the new petition ends at time nt. During this time, some cases have been added to the docket and others have been disposed of. So after the first hearing of our new petition, there are $n(1 + rt)$ pending petitions.

The second hearing of the petition finishes at time $nt(1 + rt)$ after its first hearing. In this time, there will be $rnt(1 + rt)$ new cases, making a total of $n(1 + rt)^2$ pending cases. Then, the time for all h hearings, T is calculated as

$$\text{Time for } 1st \text{ hearing } + \ldots + \text{Time for h}th \text{ hearing } = \sum_{k=0}^{h-1} (1 + rt)^k \quad (2)$$

The summation yields

$$T = (n/r)((1 + rt)^h - 1) \text{ if } r \neq 0, \text{ or } nht \text{ if } r = 0 \tag{3}$$

This equation ties together the major characteristics of the system: the number of pending cases, the number of hearings, the time taken by each hearing, the net inflow of petitions and the time taken for completing the pleadings of a petition. It can be used to predict delays, estimate judicial workload and plan ahead in order to create the requisite judicial capacity when new jurisdiction is created. It also tells us about the relations between these quantities. For example, it indicates that the time taken for the disposal of a case depends on the number of pending cases. In other words, there is an externality: each case that is filed delays all other cases. It also suggests that the total time taken for the pleadings of a petition, T is exponential in the number of hearings h. A decrease in the number of hearings could potentially have a very large impact.

Intuitively, this can be understood as follows. Let us assume that due to stricter judicial control over adjournments, the average number of hearings required for the disposal of a case comes down by half. This leads to a reduction in the time taken for the completion of a petition in two ways. Firstly, there is the straightforward effect of the number of hearings coming down, so the pleadings are completed in, say, four hearings, as compared to eight hearings earlier. Secondly, the other petitions in the queue also take fewer hearings and get disposed of sooner, so the time between consecutive hearings of the petition decreases as well. The combination of these factors means that when the number of hearings drops to half, the time taken for each petition becomes less than half.

4 Estimating NCLT Performance

We next evaluate the performance of NCLT using the indicators proposed in Sect. 3.5. Some of this analysis can be usefully compared with Bhatia et al. (2018) who studied IBC petitions till November 2017. The dataset we use differs in two important ways: it has data up to June 2018, and it contains information not only about IBC petitions but also about the entire workload of the NCLT.

4.1 Data

We use a dataset that was shared by the MCA with details for about 8076 petitions filed under IBC at the NCLT till the end of June 2018. After cleaning, the dataset provided information for about 6668 petitions. Table 1 summarises the petitions in the dataset. Here, FC means a financial creditor filed the petition; OC means the petition was filed by an operational creditor and CD means that the debtor itself approached the tribunal. 'Transfer' indicates that a petition previously filed in a High Court has been now transferred to the Tribunal. Lastly, 'Voluntary' means that the

Table 1 Status of IBC petitions at NCLT

Who filed	Inflow	Admitted	Withdrawn	Dismissed	Pending
CD	232	102	6	45	79
FC	1240	228	54	249	709
OC	4349	247	389	1250	2463
Transfer	839	18	26	677	118
Voluntary	8	0	0	3	5
All	6668	595	475	2224	3374

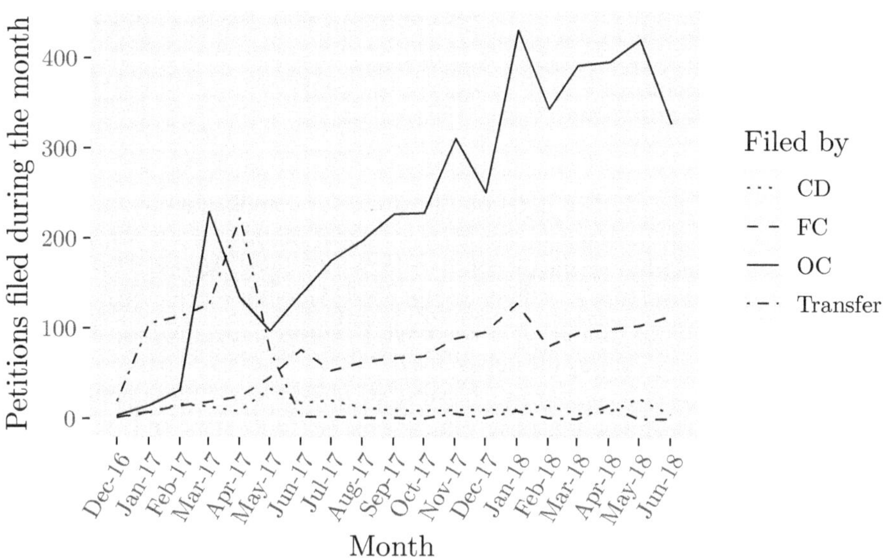

Fig. 1 Who uses IBC?

petition was filed by a firm to liquidate itself. The petitions can be disposed of by being admitted into the CIRP, being withdrawn, or being rejected.

Figure 1 illustrates the use of the IBC. It can be seen that the heaviest users of IBC are the OCs. Petitions filed by FCs, OCs and CDs, were not all equally successful in being admitted. There were a total of 2,819 petitions that were either admitted or rejected by the judge. Among these, the fraction of admitted petitions was only 21%. However, there was wide variation in this rate depending upon who filed the petition (see Table 2). The most successful among these were the CDs. More than two-thirds of their petitions were admitted. Among the creditors, FCs were thrice as successful as OCs, 48% versus 16%. Most of the transferred petitions were rejected.

Table 2 Rate of admission

Who filed	CD	FC	OC	Transfer	Overall
Admission rate (%)	69	48	16	3	21

Table 3 Duration of disposed IBC petitions

Who filed	CD	FC	OC	Transfer	Voluntary	Total
Mean time to dispose (days)	76	85	85	104	120	89

4.2 Duration

The calculation of the average duration of petitions is complicated by the fact that over half the petitions in the data available are under process. If we consider only those petitions which have been disposed of (either by being admitted or by being rejected), then the results are as in Table 3. The average petition that has been disposed of, took about 3 months from filing to disposal. Unsurprisingly, the fastest disposal is when the petition is filed by the debtor itself.

These numbers may be misleading because we consider only those petitions that were disposed of. The remaining observations were *censored* at the end of the observation period (in this case June 2018). To get an accurate picture, it is necessary to incorporate them also into our analysis which can be done through *survival analysis*, which is a field of statistics that studies the time till an event. The event could be the failure of a machine, the death of a patient, or, in our case, the disposal of a petition.

Since we need to model the effect of both categorical and continuous variables, we choose to use Accelerated Failure Time (AFT) model. Such models allow covariates to have a multiplicative effect on survival time. In other words, the life of the petition accelerates or decelerates depending on the value of its covariates. In this paper, we consider various distributions for the survival and identify the distributions that best fit the data. Some of the commonly used distributions for this purpose are the Weibull, log-logistic and log-normal distributions. The standard AFT model is[31]

$$\log(T) = x^T \beta + \sigma w \tag{4}$$

Here, T is the time to the event, x is a vector of covariates, β is a vector of regression coefficients, and the error w, drawn from some distribution W, is scaled by the shape parameter σ. The distribution of T is determined by the error. For instance, if W is the logistic distribution, then T will have a log-logistic distribution.

[31] Kleinbaum and Klein (2012).

From the discussion in Sect. 3.6, the duration of a petition is likely to depend on the number of petitions pending at the time it was admitted, the net inflow rate of petitions, the number of hearings and the time taken by each hearing. We developed a model to determine the significance of these variables on the duration of the petition.

The last two variables, the number of hearings and the time taken by each hearing, are not observed in the dataset. However, these variables are very likely to depend on the nature of the petition (whether it is filed by an FC, an OC or a CD). These variables are also likely to depend on the bench of NCLT where the petition is filed. While the rules determining the disposal of petitions are the same across different benches, there might be systematic differences in petition disposal practices between the benches, resulting in different distributions of the disposal times. For instance, one bench might favour many short hearings, another might favour a few long ones, and a third bench might prefer many long ones. We accounted for this possibility by introducing the bench as a stratifying categorical variable into the model. The filer was also included as a categorical variable.

The coefficients in Table 4 are relative to a baseline corresponding to a petition filed by a CD. It can be seen that the filer, the inflow rate and the pendency at the bench, are all highly significant. The duration also depends on the benches, and this dependence is also highly significant in almost all cases. Likelihood ratio tests show that the full models (models 4 and 5) are significantly better descriptions of the process than the nested models (models 1–3).

Models 4 and 5 differ in the treatment of the pendency variable. In Model 4, it enters untransformed, but model 5 contains the logarithm. Equation 3 predicts that fractional changes in time should be proportional to fractional changes in the pendency (with the coefficient of proportionality being 1 if the equation is exactly correct). This relation can be best modelled by taking the logarithm of the pendency, as in model 5, since the covariates are regressed against the logarithm of the time in the AFT formulation (Eq. 4). Among these two models, model 5 ranks better on Akaike Information Criteria (AIC), and it is used in the discussion that follows.

Model 5 indicates that compared to a petition filed by a CD, one filed by an FC will take longer by $e^{0.65} - 1 = 92\%$ on average. Similarly, a petition filed by an OC will be longer by 79%. An increase in the net inflow of petitions of one petition per day is predicted to increase the duration by 7%.

The model presented in Sect. 3.6 predicted that the duration of a petition at a bench would increase with the pendency and the inflow rate. It also predicted that the duration will depend on the time taken for each hearing and the number of hearings, which we have posited will vary with the type of the filer and the bench at which the petition is filed. Table 4 provides strong empirical support to the model, since all the factors in the model are seen to be statistically significant predictors (filer, bench, pendency and inflow rate).

The duration of the petition is proportional to $n^{0.47}$, roughly the square root of the pendency. This agrees only partially with our theoretical model, which predicts that the duration should increase linearly with the pendency. A possible reason for the deviation is that when petitions take too long, the chances of withdrawal increase, because the parties may come to a negotiated settlement. Thus, petitions which would

Table 4 Petition duration models

	Model 1	Model 2	Model 3	Model 4	Model 5
(Intercept)	5.30***	4.54***	4.10***	4.01***	1.44***
	(0.03)	(0.10)	(0.09)	(0.09)	(0.24)
Benches (shape)					
Ahmedabad	−0.01	−0.02	−0.22***	−0.23***	−0.25***
	(0.05)	(0.05)	(0.05)	(0.05)	(0.05)
Allahabad	−0.51***	−0.49***	−0.66***	−0.64***	−0.51***
	(0.09)	(0.09)	(0.09)	(0.09)	(0.10)
Bengaluru	−0.41***	−0.44***	−0.26***	−0.30***	−0.33***
	(0.07)	(0.07)	(0.07)	(0.07)	(0.07)
Chandigarh	−0.01	−0.07	−0.39***	−0.42***	−0.58***
	(0.06)	(0.06)	(0.06)	(0.06)	(0.06)
Chennai	−0.17*	−0.15	−0.35***	−0.29***	−0.21**
	(0.08)	(0.08)	(0.08)	(0.08)	(0.08)
Gauhati	−0.16	−0.18	−0.54*	−0.60*	−0.49*
	(0.22)	(0.22)	(0.23)	(0.24)	(0.25)
Hyderabad	−0.62***	−0.63***	−0.76***	−0.83***	−0.87***
	(0.06)	(0.06)	(0.06)	(0.06)	(0.06)
Kolkata	−0.24***	−0.23***	−0.37***	−0.38***	−0.34***
	(0.05)	(0.05)	(0.05)	(0.05)	(0.05)
Mumbai	−0.36***	−0.37***	−0.14***	−0.03	−0.06
	(0.04)	(0.04)	(0.04)	(0.05)	(0.04)
New Delhi	0.16***	0.18***	0.15***	0.13**	0.18***
	(0.04)	(0.04)	(0.04)	(0.04)	(0.04)
Principal	−0.04	−0.05	−0.18***	−0.19***	−0.17***
	(0.05)	(0.05)	(0.05)	(0.05)	(0.05)
Who filed (relative to CD)					
FC		0.73***	0.66***	0.67***	0.65***
		(0.11)	(0.10)	(0.10)	(0.10)
OC		0.82***	0.63***	0.64***	0.58***
		(0.10)	(0.10)	(0.10)	(0.09)
inflow Rate			0.18***	0.07***	0.07***
			(0.01)	(0.02)	(0.01)
start Pendency				0.00***	
				(0.00)	
log (start Pendency)					0.47***
					(0.04)

(continued)

Table 4 (continued)

AIC	27882.94	27824.07	27289.75	27203.35	27133.47
Log Likelihood	−13929.47	−13898.04	−13629.88	−13585.67	−13550.74
Num. obs.	5367	5367	5367	5367	5367

$^{***}p < 0.001$, $^{**}p < 0.01$, $^{*}p < 0.05$

Table 5 Estimated time to dispose of petitions filed by CDs—comparison of benches under current loads (as on June 2018)

Bench	Pendency	Daily Net Inflow Rate	Time to dispose (days)
Ahmedabad	587	1.9	95
Allahabad	230	0.9	58
Bengaluru	589	−0.0	83
Chandigarh	294	1.0	65
Chennai	1140	1.5	126
Gauhati	40	0.3	24
Hyderabad	652	0.6	91
Kolkata	1094	2.5	133
Mumbai	5492	14.6	660
New Delhi	1619	2.9	164
Principal	579	1.1	90

otherwise take a long time would systematically drop out of our analysis. In the dataset, sometimes it wasn't fully clear whether a petition had been dismissed by the judge on merit, or if it had been withdrawn by the parties. A competing-risks model of survival analysis might capture this phenomenon better. Another possible reason is that as the pendency increases, the judges may change their behaviour—they may reduce the number of hearings or the length of each hearing.

Using this model, it is possible to estimate the duration that a particular petition will take. In Table 5, we provide the predicted expected values for the time taken for the disposal of petitions filed by a CD. The values of pendency and inflow rate correspond to a situation where the petition is filed at the 11 different benches towards the end of June 2018. It can be seen that there is a wide variation in the average time for disposal, with Gauhati bench the fastest and Mumbai the slowest. It may be noted that in each of the benches, the predicted mean time is greater than the statutorily allowed 14 days.

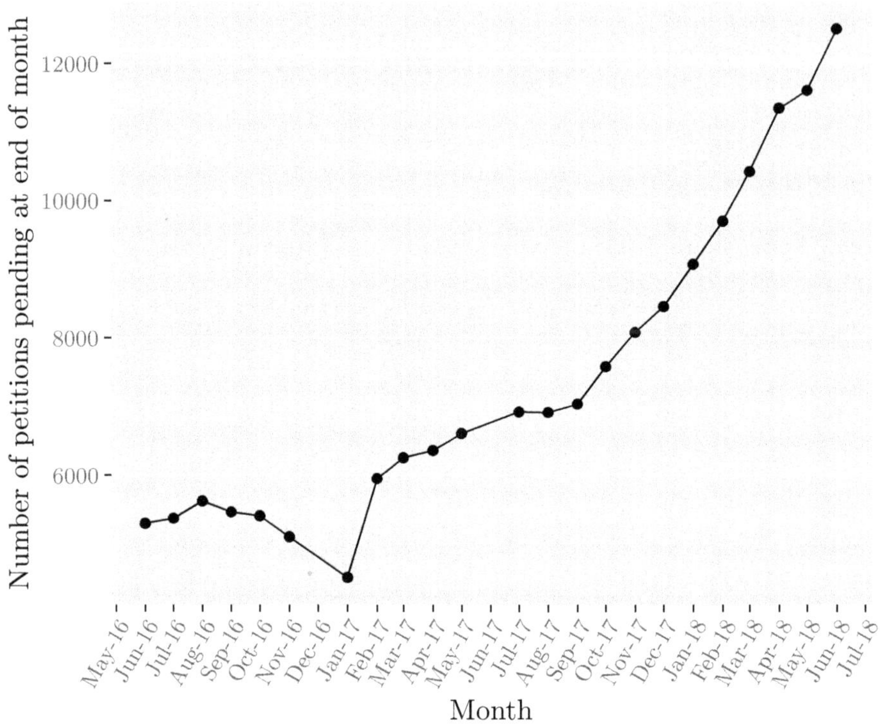

Fig. 2 Pendency of all petitions at NCLT

4.3 *Pendency*

In Fig. 2, we plot the trend of petitions filed at the NCLT. It can be seen that NCLT has developed a large backlog of about 12,500 petitions as of June 2018. It is useful to note that this is the pendency for all petitions, not only those related to IBC. If NCLT had been able to keep pace with the inflow, the pendency numbers would have been flat. Figure 2 shows that the overall pendency figures are increasing at the rate of about 600 petitions every month. Far from being able to make a dent in the backlog, NCLT is not able to keep up with the inflow.

4.4 *Outflow Rate*

As discussed earlier, the pendency figure alone is meaningless without further context. The outflow rate is presented in Fig. 3. It indicates that the outflow rate is around 10% every month. If there were no new petitions, it will take about 10 months for NCLT to finish off the pending workload.

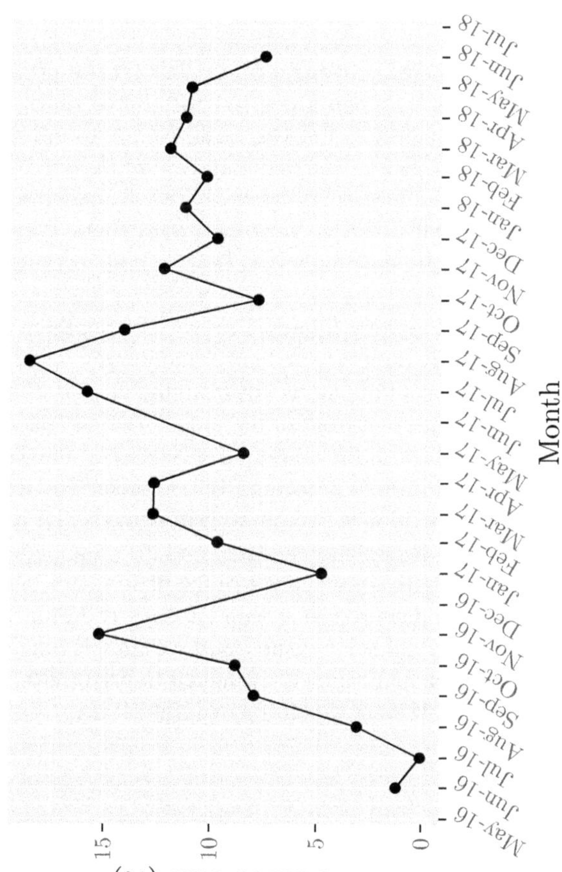

Fig. 3 Outflow rate at NCLT

Table 6 Delay in IBC petitions

(Delay is the time taken in excess of 14 days)

Who filed	CD	FC	OC	Transfer	Voluntary	Overall
Delay (days)	109	104	104	245	96	122

4.5 Delay

IBC provides time limits for different parts of the insolvency process, making it possible to define delay clearly. When a petition for admission of a CD into the insolvency process is filed at NCLT, the IBC asks NCLT to admit or reject the petition within 14 days. In our dataset, we find that 6187 of the 6668 petitions in our dataset (about 93%) have taken more than 14 days. The average delay across filers is given in Table 6. This is the situation as of the end of June 2018, and as many of the petitions are still pending, the numbers here is an underestimate of the actual average delay.

There are caveats attached to these figures. For one, the Supreme Court has held that the limit of 14 days is only directory and not mandatory.[32] Secondly, the courts have also stated that the 14 days limit starts not from the date of filing the petition, but from the date, it is first put up in front of the judge. The gap between these two is the time the petition spends with the administrative staff of the Tribunal, during which they check that the petition is procedurally complete. The dataset does not contain the date at which the petition is first put up before the NCLT judges; hence, it is not possible to estimate the administrative delay and the judicial delay separately.

If we assume that administrative verification of the petition can take up to 7 days, then the petition ought to be disposed of within 21 days of filing. In Table 7, we estimate the fraction of petitions that are disposed of within this time, given the June 2018 loads at the benches. Gauhati bench is estimated to perform the best, but even it is able to dispose of only half its new petitions within 21 days.

4.6 Cost

The cost of the judicial process should also include the cost of the delay in the court. This cost can be calculated as the time value of money for the amount at stake in the petition, for the period of the delay. We have attempted to calculate this figure for IBC petitions here.

For admitted IBC petitions, we calculated the interest cost on the amount for the period of the delay, which is defined as the excess of the petition duration over 21 days. For pending petitions, we estimated the duration and assumed that the admission of

---

[32] See Supreme Court (2017a).

Table 7 Fraction of IBC petitions disposed of within 21 days

Bench	Fraction of cases disposed of (%)
Ahmedabad	13
Allahabad	16
Bengaluru	13
Chandigarh	12
Chennai	10
Gauhati	44
Hyderabad	3
Kolkata	7
Mumbai	2
New Delhi	15
Principal	15

petitions shall follow the pattern we have seen so far (see Table 2). We use average bank lending rates for June 2018 provided by the Reserve Bank of India.[33] The cost due to the delays comes to over Rs 5400 crore.

Note that this is a very conservative estimate. Firstly, we are only considering the cost to the economy due to delay in IBC petitions. These petitions form only a part of the pending workload of NCLT. Secondly, the amount considered here is the amount claimed by the filer, which might be a small fraction of the total amount owed to all the creditors. Further, this is the cost to the creditors alone. The filing of an insolvency petition against a firm can be expected to cause some disruption to its functioning even if the petition is eventually dismissed, and this cost will increase with the delay. Further, this amount does not include the costs of other judicial delays, such as delays in the approval of the resolution plan, which may be quite high.[34] Thus, this amount, large as it is, is a very conservative lower bound on the actual cost to the economy due to the delays in NCLT. Others have estimated the cost to be as high as Rs 25,000 crore.[35]

5 Discussion

We have seen that the NCLT suffers from severe problems of delay, pendency and cost. In this section, we try to diagnose the root causes of these delays. We propose some steps to solve these problems. While the data presented above shows that the NCLT suffers from delays, that data does not allow us to easily determine the cause

[33] Reserve Bank of India (2018).

[34] Marwah and Sharma (2018).

[35] Iyengar (2018).

of the delays. A qualitative study of orders can help illustrate the reasons for delay better.

As an example, let us consider a particular petition under IBC.[36] In this petition, the financial creditor, a bank, seeks to initiate the CIRP against the corporate debtor. As on the date of writing, there are nine orders associated with this petition on the NCLT website:

1. March 7, 2018: The petition (which was filed on January 10, 2018), was first put up before the tribunal. It was ordered to be listed for arguments on March 22, 2018.
2. March 22, 2018: The pleadings were recorded to be complete. The counsel for CD stated that there is a possibility of settlement. The tribunal ordered listing on April 12, 2018.
3. April 12, 2018: Both counsels requested time for settlement. The tribunal ordered the petition to be listed on May 10, 2018.
4. May 10, 2018: Pleadings were again recorded to be complete. The tribunal ordered the petition to be listed on May 30, 2018.
5. May 30, 2018: Yet another adjournment was granted, this time because a counsel cited personal difficulties. The tribunal ordered that the petition was to be listed on June 6, 2018, with a warning that no further adjournments shall be granted.
6. June 6, 2018: Arguments were heard and the order was reserved.
7. July 23, 2018: An order was passed admitting the petition.
8. August 21, 2018: A report filed by the Resolution Professional was taken on record.
9. September 4, 2018: Another report filed by the Resolution Professional was taken on record.

The entire process took 223 days from the date of filing to the date of disposal of the petition. If we only consider the duration since the petition was first put up before the judges, it took 167 days. In either case, the time taken is far more than the 14 days provided in IBC. After the petition was filed, it took almost 2 months for it to appear before the judges. This time was spent in the registry. When the petition was first put up before the judges, it was listed for arguments after 15 days. This alone is greater than the time allowed by IBC.

5.1 Delay Due to Extra Steps

When an FC files a petition for the initiation of CIRP, section 7(1) of IBC specifies a very simple set of tests for admitting the petition:

1. Has default occurred?
2. Is the application complete?

---

[36] This is petition (IB)-59(PB)/2018, available on the NCLT website.

3. Are there any disciplinary proceedings pending against the proposed resolution professional?

In the illustration above, the delay in the petitions has been caused on account of criteria other than the three above, i.e. adjournment of hearings at least twice because the parties were discussing a settlement. This converts the tribunal proceedings in to a negotiating tactic. The petitioner gets the best of both worlds: he gets to use the overhanging petition to force the respondent into a settlement, and he benefits from the fact that the tribunal is standing ready to take the petition forward if the settlement talks fail. These requests for adjournment should have been rejected, recognising that the parties do not have the right to discuss their settlement on the tribunal's time. Such requests are wasteful not only of the time of the tribunal but also of the thousands of other petitions pending before the NCLT.

Allowing IBC petitions to be used as a negotiation tactic in a settlement discussion can have more dangerous consequences as well. A bankrupt debtor might be able to arrive at settlements with each creditor separately, and thus conceal the true situation of the business from them. A CIRP, on the other hand, forces the CD to reveal complete information about the business to all the creditors.

In addition, the judges took on record reports indicating the progress of the CIRP. The IBC does not require such detailed supervision by the NCLT.

5.2 *Delay Due to Failed Hearings*

In Regy and Roy (2017), the authors define a *failed hearing* as a hearing which meets these conditions:

1. The hearing resulted in an adjournment without transacting judicial business;
2. The adjournment was avoidable; and
3. The adjournment was not penalised.

These hearings cause delay by consuming the time of the judiciary (and, consequently, all the other petitioners and respondents waiting for judicial time) in an unproductive manner. In the example petition, of the six hearings (corresponding to orders (1) through (6)), we can identify at least two failed hearings (corresponding to orders (3) and (5)).

Both extra hearings and failed hearings increase the workload of the tribunal and increase the time other petitioners have to wait for the disposal of their petitions.

5.3 *Systems and Processes*

Judicial time is precious and should be reserved for making judicial decisions. Using judicial time for administrative purposes, or to oversee procedural steps, should be avoided as far as possible. Properly designed systems and processes can help with this.

The last couple of orders above indicates that the judges took on record a report filed by the Resolution Professional. Similarly, there have been instances where petitions have been filed without even the basic set of supporting documents.[37] These are procedural matters that could have been handled at the level of the registry, which could in turn help reduce delays in other petitions.

5.4 Capacity Constraints

There has been a long-standing assertion that one of the main reasons for judicial delays in India is the lack of sufficient judges.[38] This view seems to be favoured within the judiciary itself.[39]

It is definitely possible that capacity constraints are a significant contributor to delay, though, in the absence of better data, it is not possible to come to a clear conclusion about the degree to which capacity constraints are responsible.

It should be noted that capacity constraints may not only exist at the judicial level but also at the administrative level. High-quality support staff and technological automation can help reduce the burden on the judicial members. See Box 5.4.

The example of Singapore

The issue of adjudication capacity was a major topic of discussion at the IBBI-IGIDR Insolvency and Bankruptcy Reforms Conference held on August 3 and 4, 2018, especially the dialogue on building institutional capacity in adjudication between Justice M.M. Kumar, Chairperson and President of the NCLT, and Justice Kannan Ramesh, of the Supreme Court of Singapore. Justice Kumar highlighted judicial vacancies at the NCLT. He mentioned that out of 63 required members at the NCLT, only 28 posts had been filled. He also pointed to the paucity of support staff for judicial members at the tribunal.

Justice Ramesh suggested that strengthening bench strength was important, but that it was only one of a continuing, multi-pronged approach to improve judicial outcomes. The problem of judicial vacancies is pervasive across jurisdictions. As an example, he mentioned that there was a 40% vacancy in the UK courts.

The approach adopted in most of these jurisdictions was to strengthen the number and quality of support staff, simultaneously with the recruitment of

[37] See Piramal Enterprises Ltd. versus Sunshine Institute of Information Technology Pvt. Ltd., NCLT (2018).

[38] Department of Justice (2016); Law Commission of India (1958, 2014).

[39] Misra (2018).

judicial members. Illustratively, he described that in his own court, there are around 60 support staff for 25 judicial members.

Justice Ramesh also mentioned that a specialised case management system aids in facilitating the speedy disposal of cases. Such a system helps to separate the administrative function from the adjudication function of the judiciary, thereby reducing the administrative burden on judicial members. He emphasised that back-room support is absolutely critical to allow the judiciary to perform effectively and it is here that technology and automation may offer solutions for improving court processes.

In this regard, the organisation structure of the Singapore Supreme Court offers a good example for the delineation of the administrative function from the adjudication function of the judiciary. Judicial administration is housed within 9 distinct departments, which are overseen by a Chief Executive Officer reporting to the Chief Justice. There is an online case filing and management system that allows parties remote access to services such as filing applications, submitting support documents, monitoring case development and applying for orders.

5.5 *Ongoing Reform Efforts*

In India, given that judicial delays have been a persistent problem, there have been many attempts to solve them. These have ranged from technological to institutional. In this section, we summarise some of these attempts, with a focus on those that pertain to the NCLT.

Tribunalisation The 42nd amendment to the Constitution of India provided for the establishment of tribunals, with the objective of 'secur[ing] speedy disposal …'. While tribunalisation has been successful in many countries, it has not been as successful in India.[40] The Financial Sector Legislative Reforms Commission, chaired by Justice Srikrishna, brought some fresh thinking into this area.[41] One of its key recommendations was that a separate entity for court administration should be set up to enhance the adjudication capacity of the Financial Securities Appellate Tribunal.

Technological interventions In the 1990s, the National Informatics Centre (NIC) began computerising basic services at the Supreme Court and later the High Courts. The eCourts project envisages universal computerisation and digitisation of the subordinate judiciary in India. Software to facilitate workflow and enable e-filing is being introduced in NCLT as well.[42]

[40] Law Commission of India (2017).

[41] Financial Sector Legislative Reforms Commission (2013).

[42] National Company Law Tribunal (2018).

Increasing judicial capacity The MCA is planning to establish one bench in each High Court jurisdiction, and to recruit more judges.[43]

Legal and procedural reforms Some reform efforts have been directed at modifying laws and procedures so that delays can be reduced. For instance, the 230th Report of the Law Commission contained a list of procedural measures, such as: providing strict guidelines for the grant of adjournments, and reducing the time for oral arguments except in cases involving complicated questions of law.[44] Most jurisdictions have also adopted case management systems, annual targets for judicial officers, and performance reviews.

Recently, the MCA has sought to use statutory interventions to identify areas within corporate law where the judicial workload could be reduced.[45] Moving minor offences in the nature of procedural transgressions into a penalty-based adjudication framework will help achieve speedier disposal of petitions and in the process help de-clog the NCLT. As we saw in the preceding section, some steps are already being taken to reduce delays in the NCLT and other courts. We next synthesise the new evidence presented in previous sections into ideas towards solving the problem.

5.6 Eliminating Wasteful Hearings

In the context of the IBC, there are two kinds of hearings that waste judicial time. Firstly, there are those hearings that are extra steps taken by the tribunal, and which go beyond what is envisaged in the IBC. This is most commonly seen when the tribunal provides opportunity to the parties to settle (see Sect. 5.1). This mixing of the judicial process with a negotiation, conducted, as it were, under the auspices of the tribunal, harms the ability of the tribunal to perform its work, not only with regard to that petition but also with regard to all the other petitions. The tribunal might achieve better outcomes by ensuring that private parties are not allowed to clog the docket of the tribunal for negotiation settlements.

Secondly, judicial time is also wasted by the large number of failed hearings, those in which the judicial business planned for that hearing does not happen due to avoidable reasons (see Sect. 5.2). There is a range of reasons for these failures: the lawyers not being present, failure to produce essential documents, lack of instruction from client and so on. The tribunal generally grants adjournments in these cases. This hurts the delivery of justice to all other waiting parties and creates perverse incentives for the parties and their lawyers. Requests for adjournments would be sharply reduced by imposing costs on parties, but this is very rarely done.

Reducing wasteful hearings can make a very significant dent in judicial delay. As discussed in Sect. 3.6, the number of hearings has an outsize impact on the total

[43] Ministry of Corporate Affairs (2018b); Rajagopal (2015).

[44] Law Commission of India (2009).

[45] Ministry of Corporate Affairs (2018c).

time taken for the disposal of a petition, and consequently on judicial delay. This intervention has no budgetary implications, but it requires a mindset change in the judiciary. It might well be the most effective reform that can reduce delays.

5.7 Planning

Once a backlog is allowed to build up, it is very difficult to return to a situation without delays. Even if the disposal rate is later increased to match the inflow rate, the petitions stay pending for so long that they exceed their prescribed time limits. In the case of justice, as in many other areas, prevention is indeed better than cure.

A key method to prevent the build-up of a backlog is to estimate the future workload and to ensure that adequate judicial manpower, administrative manpower and support infrastructure are put in place to deal with that workload. This is done in many countries using what is called a Judicial Impact Assessment (JIA)—using court data to predict the resources required by the judiciary to handle future case-load. JIA requires accurate and detailed data, which is currently not available for many courts in India. Nevertheless, a JIA was attempted by Damle and Regy (2017), who predicted early on that the NCLT was too poorly equipped to handle the case-load it would face.

5.8 Rethinking Processes

A redesign of the procedures followed in the tribunal, incorporating the possibilities offered by the appropriate use of technology, can help to improve the functioning of the courts. This is distinct from 'computerisation', which often means just applying a thin veneer of technology on top of the existing processes.[46] For instance, in order to upload NCLT orders on its website, the orders are typed out on a computer, printed out, signed by the judges, scanned and uploaded. This is unnecessarily complex and time-consuming. A well-designed case management system can make this process faster and simpler. Such a system will also capture data naturally about the status of cases, without the need to separately track and consolidate data, as is done now.

This redesign should aim to ensure that the time of the judiciary is freed up to do judicial work. The registry can play a very important role in improving the performance of the tribunal. For instance, it can help ensure that petitions are put up with a minimal set of prescribed documents so that the tribunal's time is not wasted chasing after paperwork.

The Bankruptcy Legislative Reforms Committee (BLRC) proposed the idea of Information Utilities, which would contain accurate information about debts that had been verified by both the creditor and the debtor. The NCLT should work towards a

[46] Datta and Shah (2015).

future where, using Information Utilities and digital signatures, it would be possible for some classes of petitions (IBC admission petitions for instance) to be filed and disposed of entirely online, with no physical hearings required.[47]

Lastly, the tribunal should regularly publish high-quality, granular data about its functioning. It needs to recognise that data is not useful just for reporting and monitoring; it is also essential for accountability, planning and increasing productivity. Granular data is vital for understanding the performance of the judiciary and identifying possibilities for improvement.

5.9 Culture

> Adjournments are sought on the drop of a hat by the counsel .... If adjournments are granted in this manner it would tantamount to violation of rule of law and eventually turn such trials to a farce. It is legally impermissible and jurisprudentially abominable .... It is distressing to note that despite series of judgments of this Court, the habit of granting adjournment, really an ailment, continues.
>
> Chief Justice Dipak Misra, Vinod Kumar vs State Of Punjab, 2014

It is widely recognised that repeated adjournments are causing injustice and delay, but there is a deep-rooted resistance to changing this 'adjournment culture'. The authors have come across several cases (not only in NCLT but also in other courts/tribunals) where lawyers request adjournments repeatedly, claiming that they need ever more time to produce basic documents. Sometimes, lawyers are absent when their petition is scheduled to be heard, with the excuse that they were stuck in traffic, or that they were otherwise busy.[48] Such behaviour would be unacceptable in most other professions, but apparently, it is acceptable in the Indian judiciary—the judges grant the adjournments without penalty.

Perhaps part of the reason for this culture is that when young lawyers enter the profession, they are socialised into accepting adjournments and delays as normal, and they carry this attitude with them as they go on to become judges. Another reason could be that there might be perverse incentives for some lawyers who benefit from delays. In any case, the adjournment culture survives in spite of appeals and directives by the higher courts. It has also turned out to be resistant to statutory efforts for change. The CPC was amended in 1999 to limit adjournments to a maximum of three, but that does not seem to have helped matters much.

Changing the culture of an organisation or a profession is difficult. It requires a shared vision, horizontal communication, reinforcement and new systems and processes that support the new vision, rather than top-down directives. Skillsets from outside the judiciary—such as economists, business process management consultants and change management consultants—might also need to be brought in.

---

[47] Datta and Regy (2017).

[48] Regy and Roy (2017).

5.10 Future Work

The approach presented in this chapter has proven useful in determining the key factors affecting case duration, as well as in estimating the duration. However, many improvements are possible in our approach, both from the point of view of mathematical modelling, as well as from a larger policy angle.

For further improving the quality of modelling, it would be useful to distinguish between the administrative time and the judicial time spent on a petition. However, this data is not recorded as of now. Other useful data such as the number of hearings and the time taken by each hearing is not available either. We should better account for non-working days so that the duration of a petition accurately reflects the working time spent by the judiciary on it. Often, after all the hearings are done, the judges reserve their order. In some cases, the petition may be appealed in another court, and we need to identify and deal with those petitions better. These practices are not dealt with very well in our current model.

Another factor that might be useful to incorporate into the analysis is that context-switching is not free—once a judge turns to a new matter, she has to absorb the history and the issues of that matter before she can productively engage with it. This takes time, and the more the number of failed hearings, the more the time lost in this manner.

The use of other statistical modelling methods could also be investigated. As discussed earlier, the possibility of withdrawal of a petition changes with time. A competing-risks model of survival might be a better fit for such cases. Similarly, a frailty model might be useful to account for correlation due to benches or filers.[49]

From a policy point of view, it would be useful to compare these results with the results for a different tribunal or court to determine how general these findings are. We have seen how there is a wide variation in the petition duration among benches. This cries out for further study—is there a quality versus timeliness trade-off? In other words, are the faster benches able to maintain quality at par with the slower benches? If so, efforts should be made to identify the local processes and innovations that enable speed with quality, and they should be scaled up across the NCLT.

6 Conclusion

This chapter is a first attempt to think through the concept of judicial performance measurement for India. Drawbacks in achieving high judicial performance impose high costs on the citizenry and damage the institutional legitimacy of the judiciary. We reviewed the many motivations and approaches to measuring judicial performance and identified a small and widely accepted set of indicators that we propose as indicators for the NCLT. These are duration, delays, pendency, outflow rate and costs. We tried to suggest usable definitions for each of these.

[49] Kleinbaum and Klein (2012).

We used a new dataset to evaluate the performance of the NCLT using these indicators. The NCLT was established to provide a forum for the disposal of commercial disputes quickly. Our study reveals that unfortunately, the performance of the NCLT along these dimensions is poor and declining. We presented a mathematical model for court proceedings which can be used to characterise duration and delay in the judiciary. The empirical data confirms the validity of the mathematical model, allowing us to rigorously identify the factors leading to judicial delays, and allowing us to predict average case durations. It highlights that there are large delays across the benches. Only a small fraction of the petitions are disposed of within the statutory time. These delays impose a high cost on the economy of the country. Across benches, there is a high variation in the duration of similar petitions.

We then sought to identify the reasons for the poor performance: most importantly, wasted hearings, insufficient judicial staff and a culture that is permissive of delays. We suggest steps to reduce delay, including avoiding (or penalising) wasteful hearings, increasing judicial strength and augmenting the judicial members through high-quality support staff as well as technology. We also suggest that part of the solution might lie in a deeper examination of the prevailing judicial culture.

References

Aayog NITI (2017) India: three year action agenda, 2017–2018 to 2019–2020. Technical Report, NITI Aayog, New Delhi

Ahsan R (2013) Input tariffs, speed of contract enforcement, and the productivity of firms in India. J Int Econ 90(1):181–192

American Bar Association (2005) American bar association guidelines for the evaluation of judicial performance with commentary. Technical Report, American Bar Association

Baruah P, Naik S, Prakash BSS, Mandyam K (2018) Paths to justice: surveying judicial and non-judicial dispute resolution in India

Beck T, Demirgüç-Kunt A, Maksimovic V (2006) The influence of financial and legal institutions on firm size. J Bank Financ 30(11):2995–3015

Bhatia S, Marwah V, Shaikh G, Zaveri B (2018) Insolvency and Bankruptcy code: one-year report card. Bloomberg Quint

Botero JC, La Porta R, López-de Silanes F, Shleifer A, Volokh A (2003) Judicial reform. World Bank Res Obs 18(1):61–88

Casey P (1998) Defining optimal court performance: the trial court performance standards. Court Rev

Chakraborty, (2016) Judicial quality and regional firm performance: the case of Indian states. J Comp Econ 44(4):902–918

Chemin M (2010) Does court speed shape economic activity? evidence from a court reform in India. J Law Econ Organ 28(3):460–485

Choi SJ, Gulati GM (2004) Choosing the next supreme court justice: an empirical ranking of judge performance. South Calif Law Rev 78:23

Commission European (2018) The 2018 EU justice scoreboard. Technical Report, European Union

Court Supreme (2012) Judiciary transformation framework. Republic of Kenya, Technical Report

Coviello D, Moretti L, Spagnolo G, Valbonesi P (2018) Court efficiency and procurement performance. Scand J Econ 120(3):826–858

Dakolias M (1999) Court performance around the world: a comparative perspective. Yale Hum Rights Dev Law J 2(2):87
Daksh (2016) Time-and-motion study of four district and sessions courts in Bangalore, Karnataka. Technical Report, Daksh, Bengaluru. http://dakshindia.org/wp-content/uploads/2016/11/DAKSH-TIME-AND-MOTION-STUDY-OF-FOUR-DISTRICT-AND-SESSIONS-COURTS-3.pdf
Daksh (2017) Case flow management rules in India. Technical Report, Daksh, Bengaluru. http://www.dakshindia.org/wp-content/uploads/2015/11/Case-Flow-Management-Rules-in-India-by-DAKSH.pdf
Damle D, Regy P (2017) Does the NCLT have enough judges? Technical Report, The Leap Blog. https://blog.theleapjournal.org/2017/04/does-nclt-have-enough-judges.html
Datta P, Prakash BSS, Sane R (2017) Understanding judicial delay at the income tax appellate tribunal in India. Working Paper 208, National Institute of Public Finance and Policy
Datta P, Regy PV (2017) Judicial procedures will make or break the insolvency and Bankruptcy code. The Leap Blog
Datta P, Shah A (2015) How to make courts work? Technical Report, The Leap Blog. https://blog.theleapjournal.org/2015/02/how-to-make-courts-work.html
Department of Company Affairs (2000) Report of the high level committee on law relating to insolvency and winding up of companies. Technical Report, Ministry of Law, Justice and Company Affairs, Government of India, New Delhi
Department of Justice (2016) Agenda notes, joint conference of Chief Ministers of the States/UTs and chief justices of the high courts, April 24, 2016. Technical Report, Ministry of Law and Justice, Government of India
Deptartment of Economic Affairs (2018) Economic survey 2017–2018, vol 1. Technical Report, Ministry of Finance, Government of India
Djankov S, Hart O, McLiesh C, Shleifer A (2008) Debt enforcement around the World. J Polit Econ 116(6):1105–1149
E-Committee of Supreme Court (2014) Policy and action plan document: Phase II of the eCourts project. Technical Report, Supreme Court of India. https://www.sci.gov.in/pdf/ecommittee/action-plan-ecourt.pdf
E-Committee of Supreme Court (2022) National policy and action plan for implementation of information and communication technology in the Indian judiciary. Technical Report, Supreme Court of India. https://www.supremecourtofindia.nic.in/pdf/ecommittee/PolicyActionPlanDocument-PhaseII-approved-08012014-indexed_Sign.pdf
Financial Sector Legislative Reforms Commission (2013) Report of the financial sector legislative reforms commission. Technical Report, Ministry of Finance, Government of India
Fournier GM, Zuehlke TW (1996) The timing of out-of-court settlements. RAND J Econ 27(2):310–321
Ghosh A, Sanyal D, Chandrashekar R, Sekhar R (2018) Reforming the tribunals framework in india: an interim report. Technical Report, Vidhi Centre for Legal Policy. https://vidhilegalpolicy.in/s/8th-June-Final-Draft-5lgl.pdf
Gill RD, Lazos SR, Waters MM (2011) Are judicial performance evaluations fair to women and minorities? a cautionary tale from clark county, Nevada. Law Soc Rev 45(3):731–759. https://onlinelibrary.wiley.com/doi/abs/10.1111/j.1540-5893.2011.00449.x
International Consortium for Court Excellence (2013) International framework for court excellence, 2nd edn
International Consortium for Court Excellence (2018) Global measures of court performance. Technical Report, Secretariat for the International Consortium for Court Excellence, Melbourne
Iyengar SP (2018) Delay in resolving insolvency cases has cost banks Rs 25,000 cr. Business Line
Johnson S, McMillan J, Woodruff C (2002) Courts and relational contracts. J Law Econ Organ 18(1):221–277
Kagzi MCJ (1973) The Indian administrative law, 3rd edn. Metropolitan Book Co. Pvt. Ltd., Delhi
Keilitz I (2000) Standards and measures of court performance. Crim Justice 4:559–593

Kessler D (1996) Institutional causes of delay in the settlement of legal disputes. J Law Econ Organ 12(2):432–460
Kleinbaum DG, Klein M (2012) Survival analysis, 3rd edn. Springer, New York
Kondylis F, Stein M (2018) The speed of justice. Technical Report, The World Bank
Kritzer HM, Anderson JK (1983) The arbitration alternative: a comparative analysis of case processing time, disposition mode, and cost in the American arbitration association and the courts. Justice Syst J 8(1):6–19
Kumar KB, Rajan RG, Zingales L (1999) What determines firm size? Working Paper 7208, National Bureau of Economic Research
Law Commission of India (1958) Reform of judicial administration, vol 14. Technical Report, Law Commission of India
Law Commission of India (2009) Reforms in the judiciary—some suggestions, vol 230. Technical Report, Law Commission of India
Law Commission of India (2014) Arrears and backlog: creating additional judicial (wo)manpower. Technical Report, Law Commission of India. http://lawcommissionofindia.nic.in/reports/Report_No.245.pdf
Law Commission of India (2017) Assessment of statutory frameworks of tribunals in India, vol 272. Technical Report, Law Commission of India
Lewin AY, Morey RC, Cook TJ (1982) Evaluating the administrative efficiency of courts. Omega 10(4):401–411
Livemint (2022) How to make Indian courts more efficient. Livemint. https://www.livemint.com/Opinion/YbrwKToUjjADagh7biAihM/How-to-make-Indian-courts-more-efficient.html
Martin W (2008) Courts in 2020: should they do things differently? In: Australian justice system in 2020, national judicial college of Australia conference
Marwah V, Sharma A (2018) Watching the IBC: lessons from the RBI-12 cases. https://www.bloombergquint.com/insolvency/watching-the-ibc-lessons-from-the-rbi-12-casesgs.Ww6hEA0
Menon NM (2008) Evaluating judicial performance: a consumer perspective. J Indian Law Inst 50(4):468–477. http://www.jstor.org/stable/43952174
Menzies N (2015) Justice in Kenya: measuring what counts. In: Governance for Development Blog. http://blogs.worldbank.org/governance/justice-kenya-measuring-what-counts
Messick RE (1999) Judicial reform and economic development. World Bank Res Obs 14(1):117–136
Ministry of Corporate Affairs (2018) Annual report. Technical Report, Government of India, New Delhi
Ministry of Corporate Affairs (2018) Filling up of 14 (Fourteen) posts of Judicial Member in the National Company Law Tribunal (NCLT)—inviting online applications for. Technical Report, Government of India, New Delhi
Ministry of Corporate Affairs (2018) Report of the committee to review offences under the companies act. Technical Report, Government of India, New Delhi
Misra D (2018) Inaugural address. In: National initiative to reduce pendency and delay in judicial system, Supreme Court of India, pp 17–26
National Center for State Courts (1997) Trial court performance standards with commentary. Technical Report, United States Department of Justice
National Company Law Tribunal (2018) Notice. Technical Report, Government of India, New Delhi
Palumbo G, Giupponi G, Nunziata L, Sanguinetti JSM (2013) The economics of civil justice. OECD Economics Department Working Paper 1060, OECD
Piramal Enterprises Ltd. versus Sunshine Institute of Information Technology Pvt. Ltd., NCLT (2018) Piramal Enterprises Ltd versus Sunshine Institute of Information Technology Pvt. Ltd., C.P. No. (IB)-66(PB)/2018
Ponticelli J, Alencar LS (2016) Court enforcement, bank loans, and firm investment: evidence from a Bankruptcy reform in Brazil. Q J Econ 131(3):1365–1413

Porta RL, Lopez-de Silane F, Pop-Eleches C, Shleifer A (2002) The guarantees of freedom. Working Paper 8759, National Bureau of Economic Research
Posner RA (2006) Judicial behavior and performance: an economic approach. Fla State Univ Law Rev 32(4):11
Rajagopal K (2015) Centre plans NCLT bench in every state. The Hindu
Regy PV, Roy S (2017) Understanding judicial delays in debt tribunals, vol 195. Technical Report, National Institute of Public Finance and Policy. http://macrofinance.nipfp.org.in/releases/RoyRegy2017_judicial-delay-debt-tribunals.html
Reserve Bank of India (2018) Lending rates of scheduled commercial banks (Excluding RRBs)
Rosales-López V (2008) Economics of court performance: an empirical analysis. Eur J Law Econ 25(3):231–251
Schauffler RY (2007) Judicial accountability in the US State courts: measuring court performance. Utrecht Law Rev 3(1):112–128
Schneider MR (2005) Judicial career incentives and court performance: an empirical study of the German labour courts of appeal. Eur J Law Econ 20(2):127–144
Singapore Supreme Court (2017) A future-ready judiciary: annual report 2017. Technical Report, https://www.supremecourt.gov.sg/docs/default-source/default-document-library/supreme-court-2017-arb5ce3133f22f6eceb9b0ff0000fcc945.pdf
Spigelman J (2006) Measuring court performance. J Judic Adm 16(2)
Sundaresan S (2022) The problem with 'tribunalisation'. Business Standard. https://www.business-standard.com/article/opinion/the-problem-with-tribunalisation-117110101584_1.html
Supreme Court (1964) Associated Cement Companies Ltd. vs P. N. Sharma, (1965)ILLJ433SC. Technical Report, Supreme Court of India, New Delhi. https://indiankanoon.org/doc/911769/
Supreme Court (2010) Union of India versus R. Gandhi, (2010)11SCC1. Technical Report, Supreme Court of India, New Delhi. https://indiankanoon.org/doc/748977/
Supreme Court (2014a) Madras Bar Association versus Union of India, [2014]187CompCas426(SC). Technical Report, Supreme Court of India, New Delhi. https://indiankanoon.org/doc/23435981/
Supreme Court (2014b) Vinod Kumar versus state Of Punjab. Technical Report, Supreme Court of India, New Delhi. https://indiankanoon.org/doc/188951670/
Supreme Court (2017a) Surendra Trading Company versus Juggilal Kamlapat Jute Mills Company Ltd. and Ors
Supreme Court (2017b) Sustaining Judiciary Transformation (SJT): a service delivery agenda. Technical Report, Republic of Kenya. http://kenyalaw.org/kl/fileadmin/pdfdownloads/Strategic_BluePrint.pdf
Supreme Court (2018) Arcelormittal India Private Limited vs Satish Kumar Gupta and Ors., Civil Appeal Nos. 9204-9405 of 2018. Technical Report, Supreme Court of India, New Delhi. https://www.sci.gov.in/supremecourt/2018/33945/33945_2018_Judgement_04-Oct-2018.pdf
Supreme Court of India (2017) Indian judiciary annual report, 2016–2017. Technical Report, Supreme Court of India, New Delhi
Uv Lilienfeld-Toal, Mookherjee D, Visaria S (2012) The distributive impact of reforms in credit enforcement: evidence from Indian debt recovery tribunals. Econometrica 80(2):497–558
Visaria S (2009) Legal reform and loan repayment: the microeconomic impact of debt recovery tribunals in India. Am Econ J: Appl Econ 1(3):59–81
Wagner RP, Petherbridge L (2004) Is the federal circuit succeeding? an empirical assessment of judicial performance. Univ Pa Law Rev 152(3):1105–1180
Weder B (1995) Legal systems and economic performance: the empirical evidence. In: Rowat M, Malik WH, Dakolias M (ed) Judicial reform in latin america and the caribbean: proceedings of a world bank conference. World Bank, pp 21–26
White PJ (2001) Judging judges: securing judicial independence by use of judicial performance evaluations. Fordham Urban Law J 29:1053
World Bank (2019) Doing business 2019: training for reform. Technical Report, World Bank, Washington, DC

A Maximalist Approach to Data Under IBC

Adam Feibelman and Renuka Sane

1 Introduction

In May of 2016, India enacted a new comprehensive Insolvency and Bankruptcy Code (IBC) that covers commercial as well as individual debtors. IBC dramatically reforms the substantive rules of insolvency and bankruptcy law in India and creates various new important institutional actors, including the Insolvency and Bankruptcy Board of India (IBBI), financial information utilities, insolvency professionals, and insolvency professional agencies. Provisions of IBC concerning commercial debtors and related regulations have already gone into effect, and over 2,000 cases have been initiated under the system.[1] Approximately 2,000 insolvency professionals[2] and three insolvency professional agencies[3] have been registered; one information utility has been approved;[4] and IBBI has indicated that it plans to at least partially

[1] http://www.ibbi.gov.in/webadmin/pdf/press/2017/Dec/Governmentdisposes2,750casesunderInsolvencyandBankruptcyCode.pdf.
[2] http://www.ibbi.gov.in/register.html.
[3] http://www.ibbi.gov.in/ipas.html.
[4] http://www.ibbi.gov.in/webadmin/pdf/press/2017/Sep/IURegistrationPressRelease.pdf.

The work of this chapter has been used by the authors in public domain publications including blog articles (Feibelman and Sane 2019a) and university working papers (Feibelman and Sane 2019b). All opinions expressed in this chapter are the authors' own and not that of their employers.

A. Feibelman (✉)
Sumter Davis Marks Professor of Law at Tulane Law School, New Orleans, LA, USA
e-mail: afeibelm@tulane.edu

R. Sane
National Institute of Public Finance and Policy, New Delhi, India

© The Author(s), under exclusive license to Springer Nature Singapore Pte Ltd. 2022

S. Thomas (ed.), *Insolvency and Bankruptcy Reforms in India*,
India Studies in Business and Economics,
https://doi.org/10.1007/978-981-16-0854-4_5

notify and put into effect the provisions for personal debtors in the future.[5] Nearly 2 years after IBC has gone into effect, issues of first impression continue to arise with some frequency, and much preliminary work remains to be done to implement and improve aspects of the new insolvency and bankruptcy ecosystem.

As the new system took shape, the availability and reliability of data about various aspects of the system emerged as a primary topic of concern. This is, in the first instance, a challenge of implementation and institutional design. Among its numerous responsibilities, IBBI is charged with gathering and disseminating information about the insolvency and bankruptcy system. Specifically, IBC provides that IBBI must "publish such information, data, research studies and other information as may be specified by regulations; ... collect and maintain records relating to insolvency and bankruptcy cases and disseminate information relating to such cases; [and] ... maintain websites and such other universally accessible repositories of electronic information as may be necessary ... ."[6]

IBBI has taken a number of preliminary steps to perform its statutory responsibility for gathering and disseminating data. It has developed a user-friendly website where it posts regulatory materials, orders issued by tribunals and courts, and directories of insolvency professionals and insolvency professional agencies.[7] It has also begun reporting various data about the system in its quarterly newsletter, including the aggregate data on the number of cases, outcomes, proceedings initiated by type of stakeholder, voluntary liquidations, insolvency professionals per region.[8] The newsletter also reports case level data from cases yielding resolution plans regarding initiating parties, claims by financial creditors, liquidation values, and recoveries by financial creditors. It has become the repository of quantitative and qualitative information about the working of the IBC.

Thus far, the only other effort to gather and report data about the operation of the new insolvency and bankruptcy system is being conducted by independent researchers. One group of authors have analyzed relevant orders issued by the National Company Law Tribunals (NCLT), which is the adjudicating authority for cases under IBC involving commercial debtors.[9] These orders provide much illuminating information about the system. But the study also underscores the need for more comprehensive and usable data. Each order generally includes only the information relevant to its particular action or decision and does not report such information in a standardized or searchable format.

---

[5] The chairperson of the Insolvency and Bankruptcy Board stated that one of the institution's primary current goals is to "operationalise the individual insolvency regime in respect of guarantors to the corporates and the individuals having proprietary business." in *Individual Insolvency Norms a Priority, says IBBI Chairman*, Economic Times, 2 October 2017.

[6] Section 194, IBC.

[7] http://www.ibbi.gov.in/index.html.

[8] IBBI (2018).

[9] Chatterjee et al. (2018), which also discusses the importance of empirical data about the new insolvency and bankruptcy system. See also Finance Research Group (2017).

These are good and important starts, but they represent only a portion of the relevant and useful data that is, or might be, generated by the system and that could be made available to the public. And as of yet, it is impossible to assess the quality and consistency of data reported by IBBI. To date, it does not appear that IBBI has adopted a systematic approach to ensuring the quality of such data, and it has not yet announced a formal policy regarding its approach to gathering and disseminating data about the system or its goals in that regard.

The chapter proposes that IBBI take a maximalist approach to data about the new insolvency and bankruptcy system. Gathering and disseminating data about the system may seem like a regulatory function of secondary importance, and it has received scant attention thus far among policymakers and commentators. Yet the availability of comprehensive, reliable, and standardized data about the new system is essential for many purposes and very useful for many others. Without such data, regulators and public observers cannot reasonably assess how the system is performing or determine what effect it may be having on its stakeholders and on the broader society. Such data can also provide a uniquely illuminating window into the economy, highlighting economic, financial, and social trends and potential micro- and macro-vulnerabilities. Drafters of IBC were therefore wise to include a requirement regarding data. It now falls to IBBI to execute its responsibility regarding data and, hopefully, to the National Company Law Tribunals and the Debt Recovery Tribunals, which are the adjudicating authorities for cases involving individual debtors, to play cooperative roles.

As these institutions decide what information to gather and disseminate, and how to do so, IBBI and the Tribunals can draw from the experience of other jurisdictions that have struggled to determine appropriate policies and practices for making bankruptcy and insolvency data available to the public. To help frame the policy questions the new Board and the Tribunals will face, this chapter summarizes the evolution of approaches that policymakers in the United States have taken with regard to bankruptcy data and describes some of the research utilizing this data.

The American experience with bankruptcy data is, in many respects, a cautionary tale. As this chapter explains in Sect. 2, for most of the history of bankruptcy law in the U.S., bankruptcy petitions and supporting documents have been public documents; as of 2001, those documents and case docket information have been available electronically over the internet for a fee, with limited exceptions for personal information.[10] For many decades, the Administrative Office of the U.S. Courts was charged with reporting very basic aggregate data about bankruptcy cases. Debates over bankruptcy policy and major reforms in 1978 revealed, however, that available information about the system was insufficient to shed meaningful light on key questions of policy and practice.

Over the last two decades of the twentieth century, scholars and other commentators who were engaged in the empirical study of the U.S. bankruptcy system began

[10] Personal information that is omitted or redacted includes Social Security numbers, financial account numbers, the names of minors, dates of birth, and home addresses in criminal cases. See https://www.pacer.gov/.

drawing attention to the need for more and better bankruptcy data and statistics. These writers offered compelling arguments and a useful literature about how bankruptcy data can provide a window into financial and economic trends and help stakeholders and policymakers understand how the system operates, observe the impact of the system on its stakeholders, and identify areas of potential reform.

In 2005, as part of major reforms to that country's personal bankruptcy laws, the U.S. Congress significantly augmented the responsibilities of the Administrative Office of the U.S. Courts for gathering and reporting data about bankruptcy cases as well as the data collection function of bankruptcy trustees. The aggregate statistics collected and reported by the Administrative Office of the U.S. Courts now provide an essential baseline set of information about the broad scope and trends of the operation of the U.S. bankruptcy system. However, researchers continue to have concerns about the reliability of this aggregate data. Furthermore, the aggregate statistics provide rough and imperfect information about the determinants of financial distress, details of the operation of the bankruptcy system, or the impact of that system on debtors, creditors, and other stakeholders. The most useful bankruptcy data still appear to be the case-level public documents, especially the petitions and supporting schedules that debtors themselves submit, and qualitative data derived from interviews, surveys, and questionnaires. Research involving these types of data is inevitably costly and time-consuming, however, and it can be difficult to replicate and evaluate. The American experience thus not only illustrates the value of relevant and reliable aggregate data and the essential need for useful case-level data but also reflects how efforts to gather such data and make it available raise complicated issues of policy and practicality.

In these early years of the operation of India's new insolvency and bankruptcy system, both the importance and the difficulty of gathering and disseminating useful data are acute. The initial challenge in this regard is identifying precisely what types of information about the new system would be useful for policymakers, stakeholders, and researchers. Section 3.1 describes in general terms the types of aggregate and case-level data about the Indian insolvency and bankruptcy system that might be profitably gathered and made available. Section 3.2 considers whether IBBI or the tribunals might be in a better position to provide certain categories of data. As that Section explains, the tribunals are well positioned to gather and disseminate comprehensive aggregate statistics or case-level data about the cases they handle. Yet, they have not traditionally performed that role.

The Board can also gather and disseminate aggregate or case-level information without cooperation from the tribunals, but it must rely on information provided to it by insolvency professionals and insolvency professional agencies. This may be a more cumbersome process in general, but IBBI is likely in a better position to gather data about many aspects of cases that are conducted or managed by the insolvency professionals. Given that they likely have overlapping and complimentary capacities for gathering and disseminating data, it would be ideal for the tribunals and IBBI to cooperate or coordinate their efforts to make data timely, accurate, uniform, and easily accessible and usable.

Section 3.3 addresses the functionality of data gathered by IBBI or the tribunals and the need for assuring reliability and uniformity. This requires, among other things, systems for recording and retrieving information about procedural aspects of cases filed under IBC, forms designed to facilitate the extraction of data, and careful definition of terms employed in court documents and proceedings. The Board and the Ministry of Corporate Affairs have promulgated some model forms that should promote these goals. This Section also briefly discusses the challenge that policymakers will face in determining the degree and scope of access to data that it allows researchers and the public.

In conclusion, this chapter reemphasizes the institutional responsibility IBBI has to gather and disseminate data about India's new insolvency and bankruptcy system. It also underscores the great opportunity IBBI has to provide a model for transparency about the functioning of the Indian legal system and to gather extremely useful information about the financial vulnerabilities of citizens, households, retail and commercial lenders, and the broader economy. To that end, this chapter proposes that IBBI conduct or allow a study of cases brought under IBC to assess, among other things, what information the new system generates or might generate; how its model forms are utilized and the quality and uniformity of the data they reflect; whether other areas of practice warrant similar model forms; and how the data generated by the system can be most fruitfully assembled and disseminated.

2 The U.S. Experience

This part describes the evolution of the approach to bankruptcy data in the United States, which reflects the influence of scholars engaged in the empirical study of the country's bankruptcy system who have been vocal advocates for the availability of reliable and usable data. Empirical research on bankruptcy and insolvency law has become a global and international field, but as two prominent scholars have noted, "[t]raditionally, the abundance of empirical legal research in bankruptcy has been primarily a U.S. phenomenon."[11] This is attributable in large part to the historical availability of data about the U.S. bankruptcy system and to the relatively significant role of that system within the country. Section 2.1 briefly summarizes the two primary ways that data about the U.S. bankruptcy system has historically been made available to the public: first, the collection and dissemination of aggregate data by government entities in the bankruptcy system, especially the Administrative Office of the U.S. Courts and the U.S. Trustee; and second, by making court documents, records, and information publicly available. Section 2.2 describes the emergence, beginning in the 1980s, of an ever-expanding literature of empirical research of the U.S. bankruptcy system. It notes the work done by some of the leading scholars in the first wave of this literature to articulate the benefits of accurate and accessible bankruptcy

[11] Warren and Lawless (2010) describing the early empirical bankruptcy research of William O. Douglas and various studies in the 1950s and the 1960s.

data. Section 2.3. reviews scholarship and commentary that critically assesses the American approach to bankruptcy data. Section 2.4 describes the evolution of the U.S. approach to bankruptcy in provisions of the Bankruptcy Abuse Prevention and Consumer Protection Act of 2005 regarding data about the bankruptcy system, and evaluates the usefulness of the information generated by those reforms for bankruptcy scholars and policymakers.

2.1 *Starting Points*

The U.S. Congress has required various government actors to collect and disseminate bankruptcy data since it enacted the first modern bankruptcy law in 1898.[12] The U.S. Attorney General began reporting data drawn from individual bankruptcy trustee reports in 1913, a function that was taken up by the Administrative Office of the U.S. courts in the early 1940s.[13] In 1948, Congress formally assigned responsibility for collecting and disseminating general bankruptcy data to the Administrative Office of the U.S. Courts.[14] Until 2005, the Administrative Office collected limited basic data about the number and types of cases filed, some procedural actions, and debtors' assets and liabilities.[15] It regularly published aggregate statistics about the number of cases and adversary proceedings within cases drawn from this data.[16] Recently, the Administrative Office and the Federal Judicial Center, a research agency of the U.S. federal judiciary, have partnered to enable the Center to make public its integrated database of bankruptcy petitions, including data on cases filed, terminated, and pending since 2008.[17]

In the American bankruptcy system, private trustees administer almost all bankruptcy cases involving individual debtors and some bankruptcy cases of commercial debtors. The U.S. Trustee Program of the U.S. Department of Justice is charged with oversight of bankruptcy cases and private bankruptcy trustees, and it also gathers and publishes some data relating to trustees' role in bankruptcy administration in cases around the country.[18] These published data include statistics on the system's overall caseload; actions against debtors for denial of discharge and

---

[12] Sullivan et al. (1987) noting that "Congress sent out more than 15,000 letters and collected more than 20,000 constituent comments before formulating the 1903 amendments to the Bankruptcy Act".

[13] Warren and Lawless (2010).

[14] 28 U.S.C. 604(a)(2), (13) (1948); National Bankruptcy Review Commission (1997).

[15] Porter and Thorne (2006), Frasier (1996), National Bankruptcy Review Commission (1997).

[16] E.g., Business and Non-Business Cases Filed, by Chapter of the Bankruptcy Code, June 2004, http://www.uscourts.gov/sites/default/files/statistics_import_dir/1204_f2.pdf; Adversary Proceedings Commenced, Terminated and Pending, June 2004, http://www.uscourts.gov/sites/default/files/statistics_import_dir/F08Jun04.pdf.

[17] https://www.fjc.gov/research/idb.

[18] Department of Justice Executive Office for United States Trustees (2015b), Department of Justice Executive Office for United States Trustees (2004).

dismissal of cases; actions against creditors, attorneys, and other parties; criminal referrals; professional fees; objections to plan confirmations in the Chap. 11; trustee disbursements to creditors; and approval of, and fees charged by, debtor financial counseling and education providers.[19]

More significant for empirical study of bankruptcy in the United States, most documents related to bankruptcy cases in the U.S. federal court system, including bankruptcy petitions and related documents, have historically been public documents.[20] Beginning in the late 1980s, the federal courts adopted PACER, the Public Access to Courts Electronic Records program, which is operated by the Administrative Office.[21] Currently, PACER provides electronic access—for a fee—to most relevant documents and case information in bankruptcy cases, redacting certain basic personal information such as Social Security numbers and financial account numbers.[22]

2.2 *An Emerging Literature*

Although the field of empirical research on U.S. bankruptcy law stretches back at least to the late 1920s,[23] the data available from government agencies or from filings themselves had a little discernable impact on policymakers until the last quarter of the twentieth century. As Sullivan et al. (1987) wrote, "The most significant thing about the role of empirical research in bankruptcy policy has been its insignificance."[24] Debates over bankruptcy policy that began to develop and intensify in the early 1970s, culminating in major reforms in 1978, helped fuel a new interest in empirical study of the existing bankruptcy system and the impact it had on the U.S. economy and society.[25] In 1973, the Report of the Commission on the Bankruptcy Laws of the United States, which heavily influenced the development of the current Bankruptcy Code, proposed creating a national, centralized process for collecting

---

[19] Department of Justice Executive Office for United States Trustees (2015b).

[20] generally, Martin (2008).

[21] https://www.pacer.gov/about.html.

[22] LoPucki (1997) at 934.

[23] Warren and Lawless (2010) describing the early empirical bankruptcy research of William O. Douglas and various studies in the 1950 and 1960s.).

[24] See also Porter and Thorne (2006) at 965 ("Empirical research about bankruptcy is relatively young.").

[25] Sullivan et al. (1987) at 196 cites calls for empirical research in the years leading up to the 1978 amendments, while National Bankruptcy Review Commission (1997) at 925 note that the 1973 Commission report advocated "the creation of a national system of bankruptcy administration that would have among its duties the collection and dissemination of empirical data about the bankruptcy system." (citing *Report of the Commission on the Bankruptcy Laws of the United States*, H.R. Doc. No. 137, 93d Cong., 1st Sess., pt. 1, at 110–111 (1973); Dreyfus et al. (1973), Stanley and Girth (1971), Shuchman (1977).

and disseminating empirical data about the U.S. bankruptcy system.[26] In support of that proposal, it quoted these observations from a contemporaneous study: "Because of such extensive variations in local practice and financial conditions, we feel that the performance of the current bankruptcy system will continue to defy all but the crudest analysis until more uniform policies and practices are established and essential data elements can be collected as a routine part of processing each case."[27]

In fact, much of the early empirical research on U.S. bankruptcy law made similar pleas and cataloged the potential benefits of useful data about the operation of the bankruptcy system. This early literature observed, among other things, that such data can help policymakers make important administrative decisions regarding the allocation of scarce resources[28]; identify factors that impact judges' decisions in particular cases[29]; inform debates over the design of bankruptcy law and the direction of bankruptcy policy[30]; reflect the impact of bankruptcy law on the broader economy[31]; generate ideas for further empirical research and help identify what new data are needed[32]; enable stakeholders to plan around the operation of the bankruptcy system[33]; and provide critical information about the performance of an economy and its financial system.[34] As Sullivan et al. (1987) wrote,[35]

> Fundamental bankruptcy policies for both consumers and businesses are based on assumptions of fact about the behavior of debtors and creditors, credit markets, attorneys, landlords, equity holders, tort victims, trust donors, repo purchasers, stockbrokers, codebtors, shopping center lessors, labor unions, warehousemen, taxing authorities, layaway purchasers, accountants, farmers, foreign representatives, insiders, outsiders, and the rest of the cast. Some of these assumptions are tested, and some are not; likewise, some are accurate, and some undoubtedly are not.

To provide more nuanced and generalizable information about the bankruptcy system, researchers began conducting labor-intensive and cost-intensive studies of bankruptcy filings to extract and employ case-level data.[36] As the National Bankruptcy Review Commission (1997) notes, "[t]he empirical studies that do exist

---

[26] LoPucki (1997) at 925 (citing *Report of the Commission on the Bankruptcy Laws of the United States*, H.R. Doc. No.93–137, 93d Cong. 1st Sess., at 120 (1973)).

[27] Dreyfus et al. (1973).

[28] Frasier (1996) at 306 ("These statistics are critical as they determine resource allocation to bankruptcy districts and assist in docket management."); National Bankruptcy Review Commission (1997), Sullivan et al. (1987), at 222.

[29] LoPucki (1997) at 926.

[30] Frasier (1996) at 310–311 "[I]inaccurate data may lead to the adoption of inefficient laws that risk causing more harm than laws based on no statistics at all ... In addition, inaccurate data make it exceedingly difficult to evaluate the impact of bankruptcy reform measures."; Sullivan et al. (1987); Bankruptcy: The Next Twenty Years, at 926.

[31] Frasier (1996) at 308.

[32] Sullivan et al. (1987), LoPucki (1997) at 926.

[33] LoPucki (1997) at 926.

[34] Frasier (1996) at 308.

[35] Sullivan et al. (1987) at 198.

[36] LoPucki (1997) at 925; Sullivan et al. (1987).

are based on a small sampling that [have] been manually and laboriously compiled, and the conclusions of these studies cannot be updated without similar effort."[37]

In the early 1980s, Teresa Sullivan, Elizabeth Warren, and Jay Westbrook began gathering data for the Consumer Bankruptcy Project, an ongoing project that has gathered and analyzed data from cases in multiple districts and from interviews and questionnaires.[38] The first phase of the Project was conducted in the 1980s s and examined data drawn from court documents. That initial phase culminated in the ground-breaking book, *As We Forgive Our Debtors: Bankruptcy and Consumer Credit in America*.[39] A second phase of the project conducted in the early 1990s,[40] examined data drawn from court documents and questionnaires, which was described and analyzed in the *Fragile Middle Class: Americans in Debt*.[41] A third phase of the project conducted in the early 2000s,[42] involved court records, interviews, questionnaires. Data from that phase was described and analyzed in *The Two-Income Trap: Why Middle-Class Parents are Going Broke* by Elizabeth Warren and Amelia Tyagi[43] The project conducted a fourth phase in 2007[44] and began ongoing and continuous work in 2013[45] generating numerous studies and published works by its more than 10 principal investigators.[46] Perhaps most influentially, the books drawn from the data gathered by the project have focused heavily on the determinants of household financial distress among bankruptcy filers and found that most bankruptcy filings by individuals are largely attributed to a handful of external shocks, especially unemployment, medical expenses, and family crises like divorce.

In the years leading up to the major bankruptcy reforms in 2005, this group of scholars examined, among other things, the role of medical debt in household financial distress and bankruptcies[47]; evidence of under-counted business-related bankruptcies in consumer bankruptcy filings[48]; the rise in bankruptcy filings in the

[37] LoPucki (1997) at 926; Rasmussen (2007); See, e.g. U.S. Gen. Accounting Office, Bankruptcy Reform: Use of the Homestead Exemption By Chap. 7 Bankruptcy Debtors in the Northern District of Texas and the Southern District of Florida, GGD-99-142R (July 12, 1999); U.S. Gen. Accounting Office, Bankruptcy Administration: Case Receipts Paid to Creditors and Professionals, GGD-94–173 (July 13, 1994); Lawless and Ferris (1997), Lawless and Ferris (2000).

[38] The history and methodologies of the various phases of the Consumer Bankruptcy Project is described in detail in Pottow et al. (2008).

[39] Sullivan et al. (1989).

[40] Pottow et al. (2008), at 388–389.

[41] Sullivan et al. (2001).

[42] Pottow et al. (2008) at 389–391.

[43] Warren and Tyagi (2004).

[44] Pottow et al. (2008) at 391.

[45] The current investigators in the Project are Pamela Foohey, Robert Lawless, Katherine Porter, and Deborah Thorne.

[46] Porter and Thorne (2006), Warren and Tyagi (2004), at 181–188 describing Phase III of the Consumer Bankruptcy Project.

[47] Jacoby et al. (2001), Jacoby and Warren (2006).

[48] Lawless and Warren (2005).

wake of natural disasters[49]; debtors' ongoing financial distress after completion of bankruptcy cases[50]; the distinct financial hardships of rural debtors[51]; and the impact of having dependents on bankrupt debtors.[52]

During this same period, beginning in 1994, Lynn Lopucki began gathering data on bankruptcies involving public companies that became the UCLA-Lopucki Bankruptcy Research Database.[53] Lopucki's early work that drew from this data examined venue choices,[54] professional fees,[55] and outcomes[56] in large Chap. 11 cases, culminating in his book, *Courting Failure*, an influential critical assessment of large corporate reorganizations in the U.S.[57] Numerous other researchers have utilized this data[58] to shed light on such things as the financial determinant of business bankruptcies[59]; the going concern value of firms in Chap. 11;[60] the likelihood of reorganization in small-business bankruptcies,[61] additional work on professional fees[62]; courts fees[63]; the roles of examiners,[64] hedge funds,[65] and other activist investors[66] in Chap. 11 cases; instances of geographical distance between bankruptcy venue and debtor operations[67]; and the practice of asset sales.[68] In the years before BAPCPA, other researchers also gathered data independently and produced influential studies on such topics as the dischargeability of student loans[69] and impact of bankruptcy law and entrepreneurial activity in the U.S.[70]

---

49 Lawless (2005).

50 Porter and Thorne (2006) describing methodology at 125–28.

51 Porter (2005) reporting on a supplemental dataset as part of Phase III of the Consumer Bankruptcy Project to capture rural debtors.

52 Warren (2002).

53 UCLA-Lopucki Bankruptcy Research Database, available at http://lopucki.law.ucla.edu.

54 LoPucki and Eisenberg (1999).

55 LoPucki and Doherty (2004).

56 LoPucki and Kalin (2001).

57 LoPucki (2006).

58 For a list of published and unpublished research utilizing the dataset, see http://lopucki.law.ucla.edu/published_research.htm..

59 Warren and Westbrook (1999).

60 Baird and Rasmussen (2003).

61 Morrison (2007).

62 Lubben (2008).

63 LoPucki and Doherty (2009).

64 Lipson (2010), Lipson and Marrota (2016).

65 Jiang et al. (2012).

66 Ellias (2016).

67 Coordes (2015).

68 Jacoby and Janger (2014).

69 Pardo and Lacey (2005).

70 Fan and White (2003).

2.3 Critiques About Data

These ongoing projects and the advocacy of their principal investigators helped orient much of the field of bankruptcy research in the United States toward empirical inquiry.[71] As empirical research became more central to debates over bankruptcy law and policy, the availability, quality, and accuracy of data regarding the bankruptcy system emerged as increasingly important topics of scholarly interest.

As Sullivan et al. (1987) pointed out, the potential benefits of this research depend on data that are accurate, usable, and "generalizable." They and other early writers on the topic drew attention to pervasive problems with the quality of available bankruptcy data drawn from filed petitions.[72] These problems were due especially to mistakes or strategic inaccuracy by filers, flaws in the design of forms and unclear definitions of key reporting categories, and inconsistency in data input by clerks in the various districts across the country.[73] As Frasier observed, writing in 1997, "About the only data accurately reported are the number of bankruptcy cases actually filed."[74]

Sullivan et al. made an early and compelling call for improvements in the collection and dissemination of bankruptcy data. While the U.S. bankruptcy system is well-suited for data gathering,[75] they observed that doing so requires careful, expert institutional design.[76] Among other things, they called for improvements in standardized bankruptcy forms and formats to allow for routine, computerized, systematic data gathering.[77] The 1997 report of the National Bankruptcy Review Commission, an independent commission established by Congress,[78] advanced these concerns and called for making public all electronic data gathered by bankruptcy courts; a pilot effort to aggregate bankruptcy data from their various sources; the appointment of federal bankruptcy data collector; and the establishment of a comprehensive bankruptcy data system.[79]

As Frasier noted at the time, however, there was generally a lack of interest among policymakers in improving the quality, scope, and availability of bankruptcy statistics. She argued that markets and institutions tended to under-estimate the private and

[71] For a critique of this development, see Rasmussen (2007). See also articles utilizing bankruptcy statistics generated by the US Trustee's office during this period http://www.usdoj.gov/ust/eo/public-affairs/articles.

[72] Frasier (1996) at 313–17, 330–40 describing and finding data errors in characterizing the nature of cases, estimating assets and liabilities, and counting creditors, as well as transcription and judgment errors by bankruptcy clerks who convert data provided by filers into official data.

[73] Frasier (1996) at 308; see also LoPucki (1997) at 921 noting the lack of studies of the accuracy of data provided by bankruptcy filers.

[74] LoPucki (1997) at 921.

[75] LoPucki (1997).

[76] Sullivan.

[77] Sullivan, at 226–227.

[78] National Bankruptcy Review Commission (1997).

[79] National Bankruptcy Review Commission (1997) at Chap. 4; see also LoPucki (1997), Frasier (1996) at 342–343 calling for computerized bankruptcy filings and uniform definitions.

public value of public information about the bankruptcy system compared to data on, say, consumer prices, demographics, and trade, all of which are carefully studied, and generate debates about data accuracy.[80] Without pressure from these directions, and because private lenders already had access to their private information,[81] there was no real pressure for changes in the collection or dissemination of data about the U.S. bankruptcy system.

2.4 BAPCPA

In the years since Frasier's critique, the Administrative Office of the Federal Courts have significantly improved the PACER system in ways that make public bankruptcy information much more readily obtainable. This has removed at least some practical obstacles for researchers conducting district-level "episodic" studies of the operation of the bankruptcy system.[82] However, this change did not in itself address the quality of reported information or improve the ability of researchers to obtain aggregate, system-wide data. And while the availability of PACER data in electronic form may reduce threshold research costs, PACER fees can still be substantial.[83]

The Bankruptcy Abuse Prevention and Consumer Protection Act of 2005, a major and otherwise controversial set of reforms to the U.S. consumer bankruptcy system, provided an opportunity to adopt measures to improve the collection and dissemination of bankruptcy statistics.[84] Perhaps because the debates over the proposed law largely revolved around empirical claims that were difficult or impossible to resolve with available data, these data-related provisions of BAPCPA were some of the very few aspects of the law that were relatively uncontested.

Many of these provisions appear to reflect the criticism and recommendations of the National Bankruptcy Review Commission and other bankruptcy researchers. Perhaps most promising, BAPCPA increases the scope of data that the Administrative Office of the U.S. Courts must compile from the bankruptcy courts and annually make

---

[80] Frasier (1996) at 318–320; Porter and Thorne (2006).

[81] Porter and Thorne (2006).

[82] Sullivan.

[83] Porter at 981.

[84] The Act also included an aspirational but non-operational provision stating "the sense of Congress that

> (1) the national policy of the United States should be that all data held by bankruptcy clerks in electronic form, to the extent such data reflects only public records ... should be released in a usable electronic form in bulk to the public, subject to ... appropriate privacy concerns and safeguards ... and (2) there should be established a bankruptcy data system in which--(A) a single set of data definitions and forms are used to collect data nationwide; and(B) data for any particular bankruptcy case are aggregated in the same electronic record."

BAPCPA §604.

public as aggregate national and district-level statistics.[85] These data now include debtors' total assets and liabilities, including per category of assets and liabilities, as reported in debtors' filed schedules[86]; debtors' "current monthly income, average income, and average expenses as reported in debtors' filed schedules"[87]; the total amount of debt discharged[88]; the average time between the filing and the closing of cases[89]; various data related to debtors' reaffirmation of debts in bankruptcy[90]; the number of cases which creditors were sanctioned for misconduct and the amount of punitive damages awards as a result[91]; and the number of cases in which damages or sanctions were imposed against a debtor's attorney.[92] For cases filed under Chap. 13, these data include the number of cases in which property securing a claim was valued by the court; the number of cases in which such property was valued at less than the amount of the claim; the total number of dismissed cases; the number of cases dismissed because the debtor failed to make payments under the Chap. 13 plan; the total number of cases that were refiled after a dismissal, and total number of cases where the debtors' Chap. 13 plans were completed; and the total number of cases in which the debtors had filed a cases within the previous six years.[93]

BAPCPA also requires the U.S. Attorney General to issue rules requiring and standardizing final and periodic case reports by bankruptcy trustees to "facilitate compilation of data and maximum possible access of the public, both by physical inspection at one or more central filing locations, and by electronic access through the Internet or other appropriate media."[94] The Act requires that the rules provide for trustees' final reports to reflect data about the duration of each case, assets abandoned by the trustee, any assets exempted, receipt and disbursements of the debtor's estate, administrative expenses, creditors' claims asserted and allowed, distributions

[85] E.g., See http://www.uscourts.gov/statistics-reports/bapcpa-report-2016.

[86] 159(c)(3)(A), 28 U.S.C.

[87] 159(c)(3)(B), 28 U.S.C.

[88] 159(c)(3)(C), 28 U.S.C. (discharged debt is "determined as the difference between the total amount of debt and obligations of a debtor reported on the schedules and the amount of such debt reported in categories which are predominantly nondischargeable").

[89] 159(c)(3)(D), 28 U.S.C.

[90] 159(c)(3)(E), 28 U.S.C: These data include the number of cases involving a reaffirmation agreement, the total number of such agreements filed, the number of cases involving such agreements in which the debtor was not represented by an attorney, and the number of cases in which the court approved a reaffirmation agreement; 11 U.S.C. 524: A bankruptcy court is required to approve reaffirmation agreements in cases where debtors are not represented by counsel.

[91] 159(c)(3)(G), 28 U.S.C.

[92] 159(c)(3)(H), 28 U.S.C.

[93] 159(c)(3)(F), 28 U.S.C.

[94] 589b., 28 U.S.C. "The information required to be filed in the reports ... shall be that which is in the best interests of debtors and creditors, and in the public interest in reasonable and adequate information to evaluate the efficiency and practicality of the Federal bankruptcy system." In particular, the rules "shall strike the best achievable practical balance between (1) the reasonable needs of the public for information about the operational results of the Federal bankruptcy system; (2) economy, simplicity, and lack of undue burden on persons with a duty to file reports; and (3) appropriate privacy concerns and safeguards".

to creditors, "claims discharged without payment," and any failure of performance by a debtor under a plan.[95] For periodic reports under Chap. 11, the Act requires that rules provide for trustees to report on industry classification; duration of the case, the number of a debtor's employees; receipts, disbursements, and the debtor's profitability; tax payments by the debtor; professional fees approved by the court; plans of reorganization, including amounts and percentages recovered by creditors.[96] The U.S. Trustee issues annual reports reflecting at least some of this data in aggregate.[97]

The Act also requires the U.S. Trustee and the Administrative Office to develop a process for auditing information that individual debtors are required to provide under Chaps. 7 and 13.[98] It also commissioned a number of studies, including one by the U.S. Government Accountability Office (GAO), an independent agency that provides investigative assistance to Congress, on the quality and availability of bankruptcy statistics.[99]

The GAO study commissioned by the Act reported significant criticism of the BAPCPA provisions: "[F]or several reasons the statistics required under the act are likely to be of limited value. For example, many of the statistics are relatively narrow in scope and were not intended to provide certain key information, such as the causes of bankruptcy and the demographic characteristics of filers."[100] Furthermore, the study found that while some of the data reported is too narrow to offer a complete picture of facets of the system,[101] the aggregate statistics, such as those reported by the Administrative Office and the U.S. Trustee, were too broad and not as valuable as case-level data.[102] The GAO study reported that bankruptcy researchers suggested that "AOUSC to make the underlying case-level data publicly available, which would permit additional analyses of factors such as differences in debtors' income, assets, and liabilities. AOUSC currently has no plans to make these case-level data available, citing concerns about privacy and security, as well as the reliability of the data."[103]

---

[95] 589b(d), 28 U.S.C.

[96] 589b(d), 28 U.S.C.

[97] Department of Justice Executive Office for United States Trustees (2015b).

[98] 586 (BAPCPA, Sect. 603), 28 U.S.C. 586. See e.g., Department of Justice Executive Office for United States Trustees (2015a).

[99] U.S. Government Accountability Office, Report to Congressional Requesters, *Bankruptcy: Judiciary Should Take Further Steps to Make Bankruptcy Data More Accessible*, GAO-09–28, Dec. 2008, available at http://www.gao.gov/new.items/d0928.pdf. See Porter (2006).

[100] Bankruptcy: Judiciary Should Take Further Steps, at 4.

[101] Bankruptcy: Judiciary Should Take Further Steps, at 4 ("For example, the act requires AOUSC to report the number of cases in which creditors were fined for misconduct, but because courts reprimand creditors in a variety of ways, this statistic provides only a limited picture of the sanctions applied to creditors.").

[102] Bankruptcy: Judiciary Should Take Further Steps, at 4. See also, Pardo (2016) noting that the Administrative Office statistics on aggregate debt discharged are understated because they only include data from debtors' schedules and that the reliance on categories of debt results in both over- and under-inclusiveness of debt in the reported aggregate amount.

[103] Bankruptcy: Judiciary Should Take Further Steps, at 4.

2.5 Some Lessons

Given the amount of discussion about the quality and availability of bankruptcy data before BAPCPA, it is surprising that there has been little commentary on the subject since the GAO study. And it appears that little has changed since the GAO's report, and that the impact of the data provisions of BAPCPA have been limited. Those provisions do appear to have helped improved the quality and usability of the underlying data generated by the bankruptcy system and have increased the scope of available aggregate data about the U.S. bankruptcy system. Any improvement in the reliability and accuracy of such data increases the value of the resulting research and the additional aggregate data has proved at least modestly useful for certain empirical inquiries.

Yet it appears that these improvements have not dramatically expanded the ability of empirical research to shed light on crucial questions about the determinants of financial distress for firms and individuals, how system operates, or the nature of its impact on direct stakeholders. Most empirical research of the American bankruptcy system continues to be studies primarily utilizing case-level data gathered from PACER or from the UCLA-Lopucki database, sometimes supplemented with questionnaires or interviews of participants or stakeholders in the bankruptcy system. Since BAPCPA, for example, prominent research has relied on case level data and qualitative research to study whether BAPCPA itself achieved its own goal of reducing access to Chap. 7 for debtors with the ability to repay significant amounts of debt in Chap. 13[104]; the effect of a debtor's race on attorney advice regarding chapter choice[105]; the effect of attorney fees on chapter choice[106]; the particular financial costs that debtors experience before filing for bankruptcy[107]; the ways in which bankruptcy attorneys responded to BAPCPA and helped steer its impact[108]; the particular experience of religious institutions as borrowers and debtors in bankruptcy[109]; patterns in litigation over the dischargeability of student loans[110]; and the experience of pro se debtors in bankruptcy.[111]

In sum, the U.S. experience with bankruptcy data reflects that basic aggregate data is a crucial starting point, as it provides essential information about the scope of the system and activity within it. Aggregate data about case loads and chapter choice can also reveal information on general trends in the economy that may not be otherwise discernable. But the value of such aggregate data has significant limits, and case-level data—quantitative as well as qualitative—is essential for developing a useful understanding about the determinants of financial distress, how the system

[104] Pottow et al. (2008).

[105] Braucher et al. (2012).

[106] Foohey et al. (2017).

[107] Foohey et al. (2018).

[108] Littwin (2016).

[109] Foohey (2013, 2014, 2015, 2017).

[110] Pardo (2014).

[111] Pardo (2009).

operates, how certain rules within it function in particular circumstances, and what impact these rules and the system itself has on the economy. The U.S. experience also reflects that it is surprisingly difficult to ensure the quality, uniformity, and accessibility of underlying raw data generated by the system and that the definitions of relevant terms and the design of forms used by parties and courts can crucially impact the usefulness of data generated by the system.

3 Data for India's Insolvency and Bankruptcy System

It is acutely important for authorities to gather and disseminate timely and reliable data about the India's new insolvency and bankruptcy system. India's Insolvency and Bankruptcy Code essentially creates an insolvency and bankruptcy system where one did not previously exist. Information about how the system is operating and what impact it is having in its earliest phases can be extremely valuable in helping participants adjust to the system and in enabling policymakers to identify early problems and potential fixes before they become pervasive and intractable issues in the system. Not surprisingly, in the first 18 months of the operation of the system, policymakers have already made some significant adjustments to the regime. Thus far, most of these adjustments appear to have been driven by episodic challenges that have emerged in early cases and, so it seems from the outside, based on a paucity of data about how the system overall is performing. As the amount of data about the system grows, it will soon enable more sophisticated statistical or econometric analysis. Ideally, future reforms can be based on careful empirical analysis of claims made in policy debates about the functioning of the system and the need for changes.

Furthermore, the new insolvency and bankruptcy system will generate extremely useful information about the Indian economy, especially about trends in the types of financial relationships occurring in the economy and about the determinants of financial distress for various types of debtors. This is especially important due to the ongoing challenges in the country with gathering and disseminating reliable financial and economic data in general. The new insolvency and bankruptcy system represents an opportunity to start from scratch in designing an accurate source of such data. Depending on the nature and amount of data that is gathered and disseminated about the system, it could yield a broad, albeit incomplete,[112] window into commercial and consumer financial markets.

This Part first examines, generally, what data generated by the system might be profitably gathered and disseminated. It then considers the relative institutional capacity of the National Company Law Tribunals and IBBI for gathering and disseminating such data, noting some comparative advantages of each for certain types of data. Finally, it describes the importance of standardizing information generated by

[112] The obvious limit in this regard is that the system will only generate information about parties and actions that are within it.

the system, especially through the forms used by parties and through the processes by which case information is officially recorded.

3.1 What Data Should Be Collected?

In theory, everything that happens within the new insolvency and bankruptcy ecosystem is a piece of data and might be gathered and disclosed. It is impossible to anticipate all of the information about the Indian insolvency and bankruptcy system that might in the future be useful for policymakers, researchers, and private parties. But it is almost certain that some things that seem peripheral at the outset may be useful to someone down the road.[113] That said, even a maximalist approach data would require policymakers to make some basic decisions about what types of data are worth capturing in the first place.

The experience of policymakers and bankruptcy scholars in U.S. reflects that core data about the bankruptcy system include information about the procedural life of cases brought within the system; the circumstances of parties and other stakeholders throughout the process of cases that involve them; and the performance of actors and institutions that comprise the system itself, including judicial officers, bankruptcy professionals, and trustees. The discussion below identifies examples of similar or parallel subjects of core data about India's new insolvency and bankruptcy ecosystem that should ideally be gathered and disseminated—especially debtors, creditors, tribunals, and insolvency professionals.

Procedural data

Basic procedural data about cases brought under IBC provide an essential core of information about how the system operates. This data certainly includes the number of applications filed under each chapter of IBC in each jurisdiction, as well as more specific information about procedural events, such as: the number of applications accepted and rejected; the number of subsequent dismissals; the duration of cases; the number of applications that result in discharge of debt; the frequency of meetings of creditors; the number of actions to recover preferential payments, and the rate of success of such actions; various aspects of creditor voting, including outcomes; the number and nature of legal challenges and appeals of decisions made; the frequency and bases of disputes about the amount or existences of claims, and their success rate; the frequency and bases of other procedural objections made or actions taken.

Stakeholder data

Information about the primary stakeholders in the system, especially debtors and their creditors, comprise another core set of data about the system, how it operates and what impact it may be having. This data certainly includes demographic information and characteristics of the debtors who are in the system; how much debt they

[113] Choi and Gulati (2004) proposing various objective criteria to assess the quality of judges.

owe, in total and on average; the characteristics of their creditors; how prevalent are various types of claims in the system, including the nature, timing, and maturity of debtors' obligations; and what assets debtors have, including how much of those assets is exempt from creditor recovery. Furthermore, this core data include information about who utilizes the system most actively, reflected by the number of involuntary applications (filed by either financial or operational creditors) compared voluntary ones (filed by debtors), as well as other relevant information about the characteristics of the filing parties, such as the number of involuntary applications filed by financial and operational creditors.[114]

Finally, core data about stakeholders of the system include information about how they fared, including: how much value creditors recovered from their debtors, and in what form; how much debt was discharged or restructured; how frequently corporate debtors survived their cases as reorganized firms and how frequently they were liquidated; and how frequently debtors undergo subsequent insolvency or bankruptcy cases.

Institutional data

Core data about the operation of the new insolvency and bankruptcy ecosystem also includes information about the institutions and repeat professional actors within the system. Chief among these are the tribunals and their judicial officers. Judicial delay is a pervasive challenge in India, and IBC was specifically designed to streamline the institutional function in insolvency and bankruptcy cases. There is a 270-day deadline for successful adoption of an insolvency resolution plan under IBC, after which the cases are supposed to automatically go into liquidation. The capacity of the system to resolve cases within this deadline has been a primary concern about the operation of IBC from its inception. Currently, several prominent cases have exceeded this deadline, and so this is now a topic of great interest and concern. As noted above, comprehensive and system-wide information about the number and duration of cases is core data about the operation of the new system. In assessing the capacity of the tribunals and the judicial officials, it would also be essential to know such information as the number of judges in each tribunal that heard cases related to IBC; the number of cases heard per judge; and the average duration of cases by each tribunal, including the time taken between important milestones. Such data should also help the tribunals allocate resources internally.

Other pillars of the institutional machinery of IBC include the insolvency professionals, the information utilities, and IBBI itself. Core data about the system thus includes information about how many insolvency professionals are working within the system; who selects them; how often they file cases; how many cases each handles on average; how often there are objections to insolvency professionals and how those objections are resolved; the total and average fees for insolvency professionals and other administrative claims; and the instances of allegations of misconduct by insolvency professionals. It also includes information about the number and types

[114] Chatterjee et al. (2018) noting to date, it appears that most filings have been creditors, including both financial operational creditors.

of IBBI's regulatory actions, such as acts of supervision, regulation and enforcement with regard to insolvency professionals, insolvency professional agencies, and information utilities. Core data regarding information utilities will include such information as the number and scope of records they maintain; the number of requests for information they receive and for what purposes; and the average time it takes for them to provide information to parties and the tribunals.

Case-level data

The examples of core data described above are generally aggregate data which can provide some crucial baseline information about the new system and represent broad snapshots of distinct aspects of the system. As the growing body of empirical research on the US bankruptcy system reflects, more nuanced data about the parties, cases, and institutions in the new insolvency and bankruptcy system can be derived from correlative statistical information and qualitative assessment. To fully assess the function and impact of the system, it would be useful to know, for example, whether outcomes in any or all chapters differ in relation to financial or demographic attributes of debtors, their debt profiles, the types of their creditors, or who selects the insolvency professional.

Similarly, while aggregate data about the nature, timing, and maturity of debtors' obligations can provide useful information about the determinants of financial distress in India, researchers and policymakers could learn much more by assessing and comparing the full profile of particular debtors in the system. Significant data can also be generated by qualitative inquiry, perhaps through interviews or surveys of individual debtors or creditors combined with information about their insolvency or bankruptcy cases. Both types of case-level analysis—nuanced quantitative and qualitative - depend on the availability of information about particular cases; researchers must at least be able to identify individual parties in the system, even if they remain anonymous, and have some ability to access them and information about their cases. As discussed below, useful aggregate and case-level data both depend on uniformity and standardization in the ways that parties, professionals, and institutions record and report information.

3.2 *Allocating the Responsibility for Data*

Both IBBI and Tribunals could, in theory, gather all of the examples of aggregate data described above. In fact, both institutions will likely gather at least some of this information if only for internal purposes of managing and evaluating their own institutional functions. But they face significantly different challenges and enjoy some relative advantages in generating reliable and usable data, whether for internal purposes or for public use. This Part describes both institutions as sources of data and considers how they might expand their roles, including their relative advantages in this regard.

Data from IBBI

As noted above, IBC specifically requires IBBI to gather and disseminate data about the new system. It is worth noting that financial regulators in India have become increasingly attentive to the benefits of publicly available data. Financial regulators such as the Reserve Bank of India (RBI), the Securities and Exchanges Board of India (SEBI), the Pension Fund Regulatory Development Authority (PFRDA) and the Insurance Regulatory and Development Authority of India (IRDAI) release aggregate data on the markets they regulate, and their intermediaries at regular intervals. The Financial Sector Legislative Reforms Committee (FSLRC) set up by the Ministry of Finance to look at the reform of financial sector laws in India, recommended the creation of a Financial Data Management Centre (FDMC), which would be the repository of all financial regulatory data, the goal of which is "to strengthen the stability of financial system by identifying, monitoring and mitigating systemic risks." More specifically, the Committee proposed that the data center's primary goals would be

> managing the repository of financial regulatory data, to enable standardization of Data across the financial sector[,] and providing analytical support to the Financial Stability and Development Council on issues related to financial stability of the economy and matters connected therewith.[115]

When the FDMC takes shape, IBBI will presumably be required to contribute data to the FDMC.

In the meantime, as noted above, IBBI has begun publishing some information about the insolvency and bankruptcy system on its website, including a comprehensive collection of legislative and regulatory materials; basic information about insolvency professionals, insolvency professional agencies, and information utilities under its purview; and orders from cases proceeding under IBC. It has also begun publishing some aggregate and case level data in its quarterly newsletter.

It is not yet clear how IBBI will perform its full responsibility to gather and disseminate data about the insolvency and bankruptcy system. It has a full menu of possible approaches to managing data generated by the system and can presumably learn from the experiences of other jurisdictions, like the U.S., in assessing the options on this menu of approaches.

As an initial matter, IBBI does not appear to have formal authority to obtain data directly from the tribunals; it only has authority to obtain data from insolvency professionals and insolvency professional agencies. Therefore, for IBBI to obtain comprehensive aggregate data about the insolvency and bankruptcy system, it must be able to depend on these professionals and their agencies to ensure that it receives the relevant data about each and every case.

This not only requires basic compliance and participation by the professionals and their agencies, but it depends upon a system in place to make the information

[115] Department of Economic Affairs, Ministry of Finance, Report of the Committee to study the Financial Data Management Legal Framework in India, Oct. 25, 2016, at 6–7, available at https://dea.gov.in/sites/default/files/FDMCReportalongwithdraftbill_0.pdf.

provided to Board uniform such that it can be aggregated. This could be done in a variety of ways. For example, IBBI could require professionals or their agencies to gather data and report aggregate data related to the cases in which they are involved and then combine all of the data it receives from these sources into a total aggregate. Alternatively, IBBI could create a system in which it obtains raw data from the professionals and agencies and does all of the necessary analysis and aggregation itself. To conduct this second approach, IBBI might create an electronic registry of case-related documents, actions, and decisions and rely on the professionals and agencies to consistently submit documents and note case-related actions and decisions.

In any event, this relationship involves an agency problem as IBBI will be depending on parties that it regulates but does not control in the strictest sense. There are currently over 2,000 insolvency professionals in India, and this number is likely to increase when the provisions of IBC covering individual debtors go into effect. The reliability of any aggregation of data by IBBI will require a great deal of consistency and accuracy on the part of a large number of individual insolvency professionals.

Data from the judiciary

As noted above, all bankruptcy petitions and supporting court documents have long been public documents in the U.S., and these have been a primary source of data about the system for independent researchers. In contrast, the Indian system does not provide easy access to court documents. Although court documents are public documents under the Indian Evidence Act, access to them is restricted to those that have a "right to inspect" them.[116] Thus, a person would need to demonstrate her right, or her interest, in accessing the public documents.[117] One generally has to show some connection to the proceedings to seek such data.

While documents on pleadings seem to be out of the purview of public release, some information about cases, including listing dates, judgments, and orders (interim or final) is usually available to the public and is currently published on court websites for almost all judicial fora. The information, however, is usually not gathered in a database. Furthermore, the underlying data is often inconsistent. For example, courts use different definitions for basic terms, such as "case."[118] Also, accessing the data is not easy as one often requires some details of the case (such as the party name, or the bench) to retrieve it. Both issues create hurdles for empirical research; recently the Law Commission of India[119] noted that it could not obtain reliable data from trial courts on arrears and delays. The Supreme Court of India published a consolidated report of the Indian judiciary for the first time in 2015–2016.[120]

Unlike IBBI, the National Company Law Tribunals and Debt Recovery Tribunals, the adjudicating authorities under IBC, are not subject to any obligation regarding

---

[116] Section 76 of the Indian Evidence Act, 1872. "[e]very public officer having the custody of a public document, which any person has a right to inspect [emphasis supplied], shall give that person on demand a copy of it on payment of the legal fees therefore..".

[117] Papanna (1989), Arumugam (1897), Rao (1972).

[118] Kumar and Datta (2016).

[119] Law Commission of India (2014).

[120] http://supremecourtofindia.nic.in/pdf/AnnualReports/AnnualReport2016-17.pdf.

data about the new insolvency and bankruptcy system. Yet administrators and judges of these tribunals could play a crucial role in gathering and disseminating such data. The tribunals have independent and direct access to most of the data that might also be gathered by IBBI, and they will generate much of that data itself. It is not apparent whether or how the NCLT is currently gathering data internally. Like IBBI, the NCLT has published orders issued by the tribunals on its website. Chatterjee, Shaikh and Zaveri, who compiled the first data-set of such orders, observe the orders are not text search-able or machine readable, making it extremely costly for researchers to track and study the life-cycle of any case using them.[121] And, in any event, such orders only include information that is relevant for addressing the legal issue at hand.

The tribunals have similar but perhaps less imposing logistical challenges as IBBI, at least for some types of data. There are 11 National Company Law Tribunal benches across the country and 38 Debt Recovery Tribunals. Each tribunal has authority to gather data about the cases before it. In order to aggregate data across the entire system, the data gathered or produced by the various tribunals must first be gathered at the national administrator for the tribunals. Like IBBI, the tribunals could either combine aggregate data produced separately or the central administrator could conduct analysis and aggregation from raw data provided by the various tribunals.

Comparative advantages

For some types of basic case-related data—e.g., number of applications submitted, accepted, and rejected—this process can, in theory, be more easily centralized and systemized at the tribunal level than, say, within a system of insolvency professionals. First, the number of individuals who must participate and input data consistently is smaller in this context because there are fewer tribunals than insolvency professionals. Second, staff at the tribunals should not, again in theory, create the same kind of agency problems as independent insolvency professionals do in relation to IBBI.

These practical advantages erode, however, for data about aspects of the system that happen outside of the tribunals or that inevitably require some participation by insolvency professionals. Tribunals do not need to rely on outside actors to keep track of procedural actions or official docket information, but they must rely on private parties and insolvency professionals to submit almost all substantive information about each case, including about characteristics of debtors, creditors, and claims. The tribunals may still have some institutional advantage in gathering data of this nature since this information will necessarily be submitted in individual cases and does not require a separate process of submission. This institutional advantage should disappear, however, if IBBI develops an information system that captures data when it is submitted to tribunals. Furthermore, because IBBI is charged with supervising and regulating the operation of the insolvency and bankruptcy system, it should have independent motivation to gather reliable aggregate information about nature of cases and the performance of insolvency professionals.

---

[121] Also, Regy and Roy (2017) criticised the current state of data collection related to Debt Recovery Tribunals,.

An individual tribunal or an individual insolvency professional agency could make case-level data available either systematically or by granting ad hoc access. Either would likely have data from enough cases to yield a sufficient sample for meaningful analysis. The decision of insolvency professional agencies to provide such data would presumably be subject to veto from IBBI. It is also possible that case-level data could be provided under a narrowly defined set of circumstances, perhaps to researchers who are granted permission upon application. In any event, any cost charged for access to case-level data would likely impact the scope of analysis and research that could be done by parties subject to the cost.

3.3 Ensuring Standardization and Availability

Regardless of how responsibility for collecting and disseminating data is allocated between IBBI and the NCLT, the success and usefulness of those efforts depend largely on the on the data being uniform—and thus comparable—and being accessible to researchers and the broader public. These factors in turn depend, first, on the mode of generating data and, second, on the mode of dissemination. This Section describes how standardized forms can generate useful data and how a public electronic database of those forms and other court documents can maximize the access to and availability of such data.

Forms

The underlying quality of data about the insolvency and bankruptcy system—whether it is disseminated in the aggregate or made available in raw, case-level form—depends on how it is initially generated by the various actors within the system, especially the parties involved in particular cases. Much of this data is generated by the forms that parties and insolvency professionals use throughout the life of a case, including applications, reports, and resolution plans. These forms provide procedural information about the case, but also financial information about debtors and creditors and other stakeholders, and the nature of their relationships. It is thus crucial for standardizing data that these forms be carefully designed to report all potentially relevant information in uniform manner and easily searchable.

In the US, the federal judiciary has approved a large number of official bankruptcy forms[122] that must be used by private parties in bankruptcy cases.[123] Thus, parties are required to use these standardized forms for, among other things: petitions for voluntary and involuntary cases; a list of the largest creditors in Chap. 11 cases; a summary of a debtor's assets and liabilities; schedules of a debtor's property, secured and unsecured creditors, executory contracts; a statement of the debtor's financial affairs; notice given to creditors; creditors' proofs of claims; and agreements for a debtor to reaffirm debt. The federal judiciary has also promulgated standard forms for court documents that may be required under local rules or used voluntarily in other jurisdictions.

---

[122] http://www.uscourts.gov/forms/bankruptcy-forms.

[123] U.S. Bankruptcy Rule 9009.

Similarly, IBBI and the Ministry of Corporate Affairs have promulgated various standard forms for use in cases under IBC.[124] These include forms for a creditor's demand of payment before initiating a case[125]; applications to initiate a case[126]; introduction of proposed interim resolution professionals[127]; public announcement of the commencement of an insolvency case[128]; and proofs of creditors' claims.[129] The Board has also promulgated a form for resolution professionals to certify compliance with IBC for each case, which must include a significant amount of data.[130]

Yet IBBI and the MCA have not yet promulgated forms for many important actions under IBC. For example, debtors that apply for an insolvency process must furnish a statement of affairs within fourteen days of their application[131] and involuntary debtors must also submit such a document early in a case. This document will presumably contain some of the most important and comprehensive information about debtors in insolvency cases. There is no standard form for such a document, however, nor are there any rules governing the content or format of such a document. It is possible that a standard form could emerge from practice within the insolvency and bankruptcy system, but if not, or in the meantime, there is not likely to be much consistency in how the data about debtors in the insolvency and bankruptcy process are being generated. Ideally, IBBI and the Ministry of Corporate Affairs will promulgate additional forms for use by participants within the insolvency and bankruptcy system and, as suggested below, will conduct a review of the use and the design of existing standard forms by participants and the reporting of data not covered by standard forms.

Access

Assuming that the system generates reliable data, policymakers must still decide the scope of access it allows to such data. The Board and the tribunals could decide, for example, to only disseminate aggregate data generated by the system. If policymakers decide to make case level data available to researchers or other members of the public, it could do so liberally or in a restricted fashion. It could, for example, grant limited access to such data to researchers upon application. The most liberal approach would be to make data publicly available on an electronic database similar to the PACER system in the United States. Any policy in this regard must balance concerns about privacy with the benefits of widely available data about India's new insolvency and bankruptcy system.

---

[124] E.g., IBBI (2016), Ministry of Corporate Affairs (2016).

[125] Form 3, Ministry of Corporate Affairs (2016).

[126] Forms 1, 5, and 6, Ministry of Corporate Affairs (2016).

[127] Form 2, Ministry of Corporate Affairs (2016).

[128] Form A, IBBI (2016), available at http://www.ibbi.gov.in/webadmin/pdf/legalframwork/2018/Jul/187054_2018-07-0520:48:31.pdf.

[129] Form B-F and Forms C, CA, IBBI (2016).

[130] Form H, IBBI (2016).

[131] http://www.mca.gov.in/Ministry/pdf/InsolvencyRules01122016.pdf.

4 Conclusion and A Proposal

The new Insolvency and Bankruptcy Board of India has a statutory responsibility to gather and disseminate information about the insolvency and bankruptcy system—specifically, to "publish such information, data, research studies and other information as may be specified by regulations [and to] collect and maintain records relating to insolvency and bankruptcy cases and disseminate information relating to such cases ... "[132] This Article does not aim to define the content of this formal legal responsibility. Rather, it proposes that IBBI adopt a maximalist approach to data, limited only by institutional capacity and basic privacy norms.

As the ever-growing field of empirical research on bankruptcy law in the U.S. illustrates, data about an insolvency system is essential for assessing how the system functions, how it is affecting its various stakeholders and participants, and what economic and social impact it is having. Data generated by the system can also be a uniquely valuable source of information about the broader economy and society; in particular, it can provide an early indication of sources of macro-economic vulnerability and of micro-level failures plaguing certain financial products.

Such information can be valuable for public officials even if it is not widely disseminated. But it is most valuable if made available to private researchers who can provide independent analysis and generate useful proposals for policy responses to trends in how the system is operating and the private data it yields. In any event, however, the usefulness of such data depends on it being reliable, consistent, and usable.

To that end, we propose that IBBI conduct a pilot or diagnostic study of the data currently being generated by the insolvency and bankruptcy system to determine its reliability, consistency, and usability for both internal assessment and external research. Ideally, such a study would identify the numerous sources of data within the system and assess the nature and quality of data those sources generate. In particular, such a study could identify whether additional official forms might be desirable or necessary and whether existing forms might be amended to improve data entry and collection. As part of a diagnostic study, IBBI could also assess how it is currently gathering, analyzing, and disseminating data to identify flaws that may already be plaguing that process as well as opportunities for improvement.

In sum, India's new insolvency and bankruptcy system is still in its infancy, and so IBBI has a unique and fleeting opportunity to design a reliable and comprehensive approach to generating, gathering, and disseminating data about the system. Doing so would certainly help steer the system in this early period of implementation and design refinement. It could also provide a compelling model of transparency and rigorous self-examination for other institutional actors in the Indian administrative state.

---

[132] Section 196, IBC.

References

Arumugam (1897) Queen-Empress vs Arumugam and Ors., Madras High Court, (1897) ILR KAR Mad 189. Technical Report (1897) ILR KAR Mad 189, Karnataka High Court, India. https://indiankanoon.org/doc/1171829/
Baird D, Rasmussen R (2003) Chapter 11 at twilight. Stanford Law Rev 673
Braucher J, Cohen D, Lawless R (2012) Race disparity in Bankruptcy chapter choice and the role of debtors' attorneys. Am Bankruptcy Inst Law Rev 611
Chatterjee S, Shaikh G, Zaveri B (2018) Watching India's insolvency reforms: a new dataset of insolvency cases. Natl Law Sch India Rev (Forthcoming). http://ifrogs.org/releases/Chatterjeeetal2017_nclt.html
Choi S, Gulati M (2004) A tournament of judges? Calif Law Rev 299
Coordes L (2015) The geography of Bankruptcy. Vanderbilt Law Rev 381
Department of Justice Executive Office for United States Trustees (2004) United States Trustee program annual report of significant accomplishments fiscal year 2004. Tech. rep., United States Department of Justice. https://www.justice.gov/sites/default/files/ust/legacy/2011/07/13/ar2004.pdf
Department of Justice Executive Office for United States Trustees (2015a) Debtor audits by the U.S. trustee program fiscal year 2015. Technical Report, United States Department of Justice Executive. https://www.justice.gov/ust/file/debtor_audits_fy_2015_public_report.pdf/download
Department of Justice Executive Office for United States Trustees (2015b) United States trustee program annual report of significant accomplishments fiscal year 2015. Technical Report, United States Department of Justice Executive. https://www.justice.gov/ust/file/ar_2015.pdf/download
Dreyfus DJ, Greenwood PW, Fiorello MR (1973) The impact of proposed changes in Bankruptcy administration. Rand Corporation, Santa Monica, Technical Report
Ellias J (2016) Do activist investors constrain managerial moral hazard in chapter 11?: evidence from junior activist investing. J Leg Anal 493
Fan W, White MJ (2003) Personal Bankruptcy and the level of entrepreneurial activity. J Law Econ 46
Feibelman A, Sane R (2019a) A maximalist approach to data from India's new insolvency and bankruptcy system. https://www.law.ox.ac.uk/business-law-blog/blog/2019/02/maximalist-approach-data-indias-new-insolvency-and-bankruptcy-system
Feibelman A, Sane R (2019b) A maximalist approach to data from India's new insolvency and bankruptcy system. Tulane Public Law Research Paper No. 19–4. https://papers.ssrn.com/sol3/papers.cfm?abstract_id=3311195
Finance Research Group (2017) Insolvency cases dataset. Technical Report, Finance Research Group, IGIDR. https://ifrogs.org/releases/nclt_data.html
Foohey P (2013) Bankrupting the faith. Missouri Law Rev 719
Foohey P (2014) When churches reorganize. Am Bankruptcy Inst Law Rev 277
Foohey P (2015) Secured credit in religious institutions' reorganizations. Univ Ill Law Rev 51
Foohey P (2017) Lender discrimination, black churches, and Bankruptcy. Houston Law Rev 1079
Foohey P, Lawless R, Porter K, Thorne D (2017) No Money Down Bankruptcy. South Calif Law Rev 1555
Foohey P, Lawless R, Porter K, Thorne D (2018) Life in the sweatbox. Notre Dame Law Rev
Frasier JC (1996) Caught in a cycle of neglect: the accuracy of Bankruptcy statistics. 101 Com L J 307
IBBI (2016) Insolvency and Bankruptcy Board of India (Insolvency Resolution Process For Corporate Persons) Regulations. http://www.ibbi.gov.in/webadmin/pdf/legalframwork/2018/Feb/06FEB2018IBBI(INSOLVENCYRESOLUTIONPROCESSFORCORPORATEPERSONS)REGULATIONS,2016(AMENDEDUPTO06FEB2018)_2018-02-1909:31:58.pdf
IBBI (2018) Insolvency and Bankruptcy news: CoC dharma. In: The quarterly newsletter of the insolvency and Bankruptcy Board of India. http://www.ibbi.gov.in/IBBI_News_letter_2018_06_11_18_12_27

Jacoby M, Janger E (2014) Ice cube bonds: allocating the price of process in Chapter 11. Yale Law J 862
Jacoby M, Warren E (2006) Beyond hospital misbehavior: an alternative account of medical-related financial distress. North West Univ Law Rev 535
Jacoby M, Sullivan T, Warren E (2001) Rethinking the debates over health care financing: evidence from the Bankruptcy courts. N Y Univ Law Rev 375
Jiang W, Li K, Wang W (2012) Hedge funds and Chapter 11. J Finance 513
Kumar PA, Datta P (2016) Instrumenting courts in India. Technical Report, The Leap Journal Blog. https://blog.theleapjournal.org/2016/03/instrumenting-courts-in-india.html
Law Commission of India (2014) Arrears and backlog: creating additional judicial (wo)manpower. Technical Report, Law Commission of India. http://lawcommissionofindia.nic.in/reports/Report_No.245.pdf
Lawless R (2005) Bankruptcy filing rates after a major hurricane. Nevada Law J 7
Lawless R, Ferris S (1997) Professional fees and other direct costs in Chapter 7 Bankruptcies. Wash Univ Law Rev 1207
Lawless R, Ferris S (2000) The expenses of financial distress: the direct costs of Chapter 11. Univ Pittsbg Law Rev 629
Lawless R, Warren E (2005) The Myth of the disappearing business Bankruptcy. California Law Rev 743
Lipson J (2010) Understanding Failure: examiners and the bankruptcy reorganization of large public companies. Am Bankruptcy Law J 423
Lipson J, Marrota C (2016) Examining success. Am Bankruptcy Law J
Littwin A (2016) Adapting to BAPCPA. Am Bankruptcy Law J 183
LoPucki L (1997) Enhancing the accessibility and effectiveness of bankruptcy information. In: Bankruptcy: the next twenty years, national Bankruptcy reform commission
LoPucki L (2006) Courting failure. University of Michigan Press
LoPucki L, Doherty J (2004) The determinants of professional fees in large Bankruptcy reorganization cases. J Empir Leg Stud 111
LoPucki L, Doherty J (2009) Routine illegality in Bankruptcy court fee practices. Am Bankruptcy Law J 423
LoPucki L, Eisenberg T (1999) Shopping for judges: an empirical analysis of venue choice in the Bankruptcy reorganization of large. Publicly Held Co, Cornell Law Rev 967
LoPucki L, Kalin S (2001) The failure of public company Bankruptcies in delaware and New York: empirical evidence of a "Race to the Bottom" . Vanderbilt Law Rev 231
Lubben S (2008) Corporate reorganization and professional fees. Am Bankruptcy Law J 77
Martin P (2008) Online access to court records: from documents to data. Part Patterns, Villanova Law Rev 855
Ministry of Corporate Affairs (2016) The insolvency and Bankruptcy (Application to Adjudicating Authority) Rules. https://www.ibbi.gov.in/uploads/law/AArulesupdated.pdf
Morrison E (2007) Bankruptcy decision making: an empirical study of continuation bias in small business Bankruptcies. J Law Econ 381
National Bankruptcy Review Commission (1997) Bankruptcy: the next twenty years. National Bankruptcy Review Commission
Papanna M (1989) M. Papanna versus Hon'ble Chief Justice, Karnataka High Court, ILR 1989 KAR 1328. Technical Report, Karnataka High Court, India. https://indiankanoon.org/doc/180435/
Pardo R (2009) An empirical examination of access to Chapter 7 relief by pro se debtors. Emory Bankruptcy Dev J 5
Pardo R (2014) The undue hardship thicket: on access to justice, procedural noncompliance, and pollutive litigation in Bankruptcy. Florida Law Rev 2101
Pardo R (2016) Taking Bankruptcy rights seriously. Washington Law Rev 1115
Pardo R, Lacey M (2005) Undue hardship in the Bankruptcy courts: an empirical assessment of the discharge of educational debt. University Cincinnati Law Rev 405
Porter K (2005) Going broke the hard way: the economics of rural failure. Wisconsin Law Rev 969

Porter K (2006) The potential and peril of BAPCPA for empirical research. Missouri Law Rev 963
Porter K, Thorne D (2006) The failure of Bankruptcy's fresh start. Cornell Law Rev 67
Pottow J, Lawless R, Littwin A, Porter K, Thorne D, Warren E (2008) Did Bankruptcy reform fail? An Empir Study Consum Debt, Am Bankruptcy Law Rev 349
Rao MNK (1972) MN Krishna Rao versus Board of Trustees, Madras High Court, 1972(1) Mys.L.J.101, CITB. Technical Report 1972(1) Mys.L.J.101, CITB, Madras High Court, India
Rasmussen R (2007) Empirically Bankrupt. Columbia Bus Law Rev 179
Regy PV, Roy S (2017) Understanding judicial delays in debt tribunals. Technical Report 195, National Institute of Public Finance and Policy. http://macrofinance.nipfp.org.in/releases/RoyRegy2017_judicial-delay-debt-tribunals.html
Shuchman P (1977) Theory and reality in Bankruptcy: the spherical chicken. Law Contemp Probl 41(4):66–106
Stanley DT, Girth ML (1971) Bankruptcy: problem, process. Reform, Brookings Institution
Sullivan T, Warren E, Westbrook J (1987) The use of empirical data in formulating Bankruptcy policy. Law Contemp Probl 195
Sullivan T, Warren E, Westbrook J (1989) As we forgive our debtors: Bankruptcy and consumer credit in America. Beard Books
Sullivan T, Warren E, Westbrook J (2001) Fragile middle class: Americans in Debt. Yale University Press
Warren E (2002) Bankrupt children. Minnesota Law Rev 1003
Warren E, Lawless R (2010) Bankruptcy and insolvency. The Oxford Handbook of Empirical Legal Research
Warren E, Tyagi A (2004) The two-income trap: why middle-class parents are going broke. Basic Books
Warren E, Westbrook J (1999) Financial characteristics of businesses in Bankruptcy. Am Bankruptcy Law Rev 499

Prepacks Under the IBC: A Tussle Between Speed and Fair Process

Aparna Ravi

1 Introduction

The Report of the Bankruptcy Law Reform Committee (BLRC) is deliberately silent on the contents of a resolution plan and on the nature of the resolution to be arrived at by the financial creditors. The BLRC Report sets out the rationale behind being non-prescriptive on the resolution plan as follows: *"Law is not to provide guidance or limit the range of solutions that the creditors could come up with to turnaround a business."*[1] In other words, the BLRC considered the type of resolution as an issue to be determined solely by market participants and not constrained by the law. The BLRC Report further points out that the types of resolutions developed would evolve with time and depend on the circumstances of a particular case and, that the new legislation should, therefore, be open to all forms of keeping an entity as a going concern within the rest of the constraints of the law.

Following on from the BLRC Report, the Insolvency and Bankruptcy Code, 2016 (IBC or Code), in its original enactment, was broadly non-prescriptive on the nature of a resolution. Apart from specifying certain minimum requirements for a resolution plan, such as to account for the costs of the resolution process, to ensure that operational creditors receive at least liquidation value and that a resolution plan may not contravene any other law at the time in force,[2] the IBC did not mandate resolution plans to take on a particular structure or require that a specific process needed to be followed in arriving at one.

[1]Bankruptcy Law Reforms Committee (2015).
[2]In addition to these requirements, the IBC also gave powers to the Insolvency and Bankruptcy Board of India (IBBI) to prescribe other conditions for resolution plans.

The opinions expressed in this chapter are the author's own and not that of her employer.

A. Ravi (✉)
Samvad Partners, Bengaluru, India
e-mail: aparna@samvadpartners.com
© The Author(s), under exclusive license to Springer Nature Singapore Pte Ltd. 2022

S. Thomas (ed.), *Insolvency and Bankruptcy Reforms in India*,
India Studies in Business and Economics,
https://doi.org/10.1007/978-981-16-0854-4_6

However, since the IBC came into effect in December 2016, there have been two amendments to the Code as well as numerous amendments to the regulations issued under the IBC. While some of the amendments are substantive, a number of them relate to the corporate insolvency resolution process and the steps to be followed for a resolution applicant to submit a resolution plan. In light of these changes, one question that arises is whether the IBC continues to be agnostic to the type of resolution plan achieved or whether there are limits that have been imposed by laws or regulations or by market practice itself on the forms that a resolution plan can take. In this regard, one concern that has been raised by a number of stakeholders is whether the IBC permits a practice that has become increasingly commonplace in other jurisdictions–prepackaged bankruptcies, popularly known as "prepacks".

In this chapter, I consider whether prepacks are permitted under the IBC and its underlying rules and regulations, and the specific provisions and regulations that might significantly hamper or constrain the ability of financial creditors and the corporate debtor to execute a prepack under the IBC. I then look into whether it is necessary or desirable to amend any of these constraining clauses and regulations in order to make the IBC regime more conducive for prepacks, including any concerns or possible negative consequences of doing so. To inform this analysis, I consider how prepacks have evolved and been used successfully in two jurisdictions—the United States and the United Kingdom. The experience in these jurisdictions suggests that the short time period spent in the formal insolvency process makes prepacks an attractive option, in terms of minimizing costs and disruption to the debtor's business. At the same time, there is a tension between allowing for speedy resolution and ensuring a fair and transparent process for all creditors that policymakers must grapple with as they consider if changes are warranted to the IBC and its underlying regulations to facilitate prepacks.

2 What Are Prepacks?

There are broadly two different mechanisms through which a resolution plan can be arrived at for a distressed corporate debtor. One mechanism is through a consensual, out-of-court restructuring where the creditors and debtor come together to agree to a plan. This process is not specifically governed by a statute, though there are non-statutory regulatory frameworks that could govern these restructurings (for example, the framework mandated by the Reserve Bank of India for banks and financial institutions to deal with stressed assets), and offers flexibility to the stakeholders in arriving at a plan best suited to the circumstances. As there is no specific statutory or court-ordered process to be followed, an out-of-court restructuring can be achieved in a relatively short time period if the creditors and debtor are able to come to an agreement. An out-of-court restructuring also does not generally disrupt the debtor's business which can carry on as usual during the pendency of the restructuring discussions.

On the other hand, the disadvantage of an out-of-court restructuring is that it is only binding on the parties who consent to it as it is not backed by the coercive power of a statute. As such, it would not bind dissenting parties (such as financial creditors who do not agree to the plan) as well as third parties who are not part of the discussions and, therefore, do not consent to it, such as the typical trade creditors or litigating claimants. All of these non-consenting parties would be able to bring their claims even after the resolution plan has been executed with the consenting creditors. Further, an out-of-court restructuring would not give the debtor certain regulatory benefits that are available when going through the formal insolvency process. For example, companies going through the corporate insolvency resolution process under the IBC are exempt from certain compliances under securities law regulations.

The other mechanism is for the debtor or creditors to commence an in-court (or tribunal driven) process based on a collective insolvency law to arrive at a resolution. This process could take longer and may not offer the flexibility that is possible in an out-of-court restructuring as any plan arrived at would have to conform to the requirements of the statute. In the case of the IBC, for example, the amendment that introduced Sect. 29A effectively prevents the financial creditors from arriving at a resolution plan under the IBC that involves the incumbent promoters or their connected persons.[3] The formal insolvency process is also more likely to be disruptive to the debtor's business, particularly if the insolvency law provides for a creditor-in-control regime where the debtor loses possession of the business during the insolvency resolution process.

A court-driven statutory process has the advantage of providing for a holistic treatment of all claims and liabilities of the corporate debtor as the coercive power of the law allows for a cram down on dissenting creditors. A resolution plan approved through a statutory process such as the IBC would, thus, be binding on all stakeholders, including those who do not consent to it and those who are not required to consent to it (such as shareholders), thereby giving the debtor and creditors a sense of closure that would be absent in an out-of-court restructuring.

The concept of prepacks allows one to have the best of both worlds if all parties are able to reach a consensus and the debtor is willing to negotiate with creditors without the coercive force of the law. Pursuant to a prepackaged bankruptcy, the debtor and financial creditors can agree to a resolution plan prior to making an application for insolvency. The resolution plan that has been pre-agreed among creditors will then need to be formally approved through the process provided for under the insolvency law. Prepacks significantly reduce the time that a corporate debtor needs to spend in the formal insolvency process, while ensuring that the plan that is approved has the backing of the statutory process and the consequences that flow with it.

[3] Section 29A of the IBC was introduced by means of the IBC (Amendment) Ordinance, 2017 in response to the troublesome optics of promoters of a distressed corporate debtor being allowed to regain control of the business, after the creditors have had to take a haircut on the debts owed to them. Section 29A prevents various categories of persons, including their related parties and connected persons, from being resolution applicants under the IBC.

3 Are Prepacks Permitted Under the IBC?

Prepacks represent a market driven solution that has developed in the context of the interplay between in-court and out-of-court restructurings. Even in jurisdictions where they have become commonplace, the bankruptcy law itself does not explicitly allow for a prepack. Therefore, in order for prepacks to become a tool under the IBC, the law itself does not have to explicitly permit it. Rather, one would have to analyse whether there are any provisions of the IBC and the underlying regulations that prevent or would significantly hinder market participants from attempting a prepack.

The steps and requirements that need to be followed upon an admission of an application to commence the corporate insolvency resolution process (CIRP) are set out in the IBC and the related regulations, primarily the Insolvency and Bankruptcy Board of India (Insolvency Resolution Process for Corporate Persons) Regulations 2016 (*CIRP Regulations*). Under the IBC and CIRP Regulations, as originally construed, the following broad steps need to take place in order for a resolution plan to be approved:

- An interim resolution professional (IRP) is to be appointed.
- Following the appointment of an IRP, the RP is required to make a public announcement, announcing the commencement of the CIRP and inviting creditors to make claims within a specified time period (IBC, Sect. 13). Under Regulation 6(c) of the CIRP Regulations, this time period should be 14 days from the date of appointment of the IRP.
- The IRP or the resolution professional (RP) is to collate the claims submitted by creditors and constitute a committee of creditors (CoC) consisting of all financial creditors of the debtor.
- Regulation 27 of the CIRP Regulations requires the IRP or RP to appoint two valuers to determine the fair value and liquidation value of corporate debtor's assets within seven days of his appointment.
- The CoC is required to have a meeting within seven days of its constitution at which meeting it will, among other things, decide whether to appoint the IRP as the RP or appoint another RP to carry out the CIRP (IBC, Sect. 22).
- The RP is required to prepare an information memorandum for creditors to assist them in considering a resolution plan (IBC, Sect. 29).
- One of the duties of a RP is to invite resolution plans from potential resolution applicants (IBC, Sect. 25).
- Prospective resolution applicants are required to submit resolution plans to the RP, prepared on the basis of the information memorandum (IBC, Sect. 30).
- The RP must examine the resolution plan to ensure it meets certain specifications required under the IBC and put it up to the CoC for approval (IBC, Sect. 30(3)). These specifications include that the proposed resolution plan must provide for payment of insolvency resolution process costs in priority over other debts of the corporate debtors, provide for payment of at least liquidation value to operational creditors and must not contravene the provisions of any other law currently in force (IBC, Sect. 30(2)).

- CoC approves or rejects the resolution plan.
- Resolution plan approved by the CoC is submitted to the National Company Law Tribunal (NCLT) for approval (IBC, Sect. 31).

How does this process flow under the IBC fit in with a prepack? An application admitted under the IBC would have to go through the above steps. However, to the extent that a resolution plan that meets the requirements of the IBC has already been agreed by the financial creditors and preparation for some of the above steps have already been carried out (for example, preparation of an information memorandum or identification of most of the claims) prior to the filing, these steps can mostly be carried out through a condensed timeline.

An exception to this is Regulation 6(c) of the CIRP Regulations which mandates a period of 14 days for creditors to submit claims. Thus, even if a prepackaged resolution plan has been agreed to by the financial creditors, the RP would need to give potential claimants 14 days to submit claims following admission before putting up the resolution plan to a vote by the CoC. Another requirement that could similarly affect timelines is the requirement under Regulation 27 to appoint an independent valuer to arrive at the liquidation value of the corporate debtor. If this value is different from the liquidation value determined pursuant to the prepackaged resolution plan, the terms of the pre-agreed plan may have to change.

However, the requirements on the claim period and appointment of a valuer, while impacting the timeline within which a prepack may be approved following admission, do not prevent a prepack from occurring or serve as a significant disincentive to parties attempting a prepack. While it would not be possible for a resolution plan to be approved within a few days of admission in light of the 14-day claim period, it would still be possible for a prepack to be approved in a much shorter time frame (of about 30–40 days) than a typical CIRP process. As such, it would have been possible to fit in the concept of a prepack within the contours of the IBC as originally envisaged.

Over time, there have been two sets of amendments to the IBC and numerous amendments to the CIRP Regulations, which could constrain the ability of the parties to opt for a prepack or reduce the incentives for doing so. In particular, the impact of the following provisions of the CIRP Regulations on the ability to consummate a prepack is worth examining further:

- Regulation 36A requires the RP to invite expressions of interest from prospective resolution applicants, setting out the eligibility criteria for submission of bids.
- Regulation 36A(10) requires the RP to publish a provisional list of eligible resolution applicants from those who submitted expressions of interest.
- Regulation 36A(11) permits objections to be made to the provisional list of eligible applicants within five days of the RP publishing the provisional list.
- Regulation 36A(12) requires the RP to provide a final list of eligible resolution applicants within 10 days of the last date for receipt of objections.
- Regulation 36B then requires the RP to invite resolution plans from the shortlisted prospective resolution applicants by sending them the information memorandum

together with an evaluation matrix setting out the criteria on which their resolution plans will be assessed.
- Under Regulation 36B(3), resolution applicants must be given at least 30 days to submit a resolution plan from the date of the invitation requesting proposals for resolution plans.
- Regulation 40A provides a model timeline of the various steps involved in completion of a CIRP.

Regulations 36A and 36B are essentially a requirement for the RP to carry out an auction for the corporate debtor's assets and were introduced through a series of amendments to the CIRP Regulations made between February 2018 and July 2018.[4] The purpose of these amendments was to bring about greater transparency and uniformity into the resolution process by being more prescriptive on the process that a RP was to follow in inviting prospective resolution applicants to submit resolution plans. These amendments followed on the heels of concerns in some high-profile insolvency cases where resolution plans were accepted even when submitted after the ostensible bid deadline set out by the RP. A notable example of this was when the NCLT, Principal Bench allowed *Liberty House* to submit a bid for *Bhushan Power and Steel Limited* well past the deadline for submitting resolution plans established by the RP.[5]

The amendments to the CIRP Regulations that introduced Regulations 36A and 36B have generated some controversy. While it is outside the scope of this Chapter to consider this question more broadly, the requirements of Regulations 36A and 36B do significantly hamper the ability for a prepack to be executed under the IBC. These requirements would mean that even if the creditors have pre-agreed a resolution plan prior to filing an insolvency application, the RP would nevertheless have to conduct an auction and invite resolution plans from other prospective applicants. Such a structure may give little incentive for a resolution applicant to propose and agree to a plan pre-filing, as there is always a risk that it could be outbid in the auction process, thereby reducing the first mover advantage. The steps involved in conducting an auction also take several weeks, thereby significantly undoing the advantage of time involved in a prepack.

It is worth noting that in a recent decision of the NCLT, Principal Bench on 5 September 2018, the tribunal held Regulation 36A, in so far as it requires the RP to invite expressions of interest, to be ultra vires of the IBC, as it contradicted the goal of the IBC in achieving a speedy resolution. The tribunal further directed the IBBI to "frame Regulation according to its competence and the source of power granted to it by the Code."[6] The IBBI has challenged this order and the Delhi High Court has

---

[4] The first of these amendments which introduced requirements for inviting resolution plans through an auction were introduced through the CIRP (Amendment) Regulations, 2018, dated 6 February 2018. These requirements were further amended by the CIRP (Third Amendment) Regulations 2018 dated 3 July 2018, which introduced a two-tiered process for accepting prospective resolution plans—a first step involving invitations for expressions of interest, and a second step involving inviting resolution plans from shortlisted candidates who submitted expressions of interest.

[5] PNB versus Bhushan Power and Steel Ltd., NCLT, Principal Bench (2018).

[6] SBI versus Su Kam, NCLT, Principal Bench (2018).

temporarily stayed the decision of the NCLT, Principal Bench to the extent it declares Regulation 36A invalid, pending the outcome of the IBBI's petition in IBBI versus SBI and Ors., Delhi HC (2018)[7] While the Delhi High Court's decision is awaited, if the requirement to first invite expressions of interest before inviting resolution plans is done away with, the timelines for the corporate insolvency resolution process could be shortened significantly. However, the CIRP Regulations pose a hindrance to prepacks as they would still require the RP to conduct an auction before accepting a resolution plan.

4 The Experience of Prepacks in Other Jurisdictions

Even in jurisdictions where they have become common, there are many situations in which prepacks may not be a realistic solution. Prepacks are not a statutorily mandated process and, as such, require a level of consensus among financial creditors as well as a high degree of cooperation with the corporate debtor that may not be achievable in all cases. While prepacks do save time post-filing, they require significant amounts of time spent in preparatory work in the lead up to the filing. Where voluntary consensus and cooperation among the stakeholders are not forthcoming, the coercive power of the insolvency law is required to give creditors the opportunity to arrive at a resolution. Further, as the creditors and debtor will not have the benefit of a moratorium during negotiations of a prepackaged resolution plan (in contrast to an IBC filing), there is always the possibility that creditors may try to enforce other remedies, including their security interest during this period. This could be particularly risky if negotiations regarding a prepack leak to operational creditors or creditors who have not been part of the process, thereby making confidentiality prior to filing an essential pre-condition for a successful prepack. Prepacks may also not be a feasible solution where the creditors are numerous and may be hard to identify outside of the formal insolvency process.

On the other hand, prepacks may be a viable option where stakeholders generally believe that the assets have value or the business is viable, but the debtor has taken on too much debt. In such a situation, a prepack could be a valuable tool in allowing for quick restructuring while preserving the value of the assets and minimizing disruption to the business. Prepacks are also said to minimize other side effects of a long drawn out insolvency process such as the erosion of customer confidence and damage to relationships with key employees, especially in service-based companies.

The question to ask, therefore, is whether prepacks should be permitted in circumstances where all relevant stakeholders—resolution applicant, financial creditors and the corporate debtor—are desirous of using this approach, or whether there are good reasons to prevent prepacks even in such a situation. To assess this in the context of the IBC, it is worth exploring the experience of prepacks in other jurisdictions.

---

[7] The case has been posted for January 16, 2019.

United States: The prepack model of selling assets in bankruptcy has been used in the United States since the early
1980s. A prepack in the United States involves solicitations of votes from creditors in advance of filing for bankruptcy, such that the plan has been accepted by the required number of creditors prior to the bankruptcy filing. Section 1126(B) of the United States Bankruptcy Code (U.S. Bankruptcy Code) allows for votes to be solicited prior to filing as long as all the rules of solicitation regarding adequate disclosure have been complied with, or if there are no such rules, that "adequate information"[8] has been provided to creditors in connection with the pre-petition solicitation of votes. The primary action that then needs to take place upon filing then relates to the confirmation of the Chap. 11 plan of reorganization by the U.S. Bankruptcy Court. Any creditor of the debtor has the right to object to the prepack sale by filing an objection with the Bankruptcy Court, which is required to hear such objections before rendering its decision confirming or rejecting the plan of reorganization.
The experience with prepacks in the United States suggests that they are indeed must faster and less expensive than a typical Chap. 11 filing. One of the most well-known (and largest) examples of a prepack was the General Motors insolvency, where a prepackaged deal allowed General Motors to exit insolvency in 40 days. While 35–40 days post-filing is the typical time period of most prepacks, there have been prepacks where the Bankruptcy court judge has confirmed the debtor's plan of reorganization in as few as seven days after a filing.[9]An analysis of the 12 largest prepacks in the SDNY from 2012 to 2014 suggest that prepacks did not generally take longer than 80 days to complete and could be completed as quickly as 30 days from the date of the filing.[10] To this end, the local rules for the SDNY also facilitate such quick turnarounds by allowing certain steps of the Chap. 11 process to be combined. The procedural rules of the SDNY require hearings for the disclosure statement and confirmation hearings to be combined "whenever practicable," which eliminates the time and cost of having two hearings. The local rules for the SDNY also permit the waiver of the requirements to (1) file schedules and statements of financial affairs and (2) hold a meeting of creditors pursuant to Sect. 341 of the Bankruptcy Code.[11] These types of tweaks in procedures appear to be a recognition of the advantages of quick turnarounds

[8] As defined in Sect. 1125(a)(1) of the U.S. Bankruptcy Code.

[9] The plan of reorganization in the Chap. 11 filing of Roust Corporation and its affiliates in January 2017 was orally confirmed by the U.S. Bankruptcy Court for the Southern District of New York (SDNY) within 7 days of filing. (Myles McDonald, "In re Roust: Seven Steps to confirming a Plan in Seven Days" available at https://www.csbankruptcyblog.com/2017/02/articles/bankruptcy/re-roust-seven-steps-confirming-plan-seven-days/ (last accessed 29/09/2018)).

[10] Stephen D. Zide, "United States Prepackaged Bankruptcy Offers Investors a Quick Return to Liquidity" 2 December 2015, available at http://www.mondaq.com/unitedstates/x/448568/Insolvency+Bankruptcy/Prepackaged+Bankruptcy+Offers+Investors+A+Quick+\protect\penalty-\@MReturn+To+Liquidity (last accessed 28/09/2018).

[11] Stephen D. Zide, "United States Prepackaged Bankruptcy Offers nvestors a Quick Return to Liquidity" 2 December 2015, available at http://www.mondaq.com/unitedstates/x/448568/

and that some procedures required to be followed in a typical Chap. 11 process can be combined or condensed in furtherance of this goal.

At the same time, the widespread use of prepacks in the United States has not been without concerns. These concerns include whether the creditors have received sufficient disclosure and sufficient time to consider the proposal before being asked to vote on the plan. Another requirement is that in soliciting votes, the debtor must have sent solicitation materials to substantially all creditors and equity security holders of the same class.[12] However, as the plan has to ultimately be confirmed by the U.S. Bankruptcy Court and these requirements regarding disclosure and solicitation are codified in the law, prepacks in the U.S. generally do offer creditors the protections they would otherwise have in a typical Chap. 11 reorganization. The primary concern is whether these protections are significantly diluted owing to the speed at which a prepack progresses.

United Kingdom: In the United Kingdom, amendments to the UK Insolvency Act, 1986 that occurred with the enactment of the Enterprise Act, 2002 (Enterprise Act) significantly improved the landscape for prepacks. The Enterprise Act provided for a qualified floating charge holder to appoint an administrator for the debtor company out of court, whose duty was to perform functions to further the interests of the debtor company's creditors as a whole. Further, it allowed the directors of a company to appoint such an administrator out of court as well. The appointment of such out-of-court administrators made the legal environment more conducive for prepacks as it provided a mechanism recognized in the law for the out-of-court administrator to assist creditors to arrive at a restructuring plan out of court.

The significant advantages of a prepack in value creation have been recognized in the UK, with a number of businesses going for this option, particularly after the enactment of the Enterprise Act. Speed, lower costs and the advantage of running the restructuring process outside the public eye are seen by stakeholders as some of the significant benefits of prepacks to debtor companies. Service focused businesses and businesses with a lot of brand value or intellectual capital are in particular likely to benefit the "silent and fast" sale of distressed assets that a prepack allows.[13]

While there is no statute that governs prepacks in the UK, the Statement of Insolvency Practice[14] ("*SIP 16*") provides guidance to insolvency practitioners on the steps they need to take in order to decide that a prepackaged sale is the appropriate course of action in a given situation. SIP 16 provides detailed guidance to insolvency practitioners on scrutinizing prepackaged plans carefully stating:

"The administrator should provide creditors with sufficient information ("the SIP 16 statement") such that a reasonable and informed third party would conclude

---

Insolvency+Bankruptcy/Prepackaged+Bankruptcy+Offers+Investors+A+Quick+Return+To+Liquidity (last accessed 28/09/2018).

[12] Bankruptcy Rule 2018(b) under the U.S. BankruptcyCode.

[13] Kastrinou and Vullings (2018).

[14] The Statements of Insolvency Practice are a collection of guidelines that insolvency practitioners in the United Kingdom are required to maintain and follow.

that the pre-packaged sale was appropriate and that the administrator has acted with due regard for the creditors' interests. In a connected party transaction the level of detail may need to be greater."

SIP 16 also identifies potential conflicts between the roles of the insolvency practitioner as an advisor to the debtor during the negotiation of a prepackaged sale and as an administrator following his appointment upon the company entering administration and provides guidance to insolvency practitioners in this regard.

Though prepacks are popular in the UK, they have also come under fierce criticism, primarily over concerns of lack of transparency and fairness. In June 2014, an independent review report commissioned by the UK Government raised the following concerns with prepacks[15]:

- the lack of transparency disenfranchises creditors, especially unsecured creditors particularly where the purchase is being made by a connected party;
- insufficient marketing is done to maximize the return to creditors. To this end, the report recommend improvement in the quality of marketing that is both likely to improve recovery for creditors and also increase creditor confidence in the process.
- explanation of the valuation methodology for pre-pack sales needs to be improved (the report highlights the fact that the valuation attached to a business is often exactly the same final purchase price and is usually based on desktop valuations); and
- there is a lack of consideration of the viability of the new company and there is no legal requirement for insolvency practitioner to examine this as part of the pre-pack sale process. At the same time, the Graham Review Report into Prepack Administration recognized the positives of prepacks, including the flexibility they provide, and dismissed any proposal for a ban on prepacks or any need for legislative intervention. Following on some of the report's recommendations, however, SIP 16 was revised to provide enhanced disclosure requirements to creditors in connection with a prepackaged insolvency.

5 Should Prepacks Be Permitted Under the IBC?

The experience of prepacks in the United States and the United Kingdom has been a mixed bag. The principal advantages are speed and low costs both of which are crucial to the goal of a collective insolvency law to achieve a time-bound resolution to maximize the value of the debtor's assets. Another significant advantage is that a prepack could reduce the disruptive effects of the insolvency process to the debtor's business by minimizing the time spent in the statutory insolvency process. On the other hand, prepacks do also raise questions of transparency and procedural fairness, particularly on the rights of smaller creditors and unsecured creditors. They also raise the question of whether all efforts have been taken to maximize the value of the

[15] The Insolvency Services (2014).

debtor's business. In jurisdictions with a RP or administrator, prepacks also bring up questions around conflicts of interest if the same administrator is to be involved both pre- and post- filing of the insolvency petition.

While prepacks did develop out of market practice, in the United States and the United Kingdom, there have been legislative interventions as well as guidance from professional bodies to both facilitate prepacks as well as to address concerns with regard to fair process and the goal of maximizing recovery for creditors. For example, it was the enactment of the Enterprise Act in the UK that led to a surge in prepacks, while changes to the procedural rules of the SDNY facilitated prepacks by allowing for certain procedures required in Chap. 11 proceedings to be combined. On the other end, there is SIP 16 and provisions of the U.S. Bankruptcy Code on solicitation of pre-petition votes that seek to ensure that prepacks follow a transparent and fair process for all creditors. It is against this backdrop that we should examine whether the IBC regime should be more conducive towards prepacks than the current set of regulations provide.

In general, as the experience in other jurisdictions show, there appear to be some definite advantages to prepacks in terms of time and cost savings that could benefit a number of stakeholders under the IBC. The thinking and rationale behind prepacks are also in line with the objectives of the IBC of achieving a time-bound resolution process. Further, allowing for prepacks makes debtor and creditors come to the negotiation table earlier in the process to think about resolution plans, which again is consistent with the objectives of the IBC in encouraging early detection and resolution of stress. However, as discussed in Sect. 3, the auction requirements under Regulations 36A and 36B significantly constrain the ability to achieve prepacks under the IBC. The questions to consider, therefore, are, first, whether the benefits of facilitating a prepack are such as to justify an exception to the auction requirements under Regulations 36A and 36B of the CIRP Regulations, and second, if prepacks are to be permitted, whether any changes to the IBC or regulations are required to regulate prepacks.

The tension between speedy resolution and ensuring a fair and transparent process has been reflected in several cases and discussions on the implementation of the IBC to date. Some examples of this tension relate to questions such as whether the time periods under the IBC are sacrosanct and to be followed at any cost[16] and whether there could be any justification for accepting bids after the deadline has passed.[17] The purposes behind Regulations 36A and 36B appear to be to ensure a fair and transparent process for inviting and approving resolution plans and also to

---

[16] See, for example, the National Company Law Appellate Tribunal's decision in Quantum Ltd. versus Indus Finance Corp. Ltd., NCLAT (2018) where the tribunal excluded the time period during which a litigation was pending from the calculation of the 270-day period for the corporate insolvency resolution process. Even more recently, the Supreme Court (SC), in determining questions that arose on eligibility under Sect. 29A, looked at the issue of the importance of adhering to timelines in advancing the goals of the IBC. Arcelor Mittal India versus SK Gupta and Ors, SC (2018).

[17] Another example is the high-profile bidding war between Dalmia Bharat and Ultratech Cements with respect to the insolvency resolution process for Binani Cements.

ensure that resolution plans are sought through a well publicized process. Are the advantages of a prepack sufficient for the regulator to carve out an exception from these requirements for prepacks? In considering this question, one would have to look into whether Regulation 36A and 36B are essential to maintaining the integrity of the resolution process.

In my view, Regulations 36A and 36B set out the intricate procedural details of the resolution process which could be waived in certain cases in the interests of time and cost savings that a prepack might bring. However, if such an exception were to be made for prepacks, it would be important to make clear that prepacks would still be subject to the other requirements of the IBC. This includes requirements regarding provisions such as the time period for making claims (to ensure that all creditors are given sufficient notice of the CIRP process) and ensuring that any resolution plan arrived at through a prepack meets the general requirements for a plan set out in the IBC and the CIRP Regulations.

Second, if exceptions were to be made to Regulations 36A and 36B for prepacks, one must also consider if additional protections need to be in place to govern prepacks. One concern, which relates to earlier discussions on transparency, is whether creditors are provided with sufficient information in order to approve a prepackaged resolution plan. One way of addressing this concern is to require that the disclosure requirements applicable to potential resolution applicants under the IBC and CIRP Regulations, as well as the requirement for creditors to be provided with an information memorandum, apply to prepackaged resolution plans as well. In other words, creditors should have been provided with the same level of information in order to approve a prepack as they would have been provided in a typical CIRP process.

Another concern that might arise relates to the potential conflict of interest between the duties of a RP hired by creditors prior to admission and the duties of a RP appointed under the IBC. In the interests of ensuring that the prepackaged resolution plan is fair to all creditors, including smaller creditors and unsecured creditors, it might be worth considering if a different RP should be appointed upon admission. The role of this RP could be, among other things, to review the prepackaged resolution plan to assess if it is indeed in the best interests of all stakeholders. This type of independent review by a professional who has not been involved in the prepack negotiations could also increase confidence among creditors that there has been sufficient marketing during the prepack negotiations to maximize the possibility that the prepack plan brings in the best value for the debtor's business.

This type of independent review may also be important in order to make financial creditors, who in the Indian context comprise primarily of public sector banks, comfortable with the risks associated with prepacks and the lack of transparency. Officers of banks (including private sector banks) are considered to be "public servants" for purposes of the Prevention of Corruption Act, 1988.[18] Further, in 2017, the Reserve Bank of India approved the request of the Central Vigilance Commission to be permitted to investigate corruption in private sector banks. As a consequence, large banks and financial institutions are likely to be particularly risk averse and wary

[18] CBIBSFC and Ors. versus Ramesh Gelli and Ors., SC (2016).

of the opaque nature of a prepack process and the related allegations of corruption that this could bring. A report from an independent RP or restructuring expert that the prepack does indeed maximize value and benefit all stakeholders might be particularly helpful in giving bankers the comfort they would need to support a prepack. Given the gravity of these concerns, it might also be necessary for the Code or the CIRP Regulations to explicitly permit prepacks (even though this is not necessary from a statutory point of view as discussed above) in order for stakeholders, particularly banks, to explore using them when feasible.

Another thorny issue is whether a prepack must comply with Sect. 29A. In my view, exempting prepacks from complying with Sect. 29A is unlikely to be politically palatable. Such a move would also open prepacks to the charge that they provide an opportunity for collusion between incumbent promoters and financial creditors in a non-transparent process and to the detriment of other stakeholders. However, it should be borne in mind that requiring prepacks to comply with Sect. 29A could, in practice, make prepacks difficult to achieve. Before an insolvency filing is made public, how would financial creditors find potential resolution applicants outside of the incumbent promoter group? If financial creditors are to informally approach potential resolution applicants to achieve a prepack, there could be significant confidentiality concerns that could ruin the likelihood that the prepack is successful.

6 Conclusion

Prepacks, though popular in many other jurisdictions, are yet to be used under the IBC. As discussed above, there may be a number of practical considerations as to why creditors might not be in favour of a prepack at this stage of the IBC's implementation, including issues that are unique to the Indian regulatory environment, such as Sect. 29A and bankers' concerns over allegations of corruption. However, Regulations 36A and 36B of the CIRP Regulations also present an obvious regulatory hurdle to achieving a prepack by requiring the RP to conduct an auction for resolution plans. In this context, it is definitely worth considering whether, in light of the advantages of speed, cost savings and minimal disruption to the debtor's business, exceptions should be made to the auction requirement in order to make the IBC more conducive for prepacks.

At the same time, if the IBC were to permit prepacks, the concerns prepacks raise in terms of fairness, transparency and conflicts of interest would need to be addressed as well. Most importantly, in order for prepacks to be a realistic possibility under the IBC, policymakers would also need to think about how to make banks, particularly public sector banks, comfortable with the perceived loss of transparency that a prepack process might necessarily entail. While there are no definitive answers, this chapter seeks to provide a starting point to analyze if and how the time and cost savings of a prepack could be incorporated into the IBC.

Author's note: Subsequent amendments related to pre-packs in the IBC

Since the time that law was operationalised, there were significant developments on the use of prepacks under the IBC. Public debates and discussion on prepacks gained new momentum, particularly in the light of the economic stress induced by the pandemic of 2020, which led to many stakeholders to consider the possibility of a faster, more cost effective and a debtor-friendly resolution processes within and outside the IBC.[19] In October 2020, a Sub-Committee of the Insolvency Law Committee published a report (Sub-Committee Report) on what a prepack framework under the IBC might look like and also considered the broader question of whether the Indian insolvency ecosystem was "ready" to experiment with prepacks (IBBI 2020). Soon after this, on 4 April 2021, the Government enacted the Insolvency and Bankruptcy Code (Amendment) Ordinance, 2021 (subsequently the IBC (Amendment) Act, 2021) that enables prepacks for one category of corporate debtors under the IBC and those are the micro, small and medium enterprises (MSMEs).

The prepack framework in the amendment to the IBC includes a detailed set of rules governing the initiation and implementation of prepacks by MSMEs, making the prepack process significantly different from a typical CIRP. This framework provides for a debtor-in-possession regime, but with various safeguards and obligations imposed on the corporate debtor aimed at preventing misuse of prepacks. Further, a pre-pack can only be initiated by the MSME corporate debtor based on a default of at least INR 10 lakhs (as opposed to INR 1 crore for a CIRP), with the approval of the MSME's shareholders and 66% in value of unrelated financial creditors. The rules governing the process for approval of a resolution plan are fairly complex with various permutations and combinations and a limited, but important, role for the resolution professional.

Will prepacks be extended to a wider category of corporate debtors? The Sub-Committee Report indeed recommended a phased implementation of pre-packs under the IBC and the idea of introducing prepacks for MSMEs alone was most likely intended to test the waters. To date, the uptake of prepacks by MSMEs has been limited. In September 2021, the Ahmedabad Bench of the NCLT admitted the application of 'GCCL Infrastructure and Projects Limited', the first case to be admitted under the prepack framework. However, this case too is yet to be resolved (despite the lapse of over 120 days since admission) and stakeholders have questioned whether the prepack framework with is complex rules and procedures is really likely to benefit MSMEs in terms of flexibility, costs and time. Prepacks involve a significant amount of work in the preparatory phase and, perhaps, it still is not clear to MSMEs if the promised advantages of a prepack would justify this additional time and effort.

While prepacks are yet to gain much momentum, the past two years have witnessed a widespread use of out-of-court resolution mechanisms. Data on CIRPs from the IBBI as of December 2021 show that of the 1733 cases that have been resolved as a going concern, only 457 were resolved through approved resolution plans, with the remaining being withdrawn or settled outside the IBC.[20] This number itself is an

---

[19] See Ravi (2020) and Ravi (2021).

[20] See page 12 in IBBI (2021).

underestimate as it does not take into account cases that never entered the IBC process. The acceptance of out-of-court resolution mechanisms suggests that stakeholders are open to considering a range of resolution mechanisms, including prepacks.

However, for prepacks to gain acceptance, the regulatory framework will need to strike the right balance between flexibility and a fair and transparent process. It is hoped that the experience with the prepack framework for MSMEs would better inform policy makers and lead to a more flexible and less complex framework if, and when, prepacks are introduced more widely.

References

Arcelor Mittal India versus SK Gupta and Ors, SC (2018) Arcelor Mittal India versus Satish Kumar Gupta and Ors

Bankruptcy Law Reforms Committee (2015) The report of the Bankruptcy law Reforms committee volume I: rationale and design. Technical Report, Ministry of Finance. http://ibbi.gov.in/BLRCReportVol1_04112015.pdf

CBIBSFC and Ors versus Ramesh Gelli and Ors, SC (2016) Central Bureau of Investigation. Bank Securities and Fraud Cell and Others versus, Ramesh Gelli and Others

IBBI (2020) Report of the sub-committee of the insolvency law committee on pre-packaged insolvency resolution process. Online, https://www.ibbi.gov.in/uploads/resources/24c7fc03cdffff69960ce374416fa646.pdf

IBBI (2021) The quarterly newsletter of the insolvency and Bankruptcy board of India. Online, https://www.ibbi.gov.in/uploads/publication/f93d15cd01db076d3ff7931450acb4bd.pdf

IBBI versus SBI and Ors, Delhi HC (2018) Insolvency and Bankruptcy board of India versus State Bank of India and Ors

Kastrinou A, Vullings S (2018) "No Evil is Without Good": a comparative analysis of pre-pack sales in the UK and The Netherlands. Int Insolv Rev 27(3):320–339

PNB versus Bhushan Power and Steel Ltd, NCLT, Principal Bench (2018) Punjab National Bank versus Bhushan Power and Steel Limited

Quantum Ltd versus Indus Finance Corp. Ltd., NCLAT (2018) Quantum Limited versus Indus Finance Corporation Limited

Ravi A (2020) Introducing Pre-packs in India - A Useful Tool in Times of COVID-19? Oxford Business Law Blog. https://www.law.ox.ac.uk/business-law-blog/blog/2020/05/introducing-pre-packs-india-useful-tool-times-covid-19

Ravi A (2021) India Considers Introducing Pre-Packs into its Insolvency Law. Oxford Business Law Blog. https://www.law.ox.ac.uk/business-law-blog/blog/2021/01/india-considers-introducing-pre-packs-its-insolvency-law

SBI versus Su Kam, NCLT, Principal Bench (2018) State Bank of India versus Su Kam Power Systems Limited

The Insolvency Services (2014) Graham review into Pre-pack Administration. Technical Report, Government of U.K. https://www.gov.uk/government/publications/graham-review-into-pre-pack-administration

The Way Forward for Personal Insolvency

Renuka Sane

1 Introduction

In 2016, the Indian Parliament passed the Insolvency and Bankruptcy Code (IBC), which contains provisions for both corporate and personal insolvency. While corporate insolvency has been restricted to limited liability firms, the scope of personal insolvency is much wider, and covers all individuals and partnerships as well as all creditors—financial and operational, secured and unsecured, formal and informal into its fold. The Government has chosen to notify only the part on corporate insolvency. In December 2017, the insolvency regulator, the Insolvency and Bankruptcy Board of India (IBBI), published draft regulations and indicated that these would be notified for a certain class of debtors, namely individuals with business debt and personal guarantors. The draft regulations will presumably be in force after the relevant sections of the Act get notified.

This chapter makes three contributions to the discussions on personal insolvency. First, it describes the Indian credit market and presents an argument for the need for personal insolvency law. The debt to GDP ratio in India is much smaller than other emerging or developed economies. Even though NPAs on personal loans from the banking sector look small relative to those on loans to industry, they have been rising, and may continue to get bigger as individual lending expands. Personal guarantors of companies that are under corporate insolvency now find themselves under creditor action without a recourse to an insolvency law. Reports of agrarian distress indicate a serious concern regarding agricultural lending. Medium, small and micro enterprises (MSMEs) remain an important part of the economy, many of whom are organised as sole proprietorship's, and may be in financial distress. The stress stemming from informal loans remains unknown. Only institutional credit has recourse to two legal processes, the Negotiable Instruments Act (NI), 1881 and The Securitisation and

R. Sane (✉)
National Institute of Public Finance and Policy, Delhi, India
e-mail: renukas@gmail.com; renuka.sane@nipfp.org.in

© The Author(s), under exclusive license to Springer Nature Singapore Pte Ltd. 2022
S. Thomas (ed.), *Insolvency and Bankruptcy Reforms in India*,
India Studies in Business and Economics,
https://doi.org/10.1007/978-981-16-0854-4_7

Reconstruction of Financial Assets and Enforcement of Security Act (SARFAESI), 2002, for recovery, thus leaving other types of lenders without any legal channel of recovery. Poor frameworks for recovery have had an adverse impact on the credit market. These conditions emphasise the need for a personal insolvency law.

Second, it provides a brief overview of the provisions in the law. One of the biggest motivations of the Bankruptcy Law Reforms Committee (BLRC) in drafting the law was the potential impact it could have on the credit market in India, and the structure of the law is driven by this objective. The IBC provides three distinct processes for dealing with default. The "Fresh Start" process provides for a debt-waiver to debtors who meet very specific eligibility conditions in terms of their income, assets and debts, and thus is likely to apply to a small set of people. The "Insolvency Resolution Process" provides a mechanism for creditors and debtors to re-negotiate a repayment plan, while "Bankruptcy" provides for liquidation of debtors assets, but can be used only if the resolution process fails. The law designates "Debt Recovery Tribunals" (DRTs) as the adjudicating authority of the code owing to their wider presence relative to the National Company Law Tribunals which is the adjudicating authority for corporate insolvency.

Third, the chapter makes suggestions on questions of policy that need to be addressed before the law can be meaningfully implemented. It makes the case that the success of the IBC depends on the design of the subordinate legislation as well as the evolution of the institutional infrastructure. Both creditors and debtors need to perceive the processes as fair, the costs as reasonable and outcomes relatively predictable. For example, in the present scenario, it is unclear whether existing creditors will resort to immediately using the Code even if it is notified. Their interest will be based on how effectively the Code is able to reduce their costs—in terms of time and money—of recovery, and increase predictability about the process. Debtors, at least in theory, might find in the IBC a tool to obtain a complete waiver of their debts (through the Fresh Start), or to stall creditor enforcement, and bring the creditor to the negotiating table. However, debtors are a dispersed group, may have social concerns about the stigma of bankruptcy, and may generally find themselves incapable of utilising a law that they are not financially and legally literate to understand. Also, if the law is seen as creditor-friendly, or institutional processes seen as costly and cumbersome, then it will fail at providing adequate insurance to debtors, incentivising them to actually avoid the IBC at all costs.

Since the law has not been notified, this is an opportune moment to revisit questions of design on personal insolvency law, and also shape the institutional infrastructure so that it can meet the demands that will get placed on the Code. High-quality regulations, improvements in the functioning of the institutional infrastructure, setting up of advisory services for bankruptcy are critical for personal insolvency to have its effect.

This article begins with an overview of credit markets in India in Sect. 2, and the need for a personal insolvency law in Sect. 3. In Sect. 4, it describes the current framework in the IBC. Section 5 describes policy questions that need action for the successful implementation of the law. The conclusion is presented in Sect. 6.

2 The Indian Credit Market

The Indian credit market is divided into three kinds of lenders. The first are banks that include scheduled commercial banks, co-operative banks and regional rural banks regulated by the Reserve Bank of India (RBI), that are the dominant player in "institutional credit".

The second are the non-banking finance companies (NBFCs), also regulated by the RBI, and include companies in the business of housing finance, vehicle finance as well as micro-finance. The NBFCs typically do not take deposits. In recent times, P2P lending, PPI cards, fintech companies have entered this space, many of them as NBFCs. These firms are able to leverage on non-credit data of potential customers (such as spending patterns on online websites, or bill payments on phones) to evaluate credit worthiness. They have been able to drive down their on-boarding costs through the e-KYC offered by the use of Aadhaar.[1]

The third are informal entities and can range from money lenders and chit funds to friends and family. Some of these, such as chit funds and moneylenders are governed by Acts that vary across the different states in India. Little is, however, known about the efficacy of the implementation of these Acts, and it is widely believed that several of these institutions continue to be informal and unregulated.

Table 1 presents the percentage of households in the months of Jan–April 2018 who claim to have outstanding credit from various sources. The data comes from

Table 1 Percentage of households with outstanding credit (Jan–April 2018)

Source	% of HH
Any source	31.5
Any formal	13.8
Banks	8.9
SHG	3.8
NBFC	0.9
MFI	0.5
Credit cards	0.2
Any informal	20.9
Shops	8.8
Friends and family	7.9
Money lender	3.7
Chit funds	0.3
Employer	0.1
Others	1.9
Both formal and informal	3.2

Source Consumer Pyramids

[1] This may, however, change with the recent Supreme Court judgment that has held the use of Aadhaar based authentication by the private sector to be unconstitutional.

Consumer Pyramids, a pan-India household survey carried out by the Centre for Indian Economy. Consistent with the low credit-GDP ratio of India, only 31% of households claimed to have credit outstanding from any source. Overall, the presence of informal sources was higher (21% of households) than formal sources of credit (13.8% of households). However, individually it is banks that seem to be the most utilised source of credit (8.9% of households), followed by shops (8.8% of households) and friends and family (7.9% of households). Contrary to the popular narrative of the role of money lenders and micro-finance, only about 3–4% of households had credit outstanding from self-help groups and money lenders. Only 3% of households had outstanding loans from both formal and informal sectors. There are three characteristics that are worth noting.

1. *Emphasis on secured credit*: The credit market in India largely delivers capital to those who have assets to pledge. This constrains entrepreneurship,[2] especially in service, technology and knowledge industries which require a system that lends based on an assessment of future cash-flows, and not on the basis of existing collateral.[3] This can be seen from Table 2 which shows the credit outstanding by commercial banks over the decade between 2008 and 2018. The bulk of personal loans outstanding are housing, vehicle, consumer durable and education loans—all of which are collateralised.
   While secured credit continues to dominate, the share of unsecured loans has been rising in incremental credit off-take since the demonetisation event of November 2016.[4] The use of digital technology that is able to lower costs of delivering credit, and of evaluating credit worthiness of customers is also bringing in a change in access to credit.[5]
2. *Directed lending*: Credit disbursement in India is shaped by the "Priority Sector Lending" policy that mandates that all domestic scheduled commercial banks (and foreign banks with 20 or more branches) should disburse 40% of net bank credit to what are termed as "priority sectors".[6] These include agriculture, micro enterprises, weaker sections of society (which includes small and marginal farmers, artisans, self-help groups among others).[7]
   Table 3 shows the total priority sector lending and its components. The share of agriculture has risen from 37% to 40% as has the share of loans to weaker

[2] As described by Banerjee and Duflo (2014), the lack of availability of adequate and timely credit is one of the biggest problems affecting the growth of the small-scale enterprises in India.

[3] See Sane (2015).

[4] See Iyer (2018).

[5] See Khosla (2018).

[6] The genesis of PSL was a study group in 1969 that observed that while agriculture contributed 50% to the national output, it received only a third of institutional credit. This led to setting of group-wise quantity targets for disbursal of credit. Over time other groups such as village and cottage industries, weaker sections, micro-finance were added to the definition of groups eligible for priority sector lending. The drive for continuing with the quantity targets comes from the need to somehow restrict the reach of informal lenders (such as moneylenders) who are seen as exploitative.

[7] See RBI (2018).

Table 2 Outstanding non-food credit of banks

	Rs.billion		% share in total	
	2008	2018	2008	2018
Total	22,048	76,884	100	100
Agriculture	2,753	10,302	12.49	13.4
Industry	8,583	26,992	38.93	35.11
Micro/small industry	1,326	3,729	6.02	4.85
Services	5,493	20,504	24.91	26.67
Trade	1,238	4,669	5.62	6.07
NBFCs	789	4,693	3.58	6.46
Personal loans	5,217	19,084	23.67	24.82
Consumer durables	97	197	0.44	0.26
Housing	2,603	9,745	11.81	12.68
Education	205	697	0.93	0.91
Vehicle	586	1,897	2.66	2.47
Credit card	267	686	1.21	0.89
Other	966	5,080	4.39	6.61

Source CMIE Economic Outlook

Table 3 Outstanding credit of banks for priority sector

	Rs.billion		% share in total	
	2008	2018	2008	2018
Total	7,480	25,531	100	100
Agriculture	2,753	10,215	36.81	40.01
Micro industries	2,520	9,963	33.70	39.02
Micro-credit	133	263	1.78	1.03
Weaker sections	1,069	5,690	14.29	22.29

Source CMIE Economic Outlook

sections from 14% to 22% in the last decade. Most of these loans would be loans to individuals.

3. *Political influence on lending*: A less discussed aspect of Indian credit markets is the linkage between politics and credit. It is argued that large amount of credit is driven through political patronage. For example, Cole (2009) finds that agricultural credit lent by public banks is substantially higher in election years. More loans are made in districts in which the ruling state party had a narrow margin of victory (or a narrow loss), than in less competitive districts. These loans are not linked to productivity or output improvements in agriculture. To the extent that lending is a "political" activity, decisions are unlikely to be made on sound credit risk considerations, with implications for default as well as recovery.

3 The Need for Personal Insolvency

The functioning of credit markets depends on two factors. The first is the ability to solve "information asymmetry". Lenders always know less than the borrower about her true ability and motivation, and have limited ability to monitor her actions. This makes them reluctant to extend credit. The second is the ability to make recoveries should the borrower not be able to repay her debts. If recoveries are difficult, then this too can hamper the growth in credit.

India has made some progress on solving the problem of information asymmetry through the use of credit bureaus, and increasingly through the use of data from mobile phone (and other) payment records, to social media networks. The mechanisms for recovery, however, are few. This becomes especially relevant as the market grows both in size and complexity.

3.1 The Individual Credit Market Is Growing

From banking sector data, it is difficult to establish the amount of credit that is disbursed to "individuals" as opposed to limited liability companies. It is likely that agricultural loans are mostly given to individuals, as are the ones to "micro and small industry" and "personal loans". In addition it is likely that some of the loans given for "services", "trade" and "NBFCs" are also passed on to individuals. This suggests that about 43% of bank loans are given to households.

Another way of judging credit disbursements is to evaluate the size of loans. In loan sizes up to Rs.10 million, agricultural and personal loans dominate, suggesting that these may most likely be taken by individuals. In 2017, Rs. 13,903 billion (about 16% of all non-food credit disbursed) was disbursed in loan sizes below Rs. 500,000. About Rs. 15,089 billion (about 19% of all non-food credit) was between Rs. 500,000 to Rs. 5 million, and Rs. 2,954 billion (3% of all non-food credit) was between Rs. 5 million and Rs. 10 million. This suggests that 38% of all non-food credit was most likely availed by individuals—a considerable market for individual loans.

The market for personal loans is growing faster than that of corporate loans. Figure 1 shows the YoY % change in credit disbursed by banks. The only category of loans that has seen an increase in disbursements is personal loans.

It is hard to estimate the size of loans from other sources, especially informal sources such as shops and friends and family. One estimate suggests that the micro-finance market is likely to grow at a double digit CAGR between 2018–2023.[8]

[8] See TechSci Research (2018).

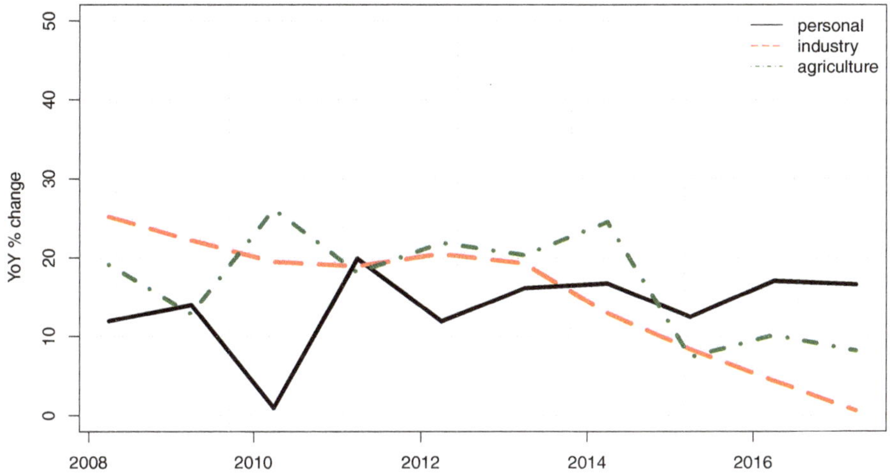

Fig. 1 YoY % change in credit disbursed by banks. *Source* CMIE Economic Outlook

3.2 Stress Is Building

It is widely believed that the NPAs in the banking sector on personal loans are small relative to those on corporate loans and hence personal insolvency is less of a concern. However, there are signs of stress for the following reasons:

1. NPAs on housing loans, as well as education loans have seen to hit 12% and 9% respectively in the last few years.[9] High growth rates in personal credit may imply higher NPAs in the near future.
2. Loans under priority sector also contribute to the total gross NPAs of the banking sector. In 2016–2017, gross NPAs on the priority sector in 2016–2017 were about 23% of the total NPAs.[10] While this may seem small relative to NPA crisis in the infrastructure and power sector space that is dominating headlines currently, this has not always been the case. In 2012–2013, priority sector NPAs accounted for 41% of total NPAs.
3. A growing cause for concern has been the lending on account of the "Kisan Credit Cards (KCC)",[11] and loans under the Mudra scheme,[12] which are likely to have significant stress.[13]

[9] See Kohli (2016) and TOI (2018).

[10] Gross Non-Performing Assets (NPAs) and Gross Advances by Priority and Non-priority Sectors: Domestic Scheduled Commercial Banks (excluding Foreign Banks), CMIE Economic Outlook.

[11] KCC scheme that was put in place in 1998, which provided farmers with easy credit without any collateral. The holder of the KCC could withdraw money up to Rs.50,000, from a bank and use it for any purpose. This also ruled out the possibility of banks monitoring the usage of the loans.

[12] Mudra loans which are given under the *Pradhan Mantri Mudra Yojana* is a Government of India initiative to provide credit support to small business.

[13] See Kapoor and Yadav (2018).

4. As the credit market expands, and households build up exposure to different lenders, the problem of collective action in recovery will also become important.

From the perspective of households, little is known about the stress in their portfolios. While the media is dominated by stories of farmer suicides owing to inability to repay loans,[14] or more recently by stories of farmer protests around the country,[15] systematic evidence on the extent of borrower over-indebtedness as well as distress is not available. One estimate from the study of financial diaries of 400 borrowers in the Krishnagiri district in Tamil Nadu points to 21% of the sample to be under serious financial stress owing to their debts.[16] At the higher income spectrum, large number of corporate promoters have accessed credit on the basis of personal guarantees,[17] that have now found themselves in the NCLT on account of corporate insolvency. These stories suggest that there is a wide range in the profile of borrowers who may be indebted, and their ability to access formal systems, or find the resources to make repayments may vary greatly.

3.3 Loan Waivers Are Rising

On recovery, India has a long history of loan waiver programs. Sensational stories about poor people burdened under large amounts of debt from exploitative lenders gain traction in the political discourse. The largest of these was a Rs.760 billion farm debt waiver in 2008. The scheme was aimed at providing relief to farmers through a complete debt-waiver to small and marginal farmers, and a partial relief to other farmers. More recently, several state governments of Uttar Pradesh, Maharashtra, Punjab have announced their own loan waiver schemes. The implementation of such schemes, however, leaves a lot to be desired. For example, a CAG report has demonstrated large-scale mismanagement in the 2008 loan waiver scheme, including problems of exclusion in beneficiary lists, tampering of records, and forging of documents to claim benefits.[18]

Besides the obvious fiscal consequences of waivers, they create moral hazard problems which are detrimental to the development of a credit culture. If debtors expect that there will be a loan-waiver announcement in the future, then there is little incentive to repay on time, as has been demonstrated by empirical research.[19] Loan waiver announcements are also believed to have caused a spike in NPAs.[20] Anecdotes suggest that loan waivers have contagion effects on other sources of credit such as

---

[14] Tiwary (2017) reports that between 2015 and 2016, farmers suicides spiked by 41% and 80% of the suicides were because of bankruptcy or debts owed to banks and micro-finance institutions.

[15] See IE (2018).

[16] See Prathap and Khaitan (2016).

[17] See Bhageria (2017).

[18] See Sane and Sapre (2017).

[19] See Kanz (2016).

[20] See The New Indian Express (2018).

micro-finance. Lenders (other than public sector banks that are forced to lend through priority sector lending targets described earlier) become wary of venturing into these markets making borrowers more credit constrained. Credit becomes more expensive for everyone, and not just those who benefited from the waiver.[21]

3.4 *Legal Processes for Recovery Are Weak*

Personal insolvency laws date back to the British times with the Presidency Towns Insolvency Act (PTIA), 1909 for Calcutta, Bombay and Madras and the Provincial Insolvency Act (PIA), 1920 for the rest of India, respectively. These laws have been used very rarely. The formal process of recovery has instead been through two legislation's[22]:

1. *Negotiable Instruments Act, 1881*: While the NI Act, 1881 has been around since British times, the Act became an important tool for credit recovery when Sect. 138 was added in 1988 which criminalised a "bounced" check.[23] The lender could collect post-dated checks from the borrower, and if the borrowers check did not clear, then the lender could pursue criminal action against the borrower. Khanna (2017) reports that lenders (in the home mortgage market) started using this provision in the mid-1990s s as there were very few other alternatives. The *process* of taking the debtor through the NI Act itself served as a deterrent to default. Even today, most NBFCs that are active in making loans to individuals—either for commercial or consumption purposes—resort to using Sect. 138 of the NI Act.
2. *SARFAESI, 2002*: The Securitisation and Reconstruction of Financial Assets and Enforcement of Security Act (SARFAESI), 2002 provided sweeping powers to banks and financial institutions to recover against non-performing loans by taking possession of collateral security without court intervention. However, SARFASEI is useful to only one class of creditors (banks and financial institutions that provide secured loans). Also, its efficiency has been falling over time—by 2013 the recovery rate was down to 22% from 61% in 2008.[24]

While the two laws have existed on paper, and Sect. 138 of the NI Act, 1881 used quite frequently, the effectiveness of the laws is hampered by the inefficiency of the Indian judicial system, which gets worse on matters related to property, contracts and mortgages.[25] For example, while SARFAESI was successful in the beginning, over time, the recovery rates had begun to decline. It is also important to note that

---

[21] See Sane (2018).

[22] While the Debt Recovery Tribunals are another mechanism, they apply only to loans worth Rs.10 lakh and more, and hence are largely used for corporate insolvency.

[23] See Malhotra (2009).

[24] RBI Report on Trends and Progress in Banking in India, 2008–2013.

[25] Khanna (2017) mentions the discussions on this issue in several Law Commission of India reports (No. 14, 79, 124, 230 and 245).

these processes are available only to a certain class of creditors—banks and financial institutions. A large category of other creditors do not find themselves with any mechanism for recovery.

3.5 Coercive Collection Is Prevalent

Ineffective legal procedures led to lenders using intimidating tactics to recover their loans. The RBI issued a circular on Guidelines on *fair practices code for lenders*, dated May 5, 2003 that dealt with matters of recovery of loans and directed that lenders should not resort to undue harassment viz. persistently bothering the borrowers at odd hours, or use muscle power for recovery of loans.[26] Such incidents resurfaced during the recession caused by the 2008 global financial crisis. Persons were hit by loss of jobs that resulted in EMI defaults on credit cards, housing mortgages, consumer and personal loans. Financial institutions resorted to recovery of loans through muscle men, who even carried out physical assault. Court Orders were passed to stop banks using muscle men. The RBI put out another circular on 26 March 2012 outlining a *fair practices code for NBFCs* that also emphasised refraining from coercive collection practices.[27]

Similar incidents on borrower distress and creditor excess have been seen in the context of micro-finance as well. In 2010, several suicides in the state of Andhra Pradesh were allegedly caused by coercive recovery practices of micro-finance institutions (MFIs), leading the state government to effectively ban MFIs in the state, and the RBI to intervene by creating a separate category for NBFC-MFIs and imposing several micro-prudential requirements on them.[28]

3.6 This Has an Adverse Impact on the Credit Market

The lack of a framework to resolve personal insolvency has had two broad effects. The first is on the structure of credit markets.[29] It is quite likely that the problem of financial exclusion is as much a result of poor frameworks for recovery as information symmetry. The cost of capital is higher if lenders do not feel confident about their ability to recover their dues, leading to informal sources such as shops, and friends as family filling the gap as was seen in Table 1. The non-existence of an insolvency framework has also led to a preponderance of collateralised lending,

[26] See RBI (2003).

[27] See RBI (2012).

[28] Sane and Thomas (2013) provide a brief overview of the micro-finance crisis and argue the need for better consumer protection frameworks in the collection of debts.

[29] World Bank (2017) presents a case on the importance of personal insolvency for the MSME sector.

which exacerbates the problems of financial exclusion. Individuals have remained credit constrained, as the market is not willing to take a chance on those without a significant credit history or collateral, thus perpetuating the cycle.

Another effect has been an emergence of businesses that modelled themselves around "joint-liability groups", where loans are given to groups as opposed to individuals. Pressure from group members solves both information asymmetry and serves as a disincentive to default, solving the collection problem. While micro-credit has, in some ways, revolutionised access to credit for those in the lower income bracket, it is not without its costs.

The second is the effect on borrowers. Coercive collection practices can have significant physical as well as psychological costs on debtors. It also leads to political pressure to take action—in the form of bans on certain forms of credit,[30] or in the form of loan waivers—which only exacerbates the problems of low credit access, and leads to further distortions in markets. Without personal insolvency procedures debtors have very limited opportunities of re-negotiation with their creditors if they see a chance of saving their businesses as a going concern.[31]

Finally, the lack of a sound process has meant that debtors have no mechanism of getting effective relief from collection, where one chapter of default can be closed, and the debtor can begin with a "clean slate", and return to productive work. The lack of such "insurance" makes debtors more likely to become risk-averse, less willing to borrow, thus having an impact on entrepreneurship in the economy.[32]

4 An Overview of Personal Insolvency in the IBC

The report of the Bankruptcy Law Reforms Committee Volume I: Rationale and Design claimed to be concerned about the adverse impact of lack of recovery frameworks on the credit market and hence, was motivated by the potential impact a personal insolvency law could have on the same.[33] Towards this end, the BLRC articulated the following goals:

1. *Providing a fair and orderly process for dealing with the financial affairs of insolvent individuals*: The BLRC suggested that active participation by stakeholders required that the process of re-negotiation is fair and orderly. This is related to the idea that the process should enable both debtor and creditor to participate with the least possible delay and expense, and there to be a certain predictability to the outcome.

[30] For example, in 2010 the Andhra Pradesh government brought an ordinance effectively banning micro-finance in the state in response to alleged suicides caused because of coercive collection by micro-finance. See Sane and Thomas (2016) for the impact of this Ordinance on consumers.

[31] An example of this is described by Ameerudheen (2018) on recovery proceedings under the SARFAESI Act, 2002 in the past two years against cashew farmers in Kerala.

[32] Feibelman (2005) presents a discussion on the insurance function of bankruptcy.

[33] See Bankruptcy Law Reforms Committee (2015).

2. *Providing effective relief or release from the financial liabilities and obligations of the insolvent*: There was recognition by the BLRC of the idea that the debtor will only meaningfully participate in the process if participation will allow for the possibility of discharging all debt. This chance at discharge might encourage households to take more risk and engage in entrepreneurial ventures.
3. *Providing the correct ex-ante incentives*: The participants in the process will naturally want to maximise their own value first. The BLRC was of the view that it was likely that either the creditors or the debtor would game the system to their own advantage. This could skew incentives and lead to a poor credit market. The processes, therefore, need to be designed such that individuals are not able to unfairly strategise during the process of bankruptcy.

These objectives have been the guiding principles behind the design of personal insolvency in the IBC. While the IBC does discuss the importance of providing the debtor with a clean discharge from debts, it seems to be less motivated by the need of bankruptcy law to also provide an element of insurance, with the emphasis being on discharged that is "earned".[34] With this background, the section turns towards a description of the defining features of personal insolvency law in the IBC.[35]

4.1 Eligibility

There are three ways to think about eligibility into the IBC process: (a) the threshold at which a filing can be made, (b) entities who make the filing and (c) the debt that qualifies for a filing.

The eligibility threshold for filing in the IBC is low—a single default of at least Rs. 1,000 would suffice. The Code makes it possible for the government to raise this to Rs. 1,00,000 but not higher.[36]

The IBC permits either the debtor defined as an individual or partnership firm, or the creditor to file for insolvency. However, for the process of "Fresh Start", discussed later in this section, only the debtor is eligible. A creditor includes a financial, operational, secured, unsecured creditor as well as a decree holder.[37] This suggests that all kinds of creditors including moneylenders, friends and family could technically file for insolvency.

Finally, a filing can be made only on default of debt that is not excluded. The IBC includes the following in its category of excluded debts—liabilities for court or tribunal fines, maintenance of any person required by law, student loans, negligence, nuisance or breach of statutory contractual or other legal obligations. The Code leaves

---

[34] See Feibelman (2005) and Feibelman (2018).

[35] Feibelman (2018) provides an excellent summary of the provisions of the Code.

[36] Section 78, IBC.

[37] Section 3(10), IBC.

open the possibility that regulations will specify other kinds of debts in the class of excluded debts.[38]

4.2 *Processes*

The IBC has two kinds of processes. The first is the route of the "insolvency resolution process" followed by "bankruptcy". The second is the route of a debt-waiver through the "fresh start". The choice of the route depends on specific eligibility criteria, and the IRP-bankruptcy route seems to be the preferred route for most insolvencies.

The IRP-bankruptcy route The Insolvency Resolution Process (IRP) is the process through which all creditors and the debtor agree on a negotiated repayment plan.[39] The IRP can be initiated by the debtor or the creditor at the relevant DRT, through an application the form and manner of which will be prescribed by regulations. The application is to be examined by a Resolution Professional (RP) who is responsible for making a recommendation of acceptance or rejection to the DRT.[40]

Once the IRP application has been accepted, a moratorium of six months would commence on all collection actions.[41] A public notice is to be issued by the DRT, and creditor claims are to be collected by the RP.[42] The debtor is required to propose a repayment plan under the supervision of a RP, which should meet the approval of majority of creditors, defined as more than three-fourth in value.[43] Once approved by the creditors and sanctioned by the adjudicating authority, the plan would be binding on the debtor and all the creditors mentioned in the plan. The IBC provides no guidance on the content of the plan, or requires the plan to provide for at least a minimum living standard for the debtor. These details might get drafted in the regulations that would govern the process. However, it requires that the consent of the debtor is mandatory for any modifications to the plan the creditors may suggest.[44] The IBC thus balances the propensity in India of the law and regulations to micro-manage every process with the welfare of the debtor.

The approved plan has to be submitted to the DRT who then passes a final order on the plan.[45] The implementation of the plan is to be supervised by the RP. A discharge order may be granted to the debtor in accordance with the content of the resolution plan.[46]

---

[38] Section 79(15), IBC.

[39] Chapter III, Part III, IBC.

[40] Section 99, IBC.

[41] Section 101, IBC.

[42] Sections 102, 103 and 104, IBC.

[43] Section 111, IBC.

[44] Section 108(3), IBC.

[45] Section 114, IBC.

[46] Section 116, IBC.

The IBC envisages three grounds for failure of the IRP which can lead to bankruptcy proceedings: (a) If the application to the IRP is not accepted due to failure to provide requisite information, (b) If creditors and the debtor cannot agree on a repayment plan and (c) If the debtor fails to implement the repayment plan within the period prescribed for such implementation in the plan.[47] The bankruptcy proceeding will not start automatically: the creditor or the debtor would have to make an application to trigger it. The rationale for this lies in the higher stigma attached to an individual's bankrupt status.

On the admission of the application for bankruptcy, an insolvency professional will be nominated as the bankruptcy trustee by the IBBI if either the debtor or creditor has failed to propose one.[48] A bankruptcy order will be passed by the DRT.[49] It will have the effect of declaring the debtor as 'bankrupt' and vesting the estate of the bankrupt with the bankruptcy trustee.[50] A certain class of assets of the debtor would remain outside the estate such as property held by the bankrupt on trust for any other person, sums due to workmen or employees from the provident or pension fund, and assets that may be specified by the Central Government or a financial sector regulator.[51] On the vesting of the estate of the bankrupt, the bankruptcy trustee will undertake the due process for registering claims, and administering them in the order of priority encapsulated in the IBC.[52]

For both of these processes, the Code does not specify fees for filing either the IRP or bankruptcy and leaves open the possibility that the fees may be prescribed later.[53] Fees to the insolvency profession in the IRP as well as bankruptcy are expected to be accommodated in the respective procedures.[54]

The Fresh Start route The IBC proposes a concept of a Fresh Start, aimed at providing debt relief to the poorest. A debtor with gross annual income of less than Rs. 60,000, assets less than Rs. 20,000, qualifying debts[55] of less than Rs. 35,000, and no home-ownership, will be eligible to get a complete waiver of debts.[56]

Only the debtor can trigger this process.[57] The default has to be on "qualifying debts". If the debtor has triggered the process through a resolution professional,

---

[47] Section 121, IBC.

[48] Section 125, IBC.

[49] Section 126, IBC.

[50] Section 128, IBC, Sect. 154, IBC.

[51] Section 155, IBC.

[52] Sections 129–137, IBC; Sect. 178, IBC.

[53] Section 94(6), IBC.

[54] Section 105(2)(b), and Sect. 178, IBC.

[55] Qualifying debt includes debt that is due for repayment provided it is not part of the excluded debt category, is not secured, and has been incurred three months before the fresh start application. See Sect. 79(19) of the IBC.

[56] These thresholds have been designed using the SECC, 2011, Deprivation Index as well as the Key Indicators of Debt and Investment in India for 2013 and will need to get revised over time.

[57] Section 80, IBC.

then the DRT will only check if there is a disciplinary proceeding against the RP, and allow the RP if no such proceeding is found. If the debtor triggers the process without an RP, then the IBBI will be required to nominate a RP for the process.[58] The Code specifies a list of particulars that must be submitted with the application.[59]

On examination of the information, the RP will make a recommendation to the DRT to accept or reject the application.[60] The DRT will accept the application based on the RPs recommendation.[61] A moratorium will become applicable on all the creditors of the applicant for a period of six months, to provide a conducive environment for the process to go through.[62] The DRT shall pass a discharge order for the qualifying debts by the end of the moratorium period.[63] The details of the discharge order will be forwarded to the IBBI for record-keeping.[64]

The motivation behind the fresh start seems to be the difficulties in the transaction costs of the IRP-bankruptcy route being larger than the debt at stake for low-income, low-asset debtors. The fresh start also provides an insurance function[65] by essentially providing a more systematic debt-waiver.

4.3 Role of Secured Creditors

In individual insolvency, secured creditors are permitted to stay out of the IRP entirely by enforcing their security interest, unlike the provisions in corporate insolvency. The secured creditors are required to submit an affidavit to this effect to the RP, and if the same lender has also extended unsecured credit, then participate in the voting process only to the extent of the same.[66] The BLRCs argument was that unlike a firm where organisational capital is better preserved when all the assets, including those put up as collateral, hang together, in the case of an individual this is less important. It is the individual herself that is the repository of the capital (human capital).

Once a bankruptcy order is passed, and the estate is vested with the bankruptcy trustee, a moratorium will begin, on all collection actions of unsecured creditors. Secured creditors will have the option to participate in the process or enforce their security outside the process.[67]

---

[58] Section 82, IBC.

[59] Section 81(4).

[60] Section 83, IBC.

[61] Section 84, IBC.

[62] Section 84, IBC.

[63] Section 92, IBC.

[64] Section 92(5).

[65] See Feibelman (2005).

[66] Section 110, IBC.

[67] Section 172, IBC.

4.4 Priority

In the IBC, there is no priority in the design of the repayment plan. There is, however, a priority in bankruptcy as follows.[68]

1. The costs and expenses incurred by the bankruptcy trustee.
2. Workmen's dues for a period of 24 months prior to the bankruptcy commencement date.
3. Wages and unpaid dues owed to employees (other than workmen) for a period of 24 months prior to the bankruptcy commencement date.
4. Amount due to the Central or State Government.
5. All other debts owed by the bankrupt include unsecured debts.

While this list provides a ranking between various classes of debt, the IBC requires that all debts within one class shall rank equally among themselves. Feibelman (2018) notes that this is problematic.

4.5 The Role of the DRT

The role of the Tribunal is wider in personal insolvency relative to corporate insolvency. For example, once the IRP has been triggered, the DRT is responsible for accepting the application on the basis of the report submitted by the RP.[69] The law does not provide any guidance on what the DRT should base its judgment on, and whether it should solely rely on the recommendations of the RP. If the RP requests, the DRT may also provide instructions for the conduct of negotiations between the debtor and creditors.[70]

Similarly when the repayment plan is submitted by the RP to the DRT, it may accept or reject the plan on the basis of the report. The DRT, in its order of approving the plan, may provide directions for implementing the plan, or may direct the RP to re-convene a meeting of creditors if it feels that the repayment plan requires modification.[71]

The DRT also has a role to play when deciding about priority of payments in a bankruptcy in specific cases related to creditor having given any indemnity or having made payments through which the bankrupt has been protected. In such an event the Code allows the DRT to give that specific creditor an advantage over other creditors.[72] Through these provisions, the DRT may actually end up playing a far greater role in the conduct of the IRP relative to the corporate insolvency process, and what was envisaged by the BLRC.

---

[68] Section 178, IBC.

[69] Section 100(1), IBC.

[70] Section 100(2), IBC.

[71] Section 114, IBC.

[72] Section 178(3), IBC.

5 The Way Forward

Personal insolvency in the IBC, when notified, will become operational in a credit market that has evolved over several decades in response to an environment with weak creditor rights on recovery, and weaker debtor rights on stalling creditor enforcement. The credit market is also politicised, especially when it comes to agricultural lending and loan waivers.

The enthusiasm of these existing creditors will depend on how the IBC affects their costs and time to recovery, as well as recovery rates. Of course, it is possible that the law leads to the evolution of new business models and new class of lenders who now feel comfortable entering the market, but this will unfold over the longer term and will also be a function of a demonstration effect based on the experience of the existing market participants.

From a debtor's perspective, the IBC provides a tool for dealing with distress that is currently unavailable. By permitting the debtor to file for insolvency, the IBC provides a legal mechanism to debtors to bring about a stay on enforcement actions. It also provides a platform for debtors to be able to re-negotiate their plan, which may be extremely useful, if the debtor has more than one creditor. The fresh start provisions, especially, may be extremely useful for the debtor to avail of a loan waiver.

For the debtors to be able to use the IBC, two facets are extremely important. First, if there is a social stigma associated with the bankruptcy process then it is unlikely that debtors will take recourse even if it might be in their economic interest to do so. Second, if the process of accessing the law is costly and cumbersome, is seen to be "creditor friendly", or if the process does not provide a reasonable mechanism of dealing with creditors while maintaining a minimum standard of living then debtors might not find it worthwhile to pursue this course of action. Much, therefore, depends on the regulatory environment and institutional infrastructure that governs the process. The section turns to issues that need to be resolved before the law can be meaningfully implemented.

5.1 Policy Issues

Personal insolvency laws affect both the creditors and debtors in different ways, and must strike a balance between both their interests. From a debtor's perspective, personal insolvency must provide a stay collection of an individual debtor's obligations, provide a scheme of repayment, and finally discharge some obligations. A process that is humane, fair, and offers debt-relief can significantly reduce psychological distress among debtors, and encourage risk taking and entrepreneurship. On the other hand, if the process provides for significant debt relief at the cost of creditors, then creditors will eventually pass on high costs of credit back to the debtors. The process also has to provide creditors with reasonable recovery rates for them to be comfortable to lend in the future. The Act and the Regulations must provide for this balance.[73] Before decisions are taken on amendments to the law or drafting of regulations, policy needs to be formulated that, at the very least, builds on the following elements[74]:

1. *Definitions of assets and income*: The selection of debtors into a fresh start, or an IRP depends on the definition of assets and income of the debtors. As of now, the thresholds for eligibility into the Fresh Start are hard coded into the law. It might be useful to take a re-look at the relevance of the thresholds from the perspective of making the process more debtor friendly, and increasing the thresholds so that a larger number of people may be eligible. It is also important to link these thresholds to some index so that the thresholds are in sync with GDP growth as well as inflation.
   For the IRP or bankruptcy process, the recovery of creditors will depend on what assets remain exempt from the insolvency process (for example, some share of property, tools of trade that allow him to gain and pursue employment, and items necessary to meet a certain minimum standard of living), and what part of the disposable income is deemed to be "reasonably necessary" for the maintenance or support of the debtor and her dependents. This requires a discussion on the definition of such assets and income.
2. *Structure of repayment plans*: The IBC provides for no structure on the repayment plan, as well as no guidance on priority in the IRP. As Feibelman (2018) has pointed out, the inconsistency in the priority in an IRP and bankruptcy might incentivise creditors to choose one over the other, which in some instances may be counter-productive, especially if there might be value in saving a small firm as a going concern. Policy also needs to consider prohibiting repayment plans from including onerous terms as well as provisions on extortionate transactions and preferential transfers.
3. *Fast track procedures through a non-judicial entity*: For a large number of cases, there might be merit in developing "fast track procedures" that involve obtaining quick relief. One example is to provide a standard "three year repayment plan", wherein debtors commit to provide a part of their income to creditors in return for a complete discharge of debts. The challenge in this procedure is going to be the design of eligibility into the plan—a demonstration that debtors have the ability to part with a share of income while still maintaining a reasonable standard of living will have to be made. This process is likely to be fraught with challenges, and disputes.
   An alternative option is to present a standardised repayment plan that promises a specified recovery rate. The debtor promises to repay this amount over a period of time. While this may imply that in some cases creditors make lower recoveries

[73] The IBBI published draft regulations on personal insolvency in December 2017. While these regulations provided the details for a broad process to be followed, they were not accompanied by a broad objective and goals that the regulations wished to achieve.

[74] World Bank (2014) provides a comprehensive analysis of the various choices regarding a personal insolvency regime.

than they otherwise would, on the whole, it reduces the cost of discovery, of negotiation and of potential litigation. It should be possible to offer this as an alternative through an administrative agency and not the court. At the very least, a policy decision on such alternatives needs to be articulated.

4. *Processes for loan waivers*: The Fresh Start process aims to provide complete debt relief to people who fall below certain asset, income and debt thresholds. This process can provide a way to carry out loan waivers in a more systematic way.[75] The details of implementing loan waivers through the fresh start process need to be thought through.
5. *Discharge and credit scores*: The IBC allows for a discharge while the repayment plan is still in progress. Similarly, it allows for availing complete debt relief for those eligible under the Fresh Start. These decisions should come at some cost to debtors to reduce the possibility of moral hazard. This can be done through a system of records where these choices of debtors are stored for a specified number of years—providing creditors with information on whether to extend credit, and at what price. The processes for the collection and maintenance of these records, and their integration with the credit bureaus need to be designed.
6. *Fees*: The IBC is silent about the fees of the two processes. It is expected that the fees to the professionals (as well as the court) will be accommodated in the repayment plan that is agreed on, or the bankruptcy estate that is liquidated. This leaves the question of how to deal with a large number of cases that have no income, and no assets and could possibly not afford the IBC processes. These may be paid out of a fund that is maintained by the IBBI from fees charged to regulated entities, through general tax revenues or alternatively such cases be not be admitted at all. The trade-offs between these alternatives need to be revisited.

5.2 *Institutional Infrastructure: Courts*

Unlike corporate insolvency, the IBC design suggests a far greater role for the DRTs in the process, placing greater demands on the judiciary. The problems with judicial inefficiency in India are not new. While tribunals were created to bypass the long-winded processes of the civil courts, they too have not lived up to their expectations.[76] The inefficiency is on account of the "quantity" of judges, as well as the "quality" of the process wherein a large proportion of the judges time is spent in administrative matters leaving little time for judicial decisions.[77]

[75] Sane (2018) for a description of how loan waivers can be carried out through the fresh start process in the IBC.

[76] The Supreme Court, in L. Chandra Kumar vs. Union of India, 1997 lamented that Indian tribunals function inefficiently since there is no authority in charge of supervising and fulfilling their administrative requirements.

[77] Damle and Regy (2017) show the shortfall in the number of judges in the NCLT in the context of the increasing case load from the IBC. Datta and Shah (2015) point out the mistakes made in India on court modernisation.

The quantity aspect assumes more importance in personal insolvency as it is expected that people from all parts of the country should be able to access the system. For example, Sane (2017) finds that the case load on existing DRTs will rise significantly even if 1% of personal loan accounts at banks in a district were to default, and just under 10% of these were to be brought under the IBC. This is a very conservative estimate as this only includes credit extended by the banking sector. The potential case load from personal insolvency cases is a concern as there were already 109,518 cases pending at the DRTs as of 30 June 2017.

Besides increasing the number of DRTs, the processes within the DRTs needs review. As has been pointed out by Datta (2016), a "Tribunal Service Agency" needs to be set up which will provide administrative support to the Tribunals. This will lead to a separation between the administrative and judicial functions, and allow the judges to spend more time on the latter.[78] These reforms are particularly important if the DRTs have to become a meaningful adjudicating authority for personal insolvency.

5.3 *Institutional Infrastructure: Information Utility*

A key problem in the implementation of any insolvency regime, and personal insolvency in particular, is that of "asset legibility". It is extremely difficult for the creditor, or the resolution professional to evaluate the exact nature and value of a debtorâŁ™s assets to arrive at an acceptable repayment plan, or liquidation value in case of bankruptcy. A core component of the BLRC recommendation was the idea of an "Information Utility" which would be a repository of information regarding debt and default. The IBBI issued regulations on IUs in March 2017. Since the regulations, only one IU, the National E-Governance Services Limited, has been established. It is extremely important to understand the reasons for the reluctance of private entities to establish IUs and make corrections in the regulations[79] in order to promote the setting up such an industry.

5.4 *Institutional Infrastructure: Intermediaries*

Individual debtors will be vulnerable to biased advice on whether to file for insolvency, the process guiding the filing, and the process for resolution, as well as in their dealings with creditors. In other sectors in retail finance in India, there have been various instances of mis-selling that have arisen from a combination of misaligned incentives that stem from high-powered sales practices combined with weak regu-

[78] A similar suggestion was made by the FSAT Task Force led by Justice N. K. Sodhi, in 2015, to provide administrative services to tribunals in financial sector.

[79] Prashant (2017) presents a critique of the IU regulations.

lation.[80] If not handled correctly, such problems are likely to occur in the field of personal insolvency as well. The IBBI will have to step up to the challenge of protecting customer interests, involving two main classes of intermediaries: the insolvency professionals and credit counsellors.

Insolvency Professionals Insolvency professionals have a very important role to play in the IBC. In the case of corporate insolvency, as "Resolution Professionals" they run the entire resolution process, and in liquidation act as the "liquidator". The role of the insolvency professional is even more important in the case of personal insolvency owing to the asymmetry in the balance of power between creditors and debtors. Several important decisions on filing, preparing a plan, preparing a statement of affairs, negotiating with creditors, which will be fundamental to the experience of the debtors in the Code, depend on the integrity and efficiency of the resolution professional.

Currently, there are about 2000 IPs registered with the IBBI for corporate insolvency. They are regulated through self-regulated organisations called the Insolvency Professional Agencies (IPA), which are in turn regulated by the IBBI.[81] There have been many challenges in the functioning of RPs in the case of corporate insolvency—from allegations of partisan behaviour, questions around appropriate timelines, to attacks and kidnappings of the RPs.[82] It is likely that frictions between the various stakeholders to the debt contract and the RPs will increase when it comes to personal insolvency. Even if the disputes end up being of small values, they are likely to be more political should misconduct be discovered.

The training and qualifications of IPs, and their regulation will require concerted efforts from the IBBI with a specific focus on the problems that can arise in personal insolvency. It is unlikely that the regulations that serve the purpose of corporate insolvency will work for personal insolvency. For example, a trade-off that the IBBI may have to evaluate is simple licensing procedure so that there are enough RPs to service individuals across India versus a minimum standard of qualifications to ensure service quality. Similarly, mechanisms to discipline a large cadre of professionals will require an enforcement capacity that may be currently missing.

Credit and insolvency advisors The decision to file under the IBC is a complex one. It is expected that debtors will require advice on questions such as whether to file for insolvency, where to file, what to expect in the process, how to find the RPs, when to expect a discharge, and the impact of the process on their credit scores and future ability to raise debt. Given the potential social stigma that may get attached to bankruptcy, the hand-holding required may be greater.

---

[80] Anagol and Kim (2012), Halan et al. (2014), Sane and Halan (2017), Anagol et al. (2017) are examples of consumer protection problems in the insurance and mutual fund industries in India.

[81] Existing professional organisations such as the Institute of Chartered Accounts of India (ICAI), Institute of Company Secretaries of India (ICSI) and Institute of Cost Accountants of India (ICWAI) have been given the license to perform as IPAs.

[82] See Vats (2018), Gopakumar and Upadhyay (2017) for more details.

In several jurisdictions, this is done through a class of intermediaries called as "credit counsellors", or "debt-advisors". In the US, for example, the Bankruptcy Abuse and Prevention and Consumer Protection Act (BAPCPA) 2005 requires the individual to obtain credit counselling from an approved counselling agency[83] within 180 days preceding a bankruptcy filing. It also requires the debtor to go through a post-petition financial management course. Failure to get counselling may lead the case to be dismissed. The agencies get regulated primarily by the Federal Trade Commission (FTC) and the US Trustee Program at the Department of Justice. In the UK, "debt advice" is not mandatory. Multiple debt advice agencies, regulated by the Financial Conduct Authority (FCA), provide help in exploring various avenues of insolvency resolution. Individuals are encouraged to go through these advisers to make an informed decision. The application for a debt-waiver in the UK (through a debt relief order which is similar to the Fresh Start in the IBC), must be made through such approved intermediaries.

The IBC is entirely silent on the need for credit and insolvency advisors. However, the draft regulations by the IBBI mention the need to have debt counsellors, but the regulations do not specify any details. It is non-trivial to get the regulations right—for example Kilborn (2011) claims that the BAPCPA reforms that made credit counselling mandatory also put a cap on fees that has resulted in "ceremonial" counselling which is ritual devoid of any substance.

6 Conclusion

Credit markets are important from the perspective of growth. A well functioning credit market allows for consumption smoothing, and facilitates entrepreneurship. Insolvency laws play an important role in facilitating the growth of credit markets.

This chapter presents an argument for the need for a personal insolvency law in India. It provides a brief overview of the provisions on personal insolvency in the Insolvency and Bankruptcy Code, 2016, that have yet to be notified. The chapter raises several policy issues that need to be addressed, and makes the case that the success of the IBC depends on the design of the subordinate legislation as well as the evolution of the institutional infrastructure. High-quality regulations, improvements in the functioning of the institutional infrastructure such as the Information Utilities and Debt Recovery Tribunals, the insolvency professionals, advisory services for bankruptcy are critical for personal insolvency to have its effect.

As has argued by Shah (2018), "state capacity building requires sequencing, where the ecosystem learns to deal with simple things before taking on the complex problems." The idea is that the reform process should always be mindful of the load-bearing capacity of public administration[84], and prematurely increasing the

[83] These are not-for-profit agencies set up to advise and educate consumers on financial portfolio management.

[84] See Shah (2017).

complexity of the ask, might actually lead to a low-equilibrium outcome.[85] These issues are extremely relevant in the context of personal insolvency where the issue is complex in and of itself, and is susceptible to political interference should there be mistakes early on. It would, therefore, be advisable to operate the system for a small subset of borrowers such as businesses, or personal guarantors before becoming operational for all individuals. Alternatively, the IBC can be made operational for granting debt relief more systematically through the Fresh Start process, before operationalising the resolution and bankruptcy processes.

Acknowledgements I thank Adam Feibelman, Josh Felman, Ajay Shah and Anjali Sharma, and participants of the round-table on personal insolvency at the National Institute of Public Finance and Policy for useful comments. This chapter draws heavily from the author's working paper—*Sane (2019), The way forward for personal insolvency in the Indian Insolvency and Bankruptcy Code. Working paper No. 251, NIPFP Working paper series. National Institute of Public Finance and Policy, New Delhi.*—and content has been re-used with permission The opinions expressed in this chapter and all errors are the author's own.

References

Ameerudheen T (2018) Despair in Kerala as banks start seizing cashew factories. Scroll.in, 27 March 2018. https://scroll.in/article/873274/despair-in-kerala-as-banks-start-seizing-cashew-factories

Anagol S, Kim HH (2012) the impact of shrouded fees: evidence from a natural experiment in the Indian mutual funds market. Am Econ Rev 102(1):576–593. http://EconPapers.repec.org/RePEc:aea:aecrev:v:102:y:2012:i:1:p:576-93

Anagol S, Cole S, Sarkar S (2017) Understanding the advice of commissions-motivated agents: evidence from the Indian life insurance market. Rev Econ Stat 99(1):1–15

Banerjee A, Duflo E (2014) Do firms want to borrow more? testing credit constraints using a directed lending program. Rev Econ Stat 81(2):572–607

Bankruptcy Law Reforms Committee (2015) The report of the Bankruptcy law reforms committee volume I: rationale and design. Technical Report, Ministry of Finance. http://ibbi.gov.in/BLRCReportVol1_04112015.pdf

Bhageria A (2017) Dealing with promoters' guarantees. LiveMint, 23 October 2017. https://www.livemint.com/Opinion/qzt9gFib7Otk47pEyRKnrJ/Dealing-with-promoters-guarantees.html

Cole S (2009) Fixing market failures or fixing elections? agricultural credit in India. Am Econ J: Appl Econ 1(1):219–250

Damle D, Regy P (2017) Does the NCLT have enough judges? Technical Report, The Leap Blog. https://blog.theleapjournal.org/2017/04/does-nclt-have-enough-judges.html

Datta P (2016) Towards a tribunal services agency. IGIDR Working Paper WP-2016-006. http://ifrogs.org/releases/Datta2016_bettercourts.html

Datta P, Shah A (2015) How to make courts work? Technical Report, The Leap Blog. https://blog.theleapjournal.org/2015/02/how-to-make-courts-work.html

Feibelman A (2005) Defining the social insurance function of consumer Bankruptcy. Am Bankruptcy Inst Law Rev 13

Feibelman A (2018) Legal shock or false start: the uncertain future of India's new personal insolvency and Bankruptcy regime. Tulane Public Law Research Paper No. 17–16. https://dx.doi.org/10.2139/ssrn.3092042

[85] Rai (2018) makes this argument in the context of the design of a privacy law.

Gopakumar G, Upadhyay JP (2017) Edelweiss ARC complains against IRP in Synergies Dooray case. liveMint, 14 September 2017. https://www.livemint.com/Industry/AF8LAo7Nc05LuEm0g6gpNM/Edelweiss-ARC-complains-against-IRP-in-Synergies-Dooray-case.html

Halan M, Sane R, Thomas S (2014) The case of the missing billions: estimating lossesto customers due to mis-sold life insurance policies. J Econ Policy Reform 17(4)

IE (2018) Farmers' march Highlights: They are not seeking gift from govt on farm loan waiver, says Rahul Gandhi. Indian Express, 30 November 2018. https://indianexpress.com/article/india/farmers-delhi-protest-live-updates-two-day-march-demanding-special-parliament-session-5470020/

Iyer A (2018) How risky is the retail loan book of banks? LiveMint, 13 March 2018. https://www.livemint.com/Money/Nracq59H6uDqwnhV4qrRQO/How-risky-is-the-retail-loan-book-of-banks.html

Kanz M (2016) What does debt relief do for development? evidence from India's bailout for rural households. Am Econ J: Appl Econ 8(4):66–99

Kapoor A, Yadav C (2018) The great Indian NPA mess: how MUDRA scheme, Kisan credit cards could pose the next round of risk for banking sector. FirstPost, 21 October 2018. https://www.firstpost.com/business/the-great-indian-npa-mess-how-mudra-scheme-kisan-credit-cards-could-pose-the-next-round-of-risk-for-banking-sector-5231341.html

Khanna VS (2017) Law, institutions and economic development: examining the development of the home mortgage market in India—can two wrongs make a right? http://dx.doi.org/10.2139/ssrn.3032632

Khosla R (2018) The changing face of Indian retail borrowing. LiveMint, 20 August 2018. https://www.livemint.com/Opinion/MgTU086kNbuc6lbpgmdgsI/The-changing-face-of-Indian-retail-borrowing.html

Kilborn JJ (2011) Former entrepreneurs in dutch personal insolvency Law: comparison with US, UK, Germany, Denmark, and France. Available at SSRN. http://dx.doi.org/10.2139/ssrn.1827004

Kohli R (2016) Will housing loans be the new NPAs? LiveMint, 2 August 2016. https://www.livemint.com/Opinion/OiaA0z7C3AfEYrkK3KNJSO/Will-housing-loans-be-the-new-NPAs.html

Malhotra V (2009) Rethinking the regime against dishonoured cheques in India. http://dx.doi.org/10.2139/ssrn.1648751

Prashant (2017) Issues with the regulation of information utilities. The Leap Blog, 12 July 2017. https://blog.theleapjournal.org/2017/07/issues-with-regulation-of-information.html

Prathap V, Khaitan R (2016) When is microcredit unsuitable? Guidelines using primary evidence from low-income households in India. Dvara Research Working Paper Series No. 2016–2. https://www.dvara.com/research/wp-content/uploads/2017/01/When-is-Microcredit-Unsuitable-Guidelines-for-Lending.pdf

Rai S (2018) A pragmatic approach to data protection. The Leap Blog, 9 February, 2018. https://blog.theleapjournal.org/2018/02/a-pragmatic-approach-to-data-protection.html

RBI (2003) Guidelines on fair practices code for lenders. DBOD. Leg. No.BC. 104 /09.07.007/2002-03. https://rbidocs.rbi.org.in/rdocs/notification/PDFs/36102.PDF

RBI (2012) Guidelines on fair practices code for NBFCs. RBI/2011-12/470, DNBS.CC.PD.No.266 /03.10.01/2011-12. https://www.rbi.org.in/scripts/NotificationUser.aspx?Id=7089

RBI (2018) Priority sector lending: targets and classification. Frequently Asked Questions, As on 1 August 2018. https://m.rbi.org.in/Scripts/FAQView.aspx?Id=87

Sane R (2015) Setting up the ecosystem for personal credit . The Leap Blog, 21 November 2015. https://blog.theleapjournal.org/2015/11/setting-up-ecosystem-for-personal-credit.html

Sane R (2017) Estimating the potential number of personal insolvency cases at the DRT. The Leap Blog, 1 December 2017. https://blog.theleapjournal.org/2017/12/estimating-potential-number-of-personal.html

Sane R (2018) Loan waivers as fresh start in bankruptcy . The Leap Blog, 12 March 2018. https://blog.theleapjournal.org/2018/03/loan-waivers-as-fresh-start-in.html

Sane R, Halan M (2017) Misled and mis-sold: Financial misbehaviour in retail banks? J Comp Econ 45:429–444. https://doi.org/10.1016/j.jce.2017.06.001
Sane R, Sapre A (2017) Implementing loan waivers: lessons from the 2008 All India Debt Waiver Scheme experience . The Leap Blog, 21 July 2017. https://blog.theleapjournal.org/2017/07/implementing-loan-waivers-lessons-from.html
Sane R, Thomas S (2013) Regulating microfinance institutions. Econ Polit Wkly 68(5)
Sane R, Thomas S (2016) The real cost of credit constraints: Evidence from micro-finance. BE J Econ Anal Policy 16(1)
Shah A (2017) Beware of premature load bearing. Business Standard, 26 June 2017. http://www.mayin.org/ajayshah/MEDIA/2017/loadbearing.html
Shah A (2018) Sequencing issues in building jurisprudence: the problems of large bankruptcy cases. online. https://blog.theleapjournal.org/2018/07/sequencing-issues-in-building.html
TechSci Research (2018) India Microfinance Market, By Types of Institution (Banks and Non-Banks), By End Use (Agriculture, Manufacturing/Production, Trade & Services, Household Finance and Others), By Company and By Geography, Forecast & Opportunities, 2024. https://www.techsciresearch.com/report/india-microfinance-market/3210.html
The New Indian Express (2018) Farm loan waiver has caused small spike in agri npas: Sbi. 16 September 2018. http://www.newindianexpress.com/states/karnataka/2018/sep/16/farm-loan-waiver-has-caused-small-spike-in-agri-npas-sbi-1872624.html
Tiwary D (2017) In 80% farmer-suicides due to debt, loans from banks, not moneylenders. Indian Express, 7 January 2017. https://indianexpress.com/article/india/in-80-farmer-suicides-due-to-debt-loans-from-banks-not-moneylenders-4462930/
TOI (2018) Education sector NPAs hit 9% in FY18. The Times of India, 13 August 2018. http://timesofindia.indiatimes.com/articleshow/65373431.cms?utm_source=contentofinterest&utm_medium=text&utm_campaign=cppst
Vats RP (2018) Insolvency professionals under the insolvency and bankruptcy code, 2016. online. http://www.mondaq.com/india/x/728508/Insolvency+Bankruptcy/Insolvency+Professionals+Under+The+Insolvency+And+Bankruptcy+Code+2016
World Bank (2014) Working group for the treatment of the insolvency of natural persons. World Bank Group. http://documents.worldbank.org/curated/en/120771468153857674/World-Working-group-for-the-treatment-of-the-insolvency-of-natural-persons
World Bank (2017) Report on the treatment of MSME insolvency. World Bank Group. http://documents.worldbank.org/curated/en/973331494264489956/Report-on-the-treatment-of-MSME-insolvency

Value Destruction and Wealth Transfer Under the Insolvency and Bankruptcy Code, 2016

Pratik Datta

1 Introduction

India experienced a major structural change with the enactment of the Insolvency and Bankruptcy Code, 2016 (IBC). Before this, it did not have any comprehensive modern statute on corporate insolvency.[1] Intermittent attempts were made at various points of time to develop a modern insolvency law framework.[2] In 2014, the Finance Minister made a budget announcement about the government's plan to usher in an entrepreneur-friendly legal bankruptcy framework.[3] Later that year, the BLRC was set up.[4] In 2015, the BLRC submitted its report along with a draft legislation, which finally culminated into the enactment of the IBC. The law was operational from the start of 2017 with a new regulator, the Insolvency and Bankruptcy Board of India (IBBI), and cases being heard at the National Companies Law Tribunal (NCLT) and National Companies Law Appellate Tribunal (NCLAT).

[1] Report of the Joint Committee on the Insolvency and Bankruptcy Code, 2015, Lok Sabha (2016)[6].
[2] See, e.g. Sengupta et al. (2016)[5–10], van Zwieten (2015)[2–5].
[3] The quote from the FM's budget speech is: "Entrepreneur friendly legal bankruptcy framework will also be developed for SMEs to enable easy exit" (Finance Minister 2014).
[4] Bankruptcy Law Reforms Committee (2015)[9].

This chapter draws from the author's working paper—*Datta (2018), Value destruction and wealth transfer under the Insolvency and Bankruptcy Code, 2016. Working paper No.247, NIPFP Working paper series. National Institute of Public Finance and Policy, New Delhi.*—and content has been re-used with permission. The opinions expressed in this chapter are the author's own and not that of his employer. This chapter is based on the position of law as on December 27, 2018.

P. Datta (✉)
Advocate, New Delhi, India
e-mail: prat.nujs@gmail.com

© The Author(s), under exclusive license to Springer Nature Singapore Pte Ltd. 2022
S. Thomas (ed.), *Insolvency and Bankruptcy Reforms in India*,
India Studies in Business and Economics,
https://doi.org/10.1007/978-981-16-0854-4_8

Since the enactment of the IBC, India's ranking under the Insolvency head in the World Bank Group's Doing Business report has sharply risen from 136 to 103.[5] India was also awarded the GRR Award for the Most Improved Jurisdiction in restructuring and insolvency regime, surpassing even European Union and Switzerland.[6] At the same time, IBC has also thrown up new challenges.

Two such challenges are particularly important. First, there are concerns that companies entering formal insolvency under the IBC often experience avoidable value destruction. For instance, a legitimate apprehension arises if insolvent companies with viable businesses on entry into formal insolvency are inadvertently pushed into liquidation instead of being successfully restructured or its business being sold as a going concern. In the context of IBC, this apprehension has been triggered due to the fact that more companies are being liquidated than successfully salvaged under the IBC. Since the enactment of IBC, out of the 1198 cases admitted to insolvency resolution process till September 30, 2018, 118 were closed on appeal or review, 52 yielded resolution, while 212 resulted in liquidation.[7] In other words, till end of September 2018, only 20% of the cases were successfully resolved, while 80% ended up in liquidation. In one particular case, allegations were made that a viable company was pushed into liquidation.[8] Value destruction could also happen if entry into formal insolvency makes it more difficult to preserve the value of an insolvent company. For instance, a company on admission into insolvency resolution process under IBC reported severe strains on its working capital and decline in level of operations, impacting the carrying value of its assets.[9] Such cases have raised apprehensions about the potential risks of value destruction under the IBC.

Second, there are wide-ranging concerns that the IBC unjustly discriminates against operational and trade creditors. The constitutionality of the IBC is currently facing legal challenges primarily on this ground.[10] The issue had gained prominence during insolvency of major real estate companies, where home buyers being

[5] Financial Stability Report, Reserve Bank of India (2017)[53].

[6] IBBI (2018a).

[7] IBBI September Newsletter (2018).

[8] Arun Kumar Jagatramka, the Chairman and Managing Director of Gujarat NRE Coke Ltd. criticised the bankers after NCLT ordered liquidation of his company. The insolvency proceeding was initiated by the company itself under Sect. 10(1) of the Code. The workers proposed a resolution plan for a going concern sale of the company. The resolution plan could not be considered by the Committee of Creditors because the statutory time limit for approving the resolution plan was exceeded. Consequently, the company had to be liquidated by the NCLT as per the Code. Gopakumar (2018) See also Re: M/s. Gujarat NRE Coke Ltd., NCLT (2018).

[9] Videocon Industries Limited (2018).

[10] Multiple writ petitions challenging the constitutionality of this feature of the statute have appeared before the Supreme Court of India. Swiss Ribbons Pvt. Ltd. versus Union of India, SC (2018), Aryan (2018) An earlier writ petition on the same ground was dismissed by the Calcutta High Court observing that the Bankruptcy Law Reforms Committee (BLRC) had given a clear rationale for differentiating between financial and operational creditors (Akshay Jhunjhunwala versus Union of India, Calcutta High Court 2018).

unsecured creditors were left without any effective remedy.[11] Subsequently, some aggrieved home buyers filed a public interest litigation in the Supreme Court challenging the constitutionality of the preference given to financial creditors under the IBC.[12] Similar concerns have arisen in the context of dissenting financial creditors too. But the decision of NCLAT in Central Bank of India versus Resolution Professional of Sirpur Paper Mills Ltd. and Ors., NCLAT (2018)[9] and a subsequent amendment to the regulations on 5 October 2018 partially addressed the problem.[13] These cases essentially highlight the risks of wealth transfer across classes of claimants under the IBC.

This article aims to apply theoretical concepts from the law and economics literature on insolvency to identify the sources of these two contemporary challenges—the *value destruction* problem and the *wealth transfer* problem. It then applies these theoretical concepts to analyse the IBC to precisely identify the unique legislative features which are responsible for these two problems in the Indian context.

This article is organised as follows: Sect. 2 provides an overview of the relevant features of the legislative scheme of the IBC. Section 3 deals with the value destruction problem. Section 4 deals with the wealth transfer problem. Finally, Sect. 4.6 summarises the main learnings from the previous two sections and concludes.

2 An Overview of IBC

The IBC classifies creditors into financial or operational, based on the nature of debt extended. 'Financial debt' is broadly defined to include credit extended against consideration for the time value of money including against payment of interest.[14] On the other hand, 'operational debt' has been defined as a claim in respect of

[11] In one such case, the NCLT held that home buyers were neither financial creditors nor operational creditors. This caused much confusion about the status of home buyers under the Code. Rubina Chandha versus AMR Infrastucture, NCLAT (2017) The ILC has now suggested that home buyers should be treated as 'financial creditors' owing to the unique nature of financing of real estate projects and the treatment of home buyers by the Supreme Court of India. Insolvency Law Committee Report (2018)[1. 1–1. 9].

[12] IDBI Bank initiated insolvency proceedings against Jaypee Infratech Limited ('Jaypee'), a real estate company. The NCLT issued an insolvency commencement order and imposed a moratorium on any individual recovery action against the company. This order left the home buyers of Jaypee without any remedy, especially since during the moratorium they could no more utilise the remedies under the Consumer Protection Act, 1986. In this backdrop, the home buyers filed a public interest litigation before the Supreme Court arguing that the differential treatment between secured financial creditors and unsecured home buyers under the Code is violative of Article 14 of the Constitution of India that guarantees equality before law as a fundamental right. Chitra Sharma versus Union of India, SC (2017).

[13] The regulations which were one of the sources of the wealth transfer problem were deleted by IBBI on 5 October 2018. IBBI (2018b).

[14] IBC (2016)[5(8)].

provision of goods or services including employment and tax dues.[15] The IBBI has subsequently created another third category of creditors—'other creditors'—who are neither financial nor operational creditors.[16] If a corporate debtor defaults on payment to any creditor, financial, operational or other creditor, the IBC allows the corporate debtor itself or any of its financial or operational creditors to make an application before the NCLT to trigger the insolvency resolution process.[17] The application (except where it is filed by an operational creditor) must also propose an insolvency professional to act as the interim resolution professional.[18]

Within 180 days from the date of commencement of the insolvency resolution process, the CoC may by 66% vote by value approve a resolution plan proposed by a resolution applicant (IBC (2016)[30(4)]).[19] The resolution plan could propose either a going concern sale or a restructuring (IBBI 2016[37]).[20] Once a resolution plan is approved by the super-majority of the CoC, the resolution applicant must submit the plan to the NCLT for its approval.[21] The NCLT must approve the resolution plan if it is satisfied that the resolution plan meets the mandatory legal requirements (including the creditor protection rules) and that the plan was approved by a vote of not less than 66% of voting share of the financial creditors.[22] Once approved

---

[15] IBC (2016)[5(21)].

[16] The IBBI is the regulator under the Code. In the initial phase of implementation of the Code, insolvency of real estate companies raised unique concerns about status of home buyers as financial or operational creditors. In view of the definitional ambiguity, IBBI amended the regulations to create a third category of creditors to cover those who are neither financial nor operational creditors. IBBI (2016)[9A].

[17] The terms 'default' and 'debt' are broadly defined such that default to any creditor could be used to trigger insolvency resolution under the Code. But, 'other creditors' do not have a specific statutory right to trigger insolvency resolution (IBC (2016)[3(11), 3(12), 7, 8, 9, 10)]).

[18] IBC (2016)[7(3)(b)].

[19] The CoC can extend the 180 days deadline by maximum of another 90 days at most. See also IBC (2016)[12(1)]. In practice, these time limits have been breached in multiple cases. Marwah and Sharma (2018) During this time, the resolution professional can raise interim finance subject to approval of the Committee of Creditors. Such interim finances are treated as part of the 'insolvency resolution process costs' and enjoy super-priority in the waterfall. See also IBC (2016)[20(2)(c), 25(2)(c), 28(1)(a), 5(13) and 53(a)].

[20] The law is unclear about the distinction between restructuring and going concern sale to third party. For instance, it is not evident why the resolution professional is under a mandatory obligation to invite resolution plans from third parties in a restructuring, although it is normal to do so in a going concern sale to third parties through auctioning. Similarly, it is unclear from where will cash be available to pay the dissenting financial creditors as required under the law, if the resolution plan proposes a restructuring that leaves the business with the company. See also IBBI (2016)[36A, 38(1)(c)].

[21] IBC (2016)[30(6)].

[22] As per the text of the IBC, the obligation on NCLT to approve such a resolution plan is mandatory. The IBC does not give any discretion to NCLT to review whether the resolution plan is unfair to the dissenting minority creditors or non-voting operational creditors. This legal position is in conformity with the policy rationale adopted by the BLRC, which observed that in the past, laws in India have brought arms of the government (legislature, executive or judiciary) to decide on the future of a defaulting firm. The BLRC wanted to avoid any such discretion being given to any organ of the state including the judiciary. It was of the view that the appropriate disposition of a defaulting firm

by NCLT, the resolution plan becomes binding on all stakeholders including the corporate debtor, its employees, members, creditors and guarantors.[23] If the NCLT rejects the resolution plan for non-compliance with mandatory legal requirements or if the resolution plan is not submitted before the NCLT within the statutory time limit, the NCLT is required to pass an order initiating the liquidation of the corporate debtor.[24]

2.1 Research Questions

The BLRC had envisaged that the assessment of viability of an insolvent firm should ideally be the outcome of collective negotiation among the claimants of the firm.[25] It acknowledged that such collective negotiations could lead to conflicts, causing destruction of value of the insolvent firm.[26] To avoid such value destruction, the BLRC tried to design a formal insolvency resolution process that would appropriately channel such conflicts to achieve a solution.[27] In designing this formal insolvency resolution process within the IBC, BLRC entrusted the power of viability assessment of an insolvent firm to a super-majority of its financial creditors instead of leaving it for collective negotiation among the different classes of claimants of the insolvent firm.[28] This chapter seeks to analyse whether entrusting financial creditors with the power to assess the viability of insolvent firms could potentially cause *value destruction*.

---

is a business decision, and only the creditors should make it (Bankruptcy Law Reforms Committee 2015[2]). The IBBI started emphasising the need for 'fairness and equity' and has observed that the CoC must not discriminate among creditors. It is unclear if the IBBI envisages a role for NCLT in ensuring such 'fairness and equity' while approving the resolution plan (IBBI June Newsletter 2018). Recently, the NCLAT held that 'any resolution plan if shown to be discriminatory against one or other financial creditor or the operational creditor, such plan can be held to be against the provision of the I&B Code'. The implication of this decision on 'out-of-money' creditors is unclear (Binani Industries Ltd. versus Bank of Baroda, NCLAT 2018[48]).

[23] IBC (2016)[31(1)].

[24] IBC (2016)[33(1)].

[25] Bankruptcy Law Reforms Committee (2015)[3. 2. 1].

[26] Bankruptcy Law Reforms Committee (2015)[3. 2. 2].

[27] Bankruptcy Law Reforms Committee (2015)[3. 2. 3].

[28] The BLRC deliberated on who should be on the creditors' committee, given the power of the creditors' committee to ultimately keep the entity as a going concern or liquidate it. The Committee reasoned that members of the creditors' committee should have the capability to assess viability, as well as the willingness to modify terms of existing liabilities in negotiations. Typically, operational creditors are neither able to decide on matters regarding the insolvency of the entity, nor willing to take the risk of postponing payments for better future prospects for the entity. Therefore, the Committee concluded that, for the process to be rapid and efficient, the law should provide that the creditors' committee should be restricted to only the financial creditors (Bankruptcy Law Reforms Committee 2015[5. 3. 1. 4]).

The BLRC was of the view that to preserve the organisational capital of insolvent firms, the insolvency process should facilitate creation of a platform for negotiation between creditors and external financiers.[29] Consequently, the regulations under IBC seek to facilitate going concern sale of the business of the corporate debtor at 'fair value' during the insolvency resolution process and not merely recover break-up 'liquidation value'.[30] Yet, the creditor protection rules under the IBC use the break-up 'liquidation value' as the benchmark for calculating the minimum amount to be paid to the operational creditors and dissenting financial creditors under a resolution plan (IBC (2016)[30(2)(b)]), IBBI (2016)[38(1)(b), 38(1)(c)]).[31] This chapter seeks to analyse the potential for abuse of these different valuation benchmarks to cause *wealth transfer* from one class of claimants to another in the absence of judicial supervision to ensure fairness of the resolution plan.

3 Value Destruction Problem

3.1 Economic Distress, Financial Distress

Making the appropriate decision about the future of a distressed company essentially hinges on correctly identifying whether the company is *economically distressed* or *financially distressed*.[32] If the present value of the company is less than the total value of the assets of the company were they to be broken up from the business and sold separately (break-up 'liquidation value'), such a company is said to be in *economic distress*.[33] Since the assets of an *economically distressed* company are worth more piecemeal than kept together in the company's business, the claimants are better off by liquidating such a company and selling its assets on a piecemeal basis. In contrast, if the company is not *economically distressed* but is unable to service its debts, such a company is said to be in *financially distress*. In terms of valuation, when the total value of debt of a company exceeds its present value, it is said to be *financially distressed*. The assets of such a company are more valuable if kept together as a functioning unit than they would be if sold off piecemeal. In other words, since a merely *financially distressed* company has *going concern surplus*, it should not be liquidated except through a process which preserves such surplus.[34]

---

[29] Bankruptcy Law Reforms Committee (2015)[3. 2. 3].

[30] This is why the resolution professional is required to appoint registered valuers to determine the 'fair value' and accordingly inform the CoC to aid in the bidding process (IBBI 2016[27, 35]).

[31] Please note that the valuation benchmark for dissenting financial creditors was applicable till 5 October 2018. IBBI has amended its regulations to remove this requirement (IBBI 2018b[6]).

[32] Baird (1998)[580].

[33] Crystal and Mokal (2006)[Part II (Bases of Valuation)].

[34] The word 'liquidation' could either refer to a break-up sale or simply entry into a liquidation procedure. The latter is not mutually inconsistent with preservation of going concern value. Such liquidation could entail a sale on going concern basis, cash proceeds could be distributed among

3.2 *Basic Objectives of Insolvency Law*

A well-designed insolvency law should have at least two objectives. First, it must facilitate the correct determination of the type of distress a company is suffering from—economic distress or financial distress. Second, it must ensure that an economically distressed company is liquidated, whereas a financially distressed company is sustained either by restructuring it among existing claimants or by selling it to new investors. Only then can the insolvency law help achieve an *ex post* efficient outcome that maximises the total value of the proceeds—measured in money terms—for the claimants.[35] In contrast, an insolvency law that pushes merely financially distressed (but not economically distressed) companies into break-up liquidation is poorly designed because it destroys the organisational value of such companies.[36] Such potentially inefficient outcome of a poorly designed insolvency law is an instance of the value destruction problem.

3.3 *Sources of Value Destruction*

The value destruction problem could arise if the insolvency law entrusts the decision regarding the future of the insolvent company to a class of claimants whose payoffs are not affected by the outcome of the decision. This could be either because the claimants are fully protected in any case or because they are not entitled to anything in the first place.[37] For instance, if the decision as to the future of the company is left to the fully secured creditors of the insolvent company, they have no incentive to recover any amount in excess of the face value of their debt. This is because, even if they recover an amount higher than the face value of their debt, the maximum amount they are entitled to is still the face value of their debt only. Therefore, if this decision is left to such secured creditors, they have an incentive to destroy value of the financially distressed company by selling it at a value less than the going concern value or to push it into immediate liquidation to realise the liquidation value (Hart 1995[27]).[38]

claimants and then the shell could be liquidated. In this article, the term 'liquidation' has been used primarily to refer to break-up liquidation, not going concern sale, unless explicitly mentioned otherwise. Similarly the term 'liquidation value' refers to break-up 'liquidation value', unless explicitly mentioned otherwise (Crystal and Mokal 2006[Part II (Bases of Valuation).]).

[35] Aghion et al. (1994)[852].

[36] A living business with established customers, knowledgeable employees and so forth will bring a higher price as a unit than would the sale of each asset class separately, even assuming that those separate sales would obtain market value for each asset (Westbrook 2004[811]).

[37] Aghion et al. (1994)[859].

[38] There could be countervailing factors like reputational costs in repeat lending, which may incentivise secured creditors not to automatically liquidate firms on payment default. For instance, there is strong evidence that UK banks do not opt for automatic liquidation on violation of debt contract (Franks and Sussman 2005[91]).

Insolvency law could also cause value destruction by delaying initiation of restructuring. Restructuring is meant to realise the *enterprise value* of the company by reorganising its capital structure.[39] The earlier the restructuring is initiated, the higher are the chances of preservation of the value of the business and its (remaining) enterprise value. If debts are not restructured early on, the corporate debtor may enter formal insolvency procedure, which may further depress the enterprise value.[40] Moreover, the lower the enterprise value, the lesser is the residual value for the equity holders, and the higher is their propensity to pursue high risk investment strategies at the expense of the creditors—the asset substitution problem.[41] Therefore, delayed initiation of restructuring could also destroy enterprise value of a company which is already, or is likely to become, financially distressed.

3.4 Value Destruction Under IBC

Liquidation of merely financially distressed companies The IBC entrusts the decision regarding the future of the insolvent company to the CoC.[42] The CoC comprises only of financial creditors, who can approve a resolution plan by 66% vote by value.[43] Therefore, if 66% or more of the financial debt of a financially distressed company is held by fully secured creditors, the future of the company is essentially entrusted with such secured creditors. If these secured creditors are fully protected against the value of the security, they are likely to have little incentive to maximise the economic value of the business of the financially distressed company. Because even if the company is sustained and the going concern surplus is realised, the secured creditors are not entitled to any of that surplus. Instead, such secured creditors are likely to have a stronger incentive to immediately liquidate the financially distressed company and realise the liquidation value, thus destroying the going concern surplus of the company. The outcome will remain the same even if the secured creditors are partially protected by the value of their securities, as long as the liquidation value is higher than the present value of their expected returns from continuing the financial distressed company.

To illustrate, let's consider a hypothetical example. Suppose a company has two types of creditors—secured financial creditors and unsecured operational trade creditors.[44] It owes \$100 to its secured financial creditors, \$30 to its unsecured operational trade creditors and the liquidation value of the company is \$90. If the company is continued as a going concern for next 6 months, there is a 0. 5

[39] See Crystal and Mokal (2006)[Part II (Bases of Valuation)].

[40] Eidenmuller and van Zwieten (2015)[655].

[41] Jensen and Meckling (1976)[334]. See also Eidenmuller and van Zwieten (2015)[655].

[42] IBC (2016)[30(4)].

[43] IBC (2016)[21(2)].

[44] In this example, I am assuming that the secured creditors are a little under-secured. If the secured creditors are fully or over secured, the effect described in this example will be even more profound.

probability that it will be worth $200 and a 0.5 probability that it will be worth $40. In other words, if the company is continued for the next 6 months, the expected going concern value of the company would be $ (0.5). (200) + (0.5). (40) = $120.[45] Since the present value ($120) is higher than the liquidation value ($90), the company is not economically distressed. It is only in financial distress because the total debt of the company ($130) exceeds its present value ($120). Therefore, the value-maximising choice would be to keep the company going, so that both the financial and operational creditors can recover a total of $120 as against only $90 if the company is liquidated. If things go well and after 6 months the company is actually worth $200, the secured financial creditors will still get only $100, the value of debt owed to them. On the other hand, if things go badly and after 6 months the company is actually worth $40, they will get the entire $40. Therefore, the expected return for secured financial creditors would be $ (0.5). (100) + (0.5). (40) = $70—far lesser than the immediate liquidation value ($90). Figure 1 summarises the returns to the creditors in the different states.

Evidently, if the future of the company is to be decided by the secured financial creditors only, they would always prefer to immediately liquidate the company for $90 even though the value-maximising decision would be to continue it.[46] Therefore, in the factual matrix described above, the IBC would fail to save a financially distressed (but not economically distressed) company from being liquidated, causing value destruction.[47]

This problem could possibly be avoided if the operational creditors and shareholders could pay off the majority secured financial creditors in exchange for the right to decide the future of the company—whether to liquidate or not.[48] Under IBC, only financial creditors could be on the CoC. Therefore, operational creditors and shareholders could possibly influence the decision as to the future of the company by entering into an agreement with majority secured financial creditors requiring the latter to vote in a certain way on the CoC. In practice, such 'side agreements' may be difficult to enter into since coordinating with a vast group of heterogenous stakeholders—financial creditors, operational creditors and shareholders—could be extremely costly. Even if such agreements are practically feasible, enforceability of such inter-creditor agreements is yet to be tested before the NCLT and NCLAT.[49]

---

[45] For convenience, we are assuming that the discount rate is 0. Therefore, the expected going concern value is also the present value of the company.

[46] This is based on the assumption that there are no countervailing factors like reputation in repeat or relationship lending (Franks and Sussman 2005[91]). This example is based on an example used by Aghion, Hart and Moore (Aghion et al. 1994[859]).

[47] The above example relates to secured creditors who are a little under-secured. If they were fully secured, the effect would be even more profound.

[48] Aghion, Hart and Moore referred to this arrangement a 'bribe' from junior creditors and shareholders to the senior creditors (Aghion et al. 1994[860]).

[49] Mr. Ajay Agarwal versus M/s. Ashok Magnetics Ltd. and Anr., NCLT (2018)[17]. The NCLT in a recent decision has called for the development of a 'Standard Operating Procedure' for CoCs to determine the suitability and viability of resolution plans. In this backdrop, it is unclear to what

Delayed restructuring Once the insolvency resolution process under the IBC is triggered, the resolution professional with the approval of the CoC can engage in debt restructuring.[50] The main advantage of restructuring within the framework of the IBC is that the law empowers the majority financial creditors (with at least 66% vote by value) to impose a restructuring plan on operational creditors as well as dissenting financial creditors—the 'cramdown' provision (IBC (2016)[28(1)(c), 30(4)]).[51] Such a potent cramdown option for restructuring is unavailable outside the IBC.[52]

The insolvency resolution process under the IBC can be triggered only post-insolvency.[53] Therefore, restructuring under the IBC is not possible pre-insolvency, when the corporate debtor is reasonably likely to default on its debt obligations and become cash flow insolvent in the foreseeable future.[54] Consequently, any attempt to restructure pre-insolvency will have to be outside the scope of the IBC, without the benefit of the cramdown provision.

Pre-insolvency debt restructuring could then potentially be executed through a scheme of arrangement under *CA, 2013*.[55] Unlike the IBC, the cramdown provision in CA, 2013 is much less potent since it does not allow cross-class cramdown.[56] CA, 2013 gives extensive discretion to the NCLT to modify the scheme.[57] There are no specific timelines for approving a scheme. Further, unlike Sect. 14 of IBC, the CA, 2013 does not provide for an automatic statutory moratorium.[58] There are various additional procedural hurdles to restructuring through

---

extent 'side agreements' between financial creditors and other claimants intended to influence the outcome of the decision of a CoC would be enforceable under Indian laws.

[50] IBC (2016)[28(1)(c)], IBBI (2016)[37(f), 37(g) and 37(i)].

[51] See also IBBI (2016)[37(f), 37(g), 37(i)].

[52] As discussed in the next paragraph, a scheme of arrangement provides a less potent cramdown option (Companies Act (2013)[230]). A cramdown provision was also available under the Guidelines on Joint Lenders' Forum (JLF) and Corrective Action Plan (CAP) issued by RBI on 26 February 2014, and subsequently amended on 5 May 2017. This framework was repealed by RBI on 12 February 2018. Under the revised framework, there is no cramdown provision.

[53] Insolvency resolution process can be triggered only after there has been a payment default by the corporate debtor. This is the case even when the corporate debtor itself is the applicant (IBC (2016)[7, 9, 10]).

[54] In UK, schemes are often used instead of administration for debt restructuring precisely because the former provides a cramdown option pre-insolvency while the latter provides a cramdown option but only post-insolvency (Payne 2014[295]).

[55] Companies Act (2013)[230].

[56] Varottil (2017)[8].

[57] Companies Act (2013)[230(7)].

[58] Under Sect. 391(6) of Companies Act (1956), a limited moratorium was available whereby the court reviewing a scheme was entitled to 'stay the commencement or continuation of any suit or proceeding against the company' pending disposal of the scheme application. This provision is absent in Companies Act (2013). It is not entirely clear whether the absence of the moratorium provision was a deliberate choice or an inadvertent omission. In any event, this is likely to adversely affect the choice of scheme by parties to effect a debt restructuring. Varottil (2017)[24]).

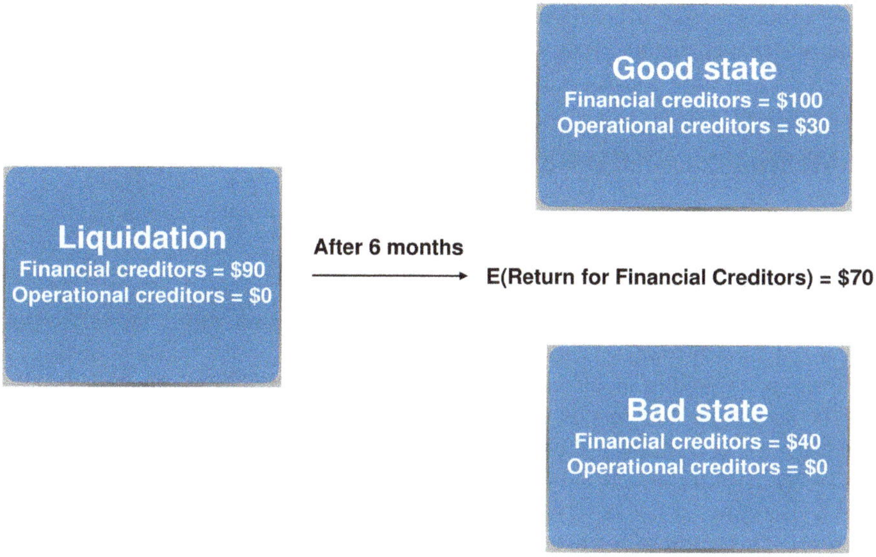

Fig. 1 Returns to creditors in different states

a scheme.[59] All these factors make debt restructuring through CA, 2013 far more difficult than through the IBC.[60]
The only other alternative to executing a pre-insolvency restructuring plan would be through private contracting. This would require consent of all the claimants—financial creditors, operational creditors and shareholders—making it extremely difficult to negotiate in practice.[61]

Overall, under the current Indian legal framework, pre-insolvency restructuring is far more difficult to execute than post-insolvency restructuring. This disparity stems from the application of the IBC to only post-insolvency restructuring. To this limited extent, by delaying restructuring to post-insolvency phase, the IBC makes it difficult

[59] For instance, any creditor with not less than 5% of the total outstanding debt has a legal right to raise an objection to the restructuring plan (in Companies Act (2013)[230(4)]).

[60] To date, schemes under Companies Act (2013) have been used sparingly in India for debt restructuring, although they have been widely used for corporate restructurings like amalgamations, mergers and demergers. Given the application of the Insolvency and Bankruptcy Code, 2016 to post-insolvency restructuring only, it remains to be seen if scheme of arrangement under Companies Act (2013) could become a viable device for pre-insolvency restructuring (Varottil 2017). One recent example where the scheme route is being used for debt restructuring is the IL&FS case (Doshi 2018).

[61] If all creditors had to agree to the restructuring that would have put significant hold-up rights into the hands of minority creditors, potentially allowing even very small creditors to derail the restructuring while they would have bargained for additional benefits or advantages. The cramdown provision helps overcome this problem (Payne 2014[284]). See also Eidenmuller and van Zwieten (2015)[632].

to preserve the value of a business which is on the verge of financial distress and enhances the risk of value destruction.[62]

4 Wealth Transfer Problem

4.1 Going Concern Sale, Restructuring

A financially distressed company has going concern surplus, which should be preserved.[63] One way of preserving the going concern surplus of a financially distressed company is by selling its business at the enterprise value.[64] Such enterprise value may be far greater than market value of asset sale (and, therefore, liquidation value) because a living business has organisational value which is lost if its assets are sold separately, even if they could be sold at market value.[65]

A going concern sale of a financially distressed company at enterprise value may not always be possible because of myriad reasons. First, the company could be in financial distress because of industry-wide factors. Its competitors in that industry may not be in a position to offer the enterprise value to expand their businesses.[66] Second, industry-wide factors may push other companies into financial distress, creating an oversupply of similar businesses in the market. This may create the risk of auctions at 'fire sale' prices, which may be equivalent to the liquidation value.[67] Third, auctions work well when there is adequate financing and competition among bidders. Countries with less developed capital markets naturally will be at a disadvantage. Even in countries with well-developed capital markets, if a very large company's business is put up for auctioning, it will be difficult to raise financing. The only solution is to raise money from some big institutional investors, who will be prepared to buy the business only at a discount because of the substantial risk they will be bearing.[68] Fourth, participating in an auction process involves transaction costs. But only the winner is able to recoup the costs. Consequently, even though there could be many potential bidders who could raise the financing, not all of them will participate. This may cause a lack of competition problem.[69]

Because of the above-mentioned reasons, sale of the financially distressed company as a going concern to new investors may not raise the enterprise value of the

62 Eidenmuller and van Zwieten (2015)[631].

63 Eidenmuller and van Zwieten (2015)[655].

64 Crystal and Mokal (2006)[Part II (Bases of Valuation)].

65 As discussed earlier, a living business with established customers, knowledgeable employees and so forth will bring a higher price as a unit (Westbrook 2004[811]).

66 Crystal and Mokal (2006)[Part II (Bases of Valuation)].

67 Crystal and Mokal (2006)[Part II (Bases of Valuation)]. See also Eidenmuller and van Zwieten (2015)[636].

68 Aghion et al. (1992)[527].

69 Aghion et al. (1992)[527].

company. In such an event, instead of selling the company to new investors, the claimants of the financially distressed company would be better of by 'selling' the company to some or all of the existing claimants themselves.[70] This 'hypothetical sale' is commonly referred to as restructuring or reorganisation.[71]

Restructuring could be implemented voluntarily if all the claimants could come to an agreement. This is difficult because of two reasons. First, when there is a dispersed set of claimants, the coordination cost is too high.[72] Moreover, a prolonged negotiation could be disadvantageous and impractical if the debtor is facing an acute liquidity crisis.[73] Second, there is a possibility that one or more claimants may hold-up the process to try and get a better deal for themselves. For instance, one or more claimants may withhold consent, file individual recovery action or petition for winding up of the company.[74] The situation is worse if the claimant holding-up restructuring efforts is an out-of-the-money claimant, who would not receive any payment or other consideration if the corporate debtor is liquidated instead.[75] State supplied insolvency laws are necessary to overcome these two specific problems—*coordination costs* and *hold-up costs*.

Insolvency law could facilitate restructuring by allowing a majority of claimants to impose a restructuring plan on a dissenting minority. This could be structured in different ways. For instance, insolvency law could allow a restructuring plan to be imposed only on dissenting claimants of a particular class if the majority of that class consents. It could also allow the restructuring plan to be imposed on whole classes of dissenting claimants—the cross-class cramdown provision (Payne 2018).[76] Such provisions help reduce the coordination and hold-up problems that make contractual restructuring difficult to achieve.

4.2 Sources of Wealth Transfer

When insolvency law provides cramdown powers to facilitate restructuring, it raises the possibility of abuse, and, in particular, of wealth transfer from one class of claimants to another.[77] The wealth transfer problem could arise when insolvency law allows majority claimants to gain control over the restructuring of the corporate

---

70 Crystal and Mokal (2006)[Part V (A case study: My Travel Group Plc)].

71 Baird (1986)[127].

72 Crystal and Mokal (2006)[Part II (Bases of Valuation)].

73 Payne (2018).

74 Payne (2018)[127]. This problem has also been referred to as the 'motivation cost'. Crystal and Mokal (2006)[Part II (Bases of Valuation)].

75 This is the reason why English courts discount dissent of those without any economic interest in the corporate debtor. Payne (2018)[138–139].

76 British policymakers are currently considering introduction of such a cramdown provision for restructuring (The Insolvency Service 2016[9. 19–9. 21]).

77 Payne (2018)[134].

debtor.[78] The majority claimants being in control of the process may be able to advantage or disadvantage different groups of beneficiaries by structuring of the securities, contract rights or other property received by each.[79] They could even abuse this control to derive disproportionate private benefits by transferring wealth away from the dissenting minority claimants through the restructuring plan.[80] Adequate safeguards are therefore necessary to protect the interests of the dissenting claimants.[81]

Insolvency laws across jurisdictions usually provide this safeguard to dissenting minority claimants through judicial supervision.[82] The main objective of such judicial supervision is to ensure that a restructuring plan does not make the dissenting creditors worse off than what they would have been in the event of liquidation of the corporate debtor.[83] The starting point for the court is to consider the counterfactual, namely, what each creditor would receive if no restructuring could be agreed upon. In that case, the company could either be liquidated on break-up basis or its business sold as a going concern and the corporate structure could be liquidated.[84] Therefore, the court could use either the break-up 'liquidation value' or the going concern 'liquidation value' as the benchmark for determining how much should be paid to the dissenting creditors. If the court uses the break-up 'liquidation value', it would obviously provide lesser protection to the dissenting creditors of a merely financially distressed company, causing wealth transfer from them.[85] It has therefore been suggested that for corporate debtors in mere financial distress, a going concern

[78] Control is the function of insolvency law. It concerns the management of the corporate debtor's assets during the recovery process after default (Westbrook 2004[800]).

[79] Westbrook (2004)[800].

[80] There are other substantial private benefits of controlling corporate decision-making. For example, in exchange for 'yes' votes, majority creditors may receive side benefits from managers or major shareholders, such as early repayment, security interest, guarantee or other business opportunities (Lee 2007[665–666]).

[81] British policymakers proposing a cramdown provision have discussed potential safeguards for creditors in the form of judicial supervision (The Insolvency Service 2016[paragraphs 9. 24–9. 28]). Even the Singaporean Insolvency Law Review Committee while recommending inclusion of a cramdown provision in the CA, 1967, was conscious of this issue. Accordingly, it recommended that 'the court should require a high threshold of proof that the dissenting class is not going to be prejudiced by the cramdown' (Insolvency Law Review Committee Singapore 2013[156]).

[82] In the US, Chap. 11 of the Bankruptcy Code relies heavily on the role of the court. This is also the policy in UK and Singapore. The 2016 EU draft Directive regarding restructuring processes and the EU Recommendation on which it is based both aim to minimise court involvement, although not remove it completely. Admittedly, judicial supervision has its disadvantages, but still it is considered better than leaving this issue to the sole discretion of the insolvency professional appointed by the senior lenders (Payne 2018[125,133–134]). For the policy in Singapore, (Insolvency Law Review Committee Singapore 2013[155–156]).

[83] For example, see European Commission (2016)[31].

[84] Since restructuring is a hypothetical sale, no actual sale of the business to third party takes place. The liquidation value on going concern basis is therefore used only for valuation purposes in this context (Clark 1981[1252]).

[85] Restructuring is a 'hypothetical sale' to preserve the going concern value or enterprise value of a financially distressed company and not merely recover the break-up 'liquidation value' (Crystal and Mokal 2006[Part II (Bases of Valuation)]).

'liquidation value' is a more appropriate benchmark than a break-up 'liquidation value'.[86]

Wealth transfer could also happen if valuation of the corporate debtor is left to one particular class of creditors. Senior creditors have an incentive to undervalue the company's business, while junior creditors have an incentive to overvalue it. For instance, in a restructuring involving conversion of debt to equity, if the value of the company is lesser than the value of the senior claims, then senior creditors could have the right to all the equity since the junior creditors would be left with no economic interest. In contrast, if the value of the company is more than the value of the senior claims, then the junior creditors will also have to be offered equity in the company. Therefore, if the issue of valuation is left to either the senior creditors or the junior creditors, they could engage in strategic valuation, leading to wealth transfer from the other.[87] Even when this issue is subject to judicial supervision, courts need to be prepared to resist any attempt at strategic valuation and instead choose the valuation method best suited to curb the wealth transfer problem.[88]

Even in cases where the court feels it appropriate to use the going concern 'liquidation value', another critical question of valuation arises, namely, how to determine the going concern value. Restructuring being a hypothetical sale to the claimants themselves, a proper market test may not be possible.[89] Therefore, it would be necessary to determine the going concern value based on valuation opinions from expert valuers. This process being subjective may generate disputes and litigation, making the valuation exercise time-consuming and messy.[90]These valuation problems have to be resolved by courts while protecting minority claimants against wealth transfer in a restructuring.

4.3 Wealth Transfer Under IBC

Inadequate protection from abusive cramdown The IBC empowers majority financial creditors with 66% vote by value in the CoC to impose a resolution plan on the dissenting minority financial creditors as well as the non-voting operational creditors.[91] Such a resolution plan could *inter alia* modify any security interest, extend the maturity date, change interest rate or other terms of a debt due from the corporate debtor.[92] In view of this broad cramdown power given to the majority financial creditors, the IBC provides three safeguards to protect the dissenting minority financial creditors as well as the non-voting operational cred-

86 Payne (2018)[139].

87 Crystal and Mokal (2006)[Part III (Sources of Valuation Uncertainty)].

88 Payne (2018)[139].

89 Restructuring is more likely when going concern sale may not fetch the enterprise value.

90 Payne (2018)[140].

91 IBC (2016)[30(4), 31(1)].

92 IBBI (2016)[37(1)].

itors. First, the resolution plan must identify specific sources of funds to pay the 'liquidation value' due to dissenting financial creditors.[93] Second, the resolution plan must provide for repayment of the debts of operational creditors which shall not be less than the amount to be paid to the operational creditors in the event of liquidation.[94] Third, the 'fair value' and 'liquidation value' of the insolvent business calculated by the registered valuers appointed by the resolution professional are expected to mitigate problems of strategic valuation.[95]

It is important to note here that there is no explicit provision in the IBC that empowers NCLT to review the fairness of the resolution plan,[96] as long as such plan provides the minimum break-up 'liquidation value' to the dissenting financial creditors and the operational creditors.[97] The ILC during its recent review of the IBC recorded stakeholders' concerns that the 'liquidation value' guaranteed to the operational creditors may be negligible as they fall under the residual category in the statutory waterfall.[98] The ILC deliberated on whether instead of 'liquidation value', a different benchmark like 'fair value', 'resolution value' or 'bid value' should be used as the floor to determine the value to be given to the operational creditors. None of them were deemed suitable.[99] Instead, the ILC went on to observe that many operational creditors get payments above the 'liquidation value' in the resolution plan.[100] Accordingly, the ILC concluded that the interests of operational creditors must be protected, not by tinkering with what minimum must be guaranteed to them statutorily, but by improving the quality

---

[93] Please note this was the legal position before October 5, 2018 (IBBI 2016[38(1)(c)]). This provision was struck down by NCLAT on 12 September 2018 for being inconsistent with the IBC (Central Bank of India versus Resolution Professional of Sirpur Paper Mills Ltd. and Ors., NCLAT 2018). Subsequently, on 5 October 2018, IBBI amended these regulations and deleted Regulations 38(1)(b) and (c) (IBBI 2018b[6]).

[94] IBC (2016)[30(2)(b)].

[95] IBBI (2016)[2(1)(hb), 2(1)(k), 35(1)(a)].

[96] The 'fairness' of a scheme is a relevant consideration for English courts while exercising their discretion to grant sanction (CA 2006[899(1)]). See also Payne (2018)[138].

[97] This protection to dissenting financial creditors is not available since 5 October 2018. There are other specific criteria that a resolution plan must satisfy including that it must not contravene any of the provisions of the law. But the law does not explicitly require a resolution plan to be 'fair' (IBC (2016)[30(2), 31(1)]). The NCLAT has recently held that 'any resolution plan if shown to be discriminatory against one or other financial creditor or the operational creditor, such plan can be held to be against the provision of the IBC'. The implication of this principle in terms of a precise valuation benchmark is not clear (Binani Industries Ltd. versus Bank of Baroda, NCLAT 2018[48]).

[98] Insolvency Law Committee Report (2018)[18. 2].

[99] Insolvency Law Committee Report (2018)[18. 3].

[100] According to data from Reserve Bank of India, over 4300 insolvency resolution applications were filed before NCLT till November 2017. Out of these cases, the ILC merely cited two instances—the *Synergies-Dooray* case and the *Hotel Gaudavan* case—to conclude that there was no empirical evidence to show that operational creditors do not receive a fair share in the resolution process. Moreover, IBBI currently does not publish data on resolution plans, and therefore it is difficult to expect private stakeholders to adduce empirical evidence on this issue (Insolvency Law Committee Report 2018[18. 4–18. 5]). See also Financial Stability Report, Reserve Bank of India (2017)[3. 27].

Table 1 Returns to holders of Debts 1 and 2

	Pre-restructuring (D1, D2)	Post-restructuring (D1, D2)
Good state	40, 80	40. 8, 79. 2
Bad state	40, 0	13. 6, 26. 4
Expected return	40, 40	27. 2, 52. 8

of resolution plans overall by efforts of regulatory bodies (like IBBI and IBA)—not the NCLT.[101] Evidently, Indian policymakers do not explicitly envisage any judicial supervision of the valuation method adopted in a resolution plan to prevent potential wealth transfer as long as the plan pays the break-up 'liquidation value' to non-voting operational and dissenting financial creditors.[102] This limitation in the creditor protection framework under the IBC creates opportunities for wealth transfer through resolution plans.

To illustrate, assume that a corporate debtor has entered insolvency resolution process under the IBC. It has a break-up 'liquidation value' of $10 and two types of financial debts—Debt 1 and Debt 2—having identical priority. The face value of Debt 1 is $40 (34% by value approx.) and its maturity is T_1; the face value of Debt 2 is $80 (66% by value approx.) and its maturity is T_2. Also, assume that the corporate debtor is likely to generate: (a) a sure cash flow of $40 at T_1 and (b) a cash flow of $80 or $0, each with a probability 0.5 in T_2. Consequently, Debt 1 will be fully repaid with certainty in T_1 (expected return = $40), while the expected return of Debt 2 in T_2 is $(80)(0.5)+(0)(0.5) = $40, which is lesser than its face value of $80. As a result, the holder of Debt 1 has no reason to consent to a restructuring, given the conflict of interest between Debt 1 and Debt 2.

Under the IBC, the holder of Debt 2 (being 66% by value) can adopt any resolution plan and impose it on the holder of Debt 1 as long as such resolution plan satisfies Sect. 30(2). Assume that the holder of Debt 2 adopts a resolution plan that extends the maturity of Debt 1 from T_1 to T_2. We know that in good state, the corporate debtor will generate $40+80 = $120; in bad state, it will generate $40+$0 = $40. Now since both Debt 1 and Debt 2 have same priority and maturity, holders of Debt 1 in good state will get $(120)(0.34) = $40.8 and in bad state will get $(40)(0.34) = $13.6; holders of Debt 2 in good state will get $(120)(0.66) = $79.2 and in bad state will get $(40)(0.66) = $26.4. Therefore, expected return of Debt 1 will now be $(0.5)(40.8)+(0.5)(13.6) = $27. 2, while expected return of Debt 2 will now be $(0.5)(79. 2)+(0.5)(26.4) = $52.8. Table 1 captures the returns for holders of Debt 1 and Debt 2, respectively, across good state and bad state both before and after restructuring.

---

[101] While IBBI is the insolvency regulator, IBA is a private association of Indian banks (Insolvency Law Committee Report 2018[18. 4]).

[102] Please note that the valuation benchmark applicable to dissenting financial creditors has been removed from the regulations since 5 October 2018.

It is evident that the restructuring will reduce the expected return of Debt 1 by \$40–\$27. 2 = \$12. 8 and increase the expected return of Debt 2 by \$52. 8–\$40 = \$12. 8. Essentially, the resolution plan in this case would lead to a wealth transfer of \$12. 8 from holders of Debt 1 to holders of Debt 2. Even after such wealth transfer, the holder of Debt 1 would get \$27. 2, which is more than the amount it would have got in a break-up liquidation, that is, \$(10)(0.34) = \$3. 4. Therefore, this resolution plan would satisfy the creditor protection rule requiring payment of break-up 'liquidation value' to dissenting financial creditors and still cause wealth transfer.[103] Moreover, since it would legitimately satisfy all the grounds in Sect. 30(2), the NCLT is not empowered to refuse approval under Sect. 31(1). This example illustrates why the IBC may fail to prevent wealth transfer from the dissenting financial creditors to the majority financial creditors in a restructuring using a break-up 'liquidation value' benchmark.[104]

Incorrect use of valuation benchmark The IBC overlooks a basic distinction between restructuring and going concern sales.[105] Restructuring, being a hypothetical sale of the corporate debtor's business to the claimants of the corporate debtor, some finite value has to be placed on the business of the corporate debtor. Otherwise, it would not be possible to calculate how much shares and other claims each claimant across each class of claimants of the corporate debtor should get in the newly restructured entity owning the business.[106] Therefore, restructuring requires a valuation benchmark, according to which the rights of each claimant in the restructured business has to be determined.[107] No such problem arises in a going concern sale for cash to a third party after proper marketing exercise. In such a sale transaction, after accounting for the expenses, the resolution professional can distribute the cash received to pay out the different claimants according to their priorities, until the money runs out.[108] Therefore, there is no need for a valuation benchmark to decide the rights of the claimants in a going concern sale. Yet, the IBC applies the same valuation benchmark to both restructuring and going concern sale.[109] Therefore, even in case of a true sale to a third party for cash at going concern value, the minimum amount to be paid out of that cash proceeds to the dissenting financial creditors and non-voting operational creditors

---

[103] It is important to note here that the NCLAT has recently struck down this creditor protection rule on the ground that it is violative of the IBC 2016. The NCLAT held that no discrimination can be made between the financial creditors in the resolution plan on the ground that one has dissented and voted against the resolution plan or the other has supported and voted in favour of the resolution plan (Central Bank of India versus Resolution Professional of Sirpur Paper Mills Ltd. and Ors., NCLAT 2018[3]).

[104] This was the legal position before 5 October 2018. Lee (2007).

[105] A resolution plan allows both possibilities (IBBI 2016[37]).

[106] Clark (1981)[1252].

[107] Clark (1981)[1252].

[108] Clark (1981)[1252–1253].

[109] Please note that the valuation benchmark applicable to dissenting financial creditors has been removed from regulations since 5 October 2018. For the legal position in this regard before 5 October 2018, see IBBI (2016)[38]. See also IBC (2016)[30(2)(b)].

under the resolution plan is to be determined according to the amount they would have received in a break-up liquidation. The remaining amount of sale proceeds could then be transferred to junior claimants.[110] Such resolution plans being in compliance with the IBC, the NCLT cannot refuse to sanction them to prevent the unfair wealth transfer from operational creditors to junior claimants.

To illustrate, assume that a corporate debtor has entered insolvency resolution process under the IBC. It has a going concern value of $130 and break-up 'liquidation value' of $110. The face value of debts owed to its financial creditors is $100 and to its operational creditors is $30. If the company is liquidated on break-up basis, then the financial creditors would get $100 and the operational creditors would get only $10. If the company is sold for cash to a third party at going concern value, then the financial creditors could get $100 and $30 will be left over. Applying the creditor protection rules under the IBC, the financial creditors could legitimately approve a resolution plan that provides only the break-up liquidation amount ($10) to the operational creditors and pays the remaining $20 to the shareholders, who feature below the operational creditors in the statutory waterfall.[111] This resolution plan would satisfy the creditor protection rule requiring payment of break-up 'liquidation value' to operational creditors and still cause wealth transfer from the operational creditors. As discussed earlier, the NCLT has no specific power to object to this resolution plan. This example illustrates why the IBC may fail to prevent wealth transfer from the operational creditors in a going concern sale because of the 'liquidation value' benchmark.

Evidently, this is an incorrect use of the valuation benchmark. Restructuring and going concern sales are two completely different concepts. For instance, Chap. 11 of the USBC (2012) deals with restructuring, which uses the valuation benchmark.[112]. On the other hand, Sect. 363 in Chap. 3 of the USBC (2012) deals with going concern sales, which does not use any such valuation benchmark. The IBC inadvertently fused both these features into the insolvency resolution process and consequently, applied the break-up 'liquidation value' benchmark to both.[113] As illustrated above, this creates unnecessary risks of wealth transfer in going concern sales under IBC.

---

110 This is antithetical to the *absolute priority principle*, which requires most senior creditors to be paid off in full before anything could be given to the next most senior creditors and so on down the ladder (Aghion et al. 1994[852–853]). Under the IBC 2016, the *absolute priority principle* is applicable to proceeds from the sale of liquidation assets. There is no specific statutory provision that extends this rule to the proceeds from a going concern sale through a resolution plan (IBC (2016)[30, 31, 53(3)(i)]). For instance, as reported by the Economic Times, when Tata Steel purchased insolvent Bhushan Steel, the banks took a 37% haircut and yet the shareholders retained the residual interests (Mehta 2018).

111 IBC (2016)[53(1)].

112 USBC (2012)[1129(a)(7)(A)(ii)].

113 Please note that the valuation benchmark applicable to dissenting financial creditors has been removed from regulations since 5 October 2018. For the legal position in this regard before 5 October 2018, see IBBI (2016)[38(1)(c)].

The NCLAT in Central Bank of India versus Resolution Professional of Sirpur Paper Mills Ltd. and Ors., NCLAT (2018) made an attempt to resolve this issue. In this case, the resolution plan for a going concern sale was approved by the NCLT. The plan provided the dissenting financial creditors an amount equal to that provided to the majority financial creditors. This particular aspect of the plan was challenged by one of the majority financial creditors before the NCLAT on the ground that it violates the creditor protection rule under Regulation 38(1)(c) of the IBBI (2016) since an amount more than 'liquidation value' was provided to the dissenting financial creditors under the resolution plan. The NCLAT rejected this argument and dismissed the appeal. It held that no discrimination can be made under IBC between the financial creditors in a resolution plan on the ground that one has dissented and voted against the resolution plan or the other has supported and voted in favour of the resolution plan.[114] The tribunal also struck down the above regulation as ultra vires the IBC.[115] Subsequently, on 5 October 2018, the IBBI deleted Regulations 38(1)(b) and (c) of the IBBI (2016).[116]

This decision of NCLAT and the subsequent amendment of regulations by IBBI do not resolve the problem of incorrect use of the valuation benchmark.

First, although Regulation 38(1)(b) (applicable to operational creditors) and Regulation 38(1)(c) (applicable to dissenting financial creditors) now stand deleted, the creditor protection rule applicable to operational creditors under Sect. 30(2)(b) of IBC is still in force. This statutory provision still uses the break-up 'liquidation value' benchmark for operational creditors.[117] Consequently, neither the decision of the NCLAT nor the amendment to the regulations may actually alter the valuation benchmark as far as operational creditors are concerned.

Second, although the NCLAT in Central Bank of India versus Resolution Professional of Sirpur Paper Mills Ltd. and Ors., NCLAT (2018) was dealing with a going concern sale, the decision did not differentiate between going concern sales and restructurings. Subsequently, the IBBI deleted the valuation benchmark altogether from its regulations. Therefore, there is at present no applicable valuation benchmark for dissenting financial creditors in restructurings during the corporate insolvency resolution process. This is problematic since restructurings require a valuation benchmark, according to which the rights of each claimant in the

114 Central Bank of India versus Resolution Professional of Sirpur Paper Mills Ltd. and Ors., NCLAT (2018)[3].

115 The NCLAT struck down both Regulation 38(1)(b) applicable to operational creditors and Regulation 38(1)(c) applicable to dissenting financial creditors. It is submitted that this was the result of a wrong interpretation by NCLAT. The regulations only provided for a minimum value to be paid to the operational and dissenting financial creditors. Consequently, any higher amount paid to such creditors was not violative of these regulations (Central Bank of India versus Resolution Professional of Sirpur Paper Mills Ltd. and Ors., NCLAT 2018[9]).

116 IBBI (2018b).

117 The section does not specifically mention that the valuation benchmark should be the break-up 'liquidation value'. The ILC in its report has used break-up 'liquidation value' as the minimum amount to be paid to operational creditors in a resolution plan (Insolvency Law Committee Report 2018[18. 2–18. 3]).

restructured business has to be determined. For instance, Sect. 1129(a)(7)(A)(ii) in Chap. 11 of the USBC (2012) uses liquidation value as the minimum benchmark for restructurings. The recent SCA (2017) in Singapore has also provided for valuation benchmark to ensure that a restructuring plan imposed on dissenting classes of creditors using the cramdown provision is fair and equitable.[118] Similarly, a critical issue in the ongoing insolvency law reforms in UK has been about the appropriate valuation benchmark to be used in restructurings.[119] Therefore, the present Indian position on this issue is at odds with the position adopted across advanced jurisdictions.

Third, the NCLAT in a subsequent decision in Binani Industries Ltd. versus Bank of Baroda, NCLAT (2018) held that 'any resolution plan if shown to be discriminatory against one or other financial creditor or the operational creditor, such plan can be held to be against the provision of the IBC'.[120] In the absence of any specific valuation benchmark in the law or regulations, this broad principle of non-discrimination could dilute the cross-class cramdown provision under IBC. Cramdown powers are necessary in restructurings to overcome potential hold-ups by dissenting claimants. The valuation benchmark provides a precise level of minimum protection to the dissenting claimants from potential abuse of cramdown powers by the majority claimants.[121] In contrast, non-discrimination is a broad principle that could be misused by dissenting out-of-the-money minority claimants to engage in hold-ups to extract a better deal for themselves. Such misuse could dilute the efficacy of the cramdown provision under the IBC and cause unnecessary litigation.

Fourth, although the principle of non-discrimination is the correct intuition, it is not a precise standard. For this principle to be implementable in practice, it has to be translated into an appropriate valuation benchmark, ideally codified in law as is the case currently in US and Singapore.[122] Therefore, Indian policymakers still need to decide whether the going concern 'liquidation value', the break-up 'liquidation value' or 'next best alternative' value is the appropriate valuation benchmark to ensure non-discrimination in restructurings.

The Indian judiciary could potentially address this issue through judicial interpretation. This could be tricky given the lack of an explicit provision for judicial supervision of the fairness of a resolution plan. In any case, Indian courts do not necessarily have a great track record of managing creditor oppression in the con-

[118] SCA (2017)[211H(4)].

[119] UK has proposed to use the 'next best alternative' valuation benchmark (Department of Business, Energy and Industrial Strategy 2018[5. 169–5. 176]).

[120] Binani Industries Ltd. versus Bank of Baroda, NCLAT (2018)[48].

[121] Policymakers in Singapore discussed this issue in detail and finally agreed to introduce the cramdown provision in the statute along with necessary safeguards including valuation benchmark (Insolvency Law Review Committee Singapore 2013[154–156]).

[122] USBC (2012)[1129(a)(7)(A)(ii)], SCA (2017)[211H(4)].

text of corporate insolvency, as is evident from the history of Board for Industrial and Financial Reconstruction (BIFR).[123]

Strategic Valuation The valuation of the insolvent company under the IBC is done by registered valuers, appointed by the resolution professional, who in turn is appointed by the CoC.[124] Therefore, it is likely that these valuers would be influenced by the interests of the majority financial creditors on the CoC.[125] This could create scope for strategic valuation under the IBC in favour of the majority financial creditors. If these financial creditors are secured, they have an incentive to depress the valuation in a restructuring, so that they can capture more equity in the restructured company. This could create further risks of wealth transfer to the majority financial creditors.

5 Conclusion

India experienced a major structural change with the enactment of the IBC. Although it has vastly improved India's corporate insolvency framework, it has also raised two important challenges—the value destruction problem and wealth transfer problem. This article applied theoretical concepts from the law and economics literature on insolvency to identify the sources of these two problems in the IBC.

The article identified two potential sources of value destruction under the IBC. First, the law entrusts the decision about the future of a financial distressed corporate debtor with a super-majority of financial creditors, whose payoffs may not necessarily be affected by the outcome of that decision. Therefore, they may not have the right incentive to preserve the value of the business of the corporate debtor. Second, by limiting the benefits of the cramdown provision only to post-insolvency restructuring, the law delays restructuring and enhances the risk of value destruction of the corporate debtor.

The article identified four potential sources of wealth transfer under the IBC. First, the law does not expressly provide for judicial supervision to ensure fairness in a resolution plan adopted by cramming down the minority financial creditors. Consequently, till 5 October 2018, a resolution plan that paid only the break-up 'liquidation value' to such dissenting minority financial creditors would have been perfectly legal under the regulations and had to be approved by NCLT. This created potential risks of wealth transfers from dissenting minority financial creditors through resolution plans. After 5 October 2018, in the absence of a specific valuation benchmark for dissenting financial creditors in the law or regulations, it remains to be seen what valuation benchmark could be successfully used in this regard. Second, the regulations

[123] van Zwieten (2015).

[124] Even if not formally appointed by the Committee of Creditors initially, an interim resolution professional can be replaced by 66% vote by value of the Committee. Therefore, for all practical purposes, the resolution professional will be answerable to the Committee (IBC (2016)[27]).

[125] At the very least, it will impact on the perception that the valuation is unbiased (Payne 2018).

before 5 October 2018 used the break-up 'liquidation value' instead of going concern 'liquidation value' as the benchmark for restructuring of a financially distressed company, reducing the valuation of the claims of the dissenting minority financial creditors in the restructured company. After 5 October 2018, in the absence of a specific valuation benchmark for dissenting financial creditors in restructuring cases, it remains to be seen what valuation benchmark could be successfully used in this regard. Third, the law incorrectly applies the 'liquidation value' benchmark used in restructurings to going concern sales for cash to third parties, creating opportunities for wealth transfer from operational creditors to junior claimants in such sales transactions. Fourth, the appointment process of registered valuers could create scope for strategic valuation favouring wealth transfer to majority financial creditors.

Indian policymakers need to revisit these fundamental legislative design choices embedded within the IBC to successfully address the contemporary concerns regarding the value destruction and wealth transfer problems.

Acknowledgements An earlier version was submitted as a dissertation in partial satisfaction of the MSc Law and Finance degree at Faculty of Law, University of Oxford. I would like to thank my dissertation supervisor, Prof. Kristin van Zwieten, for her detailed comments and extensive feedback on multiple earlier drafts of this article. I would also like to thank Mr. Arpan N. Chowdhury, Prof. Ajay Shah, various participants at the IBBI-IGIDR Insolvency and Bankruptcy Conference (August 2018) and an anonymous referee, for their valuable comments and feedback. I am grateful to Chevening Scholarships, the UK government's global scholarship programme, funded by the Foreign and Commonwealth Office (FCO) and partner organisations, including the Weidenfeld-Hoffmann Trust, for providing financial assistance.

References

Aghion P, Hart O, Moore J (1992) The economics of Bankruptcy reforms. J Law Econ Organ 8:523–546

Aghion P, Hart O, Moore J (1994) Improving bankruptcy procedure. Wash Law Univ Q 72(3):849–872

Akshay Jhunjhunwala versus Union of India, Calcutta High Court (2018) Akshay Jhunjhunwala versus Union of India

Aryan A (2018) Operational creditors should get a say, vote in insolvency process: SC. https://www.business-standard.com/article/companies/operational-creditors-should-get-a-say-vote-in-insolvency-process-sc-118121300923_1.html

Baird D (1986) The uneasy case for corporate reorganizations. J Leg Stud 5:127

Baird D (1998) Bankruptcy's uncontested axioms. Yale LJ 108:573

Bankruptcy Law Reforms Committee (2015) The report of the Bankruptcy Law Reforms Committee Volume I: Rationale and Design. Technical Report, Ministry of Finance. http://ibbi.gov.in/BLRCReportVol1_04112015.pdf

Binani Industries Ltd versus Bank of Baroda, NCLAT (2018) Binani Industries Ltd. versus Bank of Baroda

CA (2006) Companies Act

Central Bank of India versus Resolution Professional of Sirpur Paper Mills Ltd and Ors, NCLAT (2018) Central Bank of India versus Resolution Professional of Sirpur Paper Mills Ltd. and Ors

Chitra Sharma versus Union of India, SC (2017) Chitra Sharma versus Union of India. https://barandbench.com/wp-content/uploads/2017/09/Jaypee-Petition.pdf

Clark R (1981) The interdisciplinary study of legal evolution. Yale Law J 90:1238
Crystal M, Mokal R (2006) The valuation of distressed companies—a conceptual framework. Int Corp Rescue 3(63):123
Department of Business (2018) Energy and Industrial Strategy. Insolvency and Corporate Governance, Government response
Doshi M (2018) Why IL& FS Picked This Route To Solvency. https://www.bloombergquint.com/business/why-ilfs-picked-this-route-to-solvency#gs.8UOHopA
Eidenmuller H, van Zwieten K (2015) Restructuring the European business enterprise: the European Commission's recommendation on a new approach to business failure and insolvency. Eur Bus Organ Law Rev 16:625
European Commission (2016) Proposal for a directive of the European parliament and of the council
Finance Minister (2014) Budget speech, paragraph 106. https://www.indiabudget.gov.in/budget2014-2015/ub2014-15/bs/bs.pdf
Financial Stability Report, Reserve Bank of India (2017) Financial Stability Report
Franks J, Sussman O (2005) Financial distress and bank restructuring of small to medium size UK companies. Rev Finance 9:65
Gopakumar G (2018) Insolvency code: Gujarat NRE Coke CMD seeks more accountability from bankers. https://www.livemint.com/Companies/045S6mr9BoGeEAe5tI8AYL/Insolvency-code-Gujarat-NRE-Coke-CMD-seeks-more-accountabil.html
Hart O (1995) Bankruptcy procedure. Clarendon Press
IBBI (2016) Insolvency and Bankruptcy Board of India (Insolvency Resolution Process For Corporate Persons) Regulations. http://ibbi.gov.in/webadmin/\protect\penalty-\@Mpdf/legalframwork/2018/Feb/06FEB2018IBBI(INSOLVENCYRESOLU\protect\penalty-\@MTIONPROCESSFORCORPORATEPERSONS)REGULATIONS,2\protect\penalty-\@M016(AMENDEDUPTO06202018)_2018-02-1909:31:58.pdf
IBBI (2018a) India wins the GRR Award for the Most Improved Jurisdiction. http://ibbi.gov.in/webadmin/pdf/press/2018/Jun/GlobalRestructuringReview(1).pdf
IBBI (2018b) Insolvency and Bankruptcy Board of India (Insolvency Resolution Process for Corporate Persons) (Fourth Amendment) Regulations
IBBI June Newsletter (2018) Insolvency and Bankruptcy News: CoC Dharma. http://ibbi.gov.in/webadmin/pdf/whatsnew/2018/Sep/Newsletter_IBBI_April-June,2018_2018-09-1819:28:22.pdf
IBBI September Newsletter (2018) Insolvency and Bankruptcy news: automating the wheels of commerce. https://ibbi.gov.in/QUARTERLY_NEWSLETTER_FOR_JUL_SEP_2018.pdf
Insolvency Law Committee Report (2018) Report of the insolvency law committee
Insolvency Law Review Committee (Singapore) (2013) Report of the insolvency law review committee
Jensen M, Meckling W (1976) Theory of the firm: Managerial behaviour, agency costs and ownership structure. J Financ Econ 3:305
Lee H (2007) Efficient and inefficient debt restructuring: a comparative analysis of voting rules in workouts. Cornell Int'l LJ 40:661
Marwah V, Sharma A (2018) Watching The IBC: Lessons From The RBI-12 Cases. https://www.bloombergquint.com/insolvency/watching-the-ibc-lessons-from-the-rbi-12-cases#gs.Ww6hEA0
Mehta S (2018) Tata Steel completes Rs 35,200 crore purchase of bankrupt Bhushan Steel. https://economictimes.indiatimes.com/industry/indl-goods/svs/steel/tata-steel-completes-5-2-billion-purchase-of-bankrupt-bhushan-steel/articleshow/64224367.cms
Mr Ajay Agarwal versus M/s Ashok Magnetics Ltd and Anr, NCLT (2018) Mr. Ajay Agarwal versus M/s. Ashok Magnetics Limited and Anr
Payne J (2014) Debt restructuring in English law: lessons from the United States and the need for reform. LQR 130:282
Payne J (2018) The role of the court in debt restructuring. CLJ 77:124
Re: M/s Gujarat NRE Coke Ltd, NCLT (2018) Re: M/s. Gujarat NRE Coke Ltd

Report of the Joint Committee on the Insolvency and Bankruptcy Code, 2015, Lok Sabha (2016) Report of the Joint Committee on the Insolvency and Bankruptcy Code, 2015
Rubina Chandha versus AMR Infrastucture, NCLAT (2017) Rubina Chandha versus AMR Infrastucture
SCA (2017) Singapore Companies (Amendment) Act
Sengupta R, Sharma A, Thomas S (2016) Evolution of the insolvency framework for non-financial firms in India. http://www.igidr.ac.in/pdf/publication/WP-2016-018.pdf,urldate=2018-04-26
Swiss Ribbons Pvt Ltd. versus Union of India, SC (2018) Swiss Ribbons Pvt. Ltd. versus Union of India
The Insolvency Service (2016) A review of the corporate insolvency framework
USBC (2012) U.S. Bankruptcy Code
Varottil U (2017) The scheme of arrangement as a debt restructuring tool in India: problems and prospects. https://law.nus.edu.sg/wps/pdfs/005_2017_Umakanth.pdf
Videocon Industries Limited (2018) Un-audited financial results for the quarter ended 30th June, 2018 and changes in key managerial personnel of the company
van Zwieten K (2015) Corporate rescue in India: the influence of the courts. J Corp Law Stud 15:1
Westbrook J (2004) The control of wealth in Bankruptcy. Tex L Rev 82:795

GPSR Compliance
The European Union's (EU) General Product Safety Regulation (GPSR) is a set of rules that requires consumer products to be safe and our obligations to ensure this.

If you have any concerns about our products, you can contact us on

ProductSafety@springernature.com

In case Publisher is established outside the EU, the EU authorized representative is:

Springer Nature Customer Service Center GmbH
Europaplatz 3
69115 Heidelberg, Germany

www.ingramcontent.com/pod-product-compliance
Ingram Content Group UK Ltd.
Pitfield, Milton Keynes, MK11 3LW, UK
UKHW022211051026
15624UKWH00001B/104
* 9 7 8 9 8 1 1 6 0 8 5 3 7 *